William Dickson, Jean Baptiste Massillon

Sermons by J. B. Massillon, Bishop of Clermont

William Dickson, Jean Baptiste Massillon

Sermons by J. B. Massillon, Bishop of Clermont

ISBN/EAN: 9783337160470

Printed in Europe, USA, Canada, Australia, Japan

Cover: Foto ©Lupo / pixelio.de

More available books at **www.hansebooks.com**

SERMONS

BY

J. B. MASSILLON,

BISHOP OF CLERMONT.

SELECTED AND TRANSLATED

BY

WILLIAM DICKSON;

AND

DEDICATED, BY PERMISSION, TO

HER GRACE

THE DUTCHESS OF BUCCLEUGH.

VOLUME THIRD.

EDINBURGH:
PRINTED FOR ROBERT MORISON AND SON, BOOKSELLERS, PERTH;
ARCHIBALD CONSTABLE, EDINBURGH; AND BRASH
AND REID, GLASGOW.

1798.

CONTENTS.

SERM.		PAGE.
I.	The Truth of Religion,	9
II.	Doubts upon Religion,	49
III.	Evidence of the Law of God,	88
IV.	Immutability of the Law of God,	127
V.	For Christmas Day,	157
VI.	For the Day of the Epiphany,	189
VII.	The Divinity of Jesus Christ,	237
VIII.	On the Resurrection of Lazarus,	293
IX.	On the Day of Judgment,	334
X.	The Happiness of the Just,	376
XI.	On the Dispositions for the Communion,	412

SERMON I.

THE TRUTH OF RELIGION.

MATTHEW viii. 10.

Verily I say unto you, I have not found so great faith, no not in Israel.

WHENCE came then the incredulity with which Jesus Christ at present reproaches the Jews; and what cause could they still have for doubting the sanctity of his doctrine and the truth of his ministry? They had demanded miracles, and, before their eyes, he had wrought such evident ones, that no person before him had done the like. They had wished that his mission were authorised by testimonies; Moses and the prophets had amply borne them to him; the precursor had openly proclaimed, Behold the Christ and the Lamb of God, which taketh away the sin of the world; a gentile renders glory in our gofpel to his almightinefs; the heavenly Father had declared from on high, that it was his well-beloved Son; laftly, the demons themfelves, ftruck with his fanctity, quitted the bodies, in confeffing that he was the Holy, and the Son of the living God. What could the incredulity of the Jews ftill oppofe to fo many proofs and prodigies?

Behold, my brethren, what, with much greater furprife, might be demanded at thofe unbelieving minds, who, after the fulfilment of all that had been foretold, after the confummation of the myfteries of Jefus Chrift, the exaltation of his name, the manifeftation of his gifts, the calling of his people, the deftruction of idols, the converfion of Cefars, and the agreement of the univerfe, ftill doubt, and take upon themfelves to confute and to overthrow what the toils of the apoftolic men, the blood of fo many martyrs, the prodigies of fo many fervants of Jefus Chrift, the writings of fo many great men, the aufterities of fo many holy anchorites, and the religion of feventeen hundred years, have fo univerfally and fo divinely eftablifhed in the mind of almoft all people.

For, my brethren, amid all the triumphs of faith, children of unbelief ftill privately fpring up among us, whom God hath delivered up to the vanity of their own thoughts, and who blafpheme what they know not; impious men, who change, as the apoftle fays, the grace of our God into wantonnefs,

defile

defile their flesh, contemn all rule, blaspheme majesty, corrupt all their ways like the animals not gifted with reason, and are set apart to serve one day as an example of the awful judgments of God upon men.

Now if, among so many believers assembled here through religion, any soul of this description should happen to be, allow me, you, my brethren, who preserve with respect the sacred trust of the doctrine which you have received from your ancestors and from your pastors, to seize this opportunity, either of undeceiving them, or of confuting their incredulity. Allow me, for once, to do here what the first pastors of the church so often did before their assembled people, that is to say, to take upon myself the defence of the religion of Jesus Christ against unbelief; and, before entering into the particulars of your duties during this long term, allow me to begin by laying the first foundations of faith. It is so consoling for those who believe to find how reasonable their submission is, and to be convinced that faith, which is apparently the rock of reason, is however its only consolation, guide, and refuge!

Here then is my whole design. The unbeliever refuses submission to the revealed truths, either through a vain affectation of reason, or through a false sentiment of pride, or through an ill-placed love of independance.

Now, I mean at present to shew, that the submission which the unbeliever refuses, through a vain affectation

affectation of reason, is the most prudent use which he can make even of reason; that the submission which he refuses through a false sentiment of pride, is the most glorious step of it; and, lastly, that the submission which he rejects through an ill-placed love of independance, is the most indispensible sacrifice of it. And from thence I shall draw the three great characters of religion: It is reasonable, it is glorious, it is necessary.

O my Saviour, eternal author and finisher of our faith, defend thyself, thy doctrine. Suffer not that thy cross, by which the universe hath been submitted to thee, be still the folly and the scandal of proud minds. Once more triumph at present, through the secret wonders of thy grace, over that same unbelief which thou formerly triumphedst over through the striking operations of thy power; and by those lively lights, which enlighten hearts, more efficacious than all our discourses, destroy every sentiment of pride which may still rise up against the knowledge of thy mysteries.

PART I. Let us begin with admitting that it is faith, and not reason, which makes Christians; and that the first step exacted of a disciple of Jesus Christ, is to captivate his mind, and to believe what he may not comprehend. Nevertheless, I say, that we are led to that submission by reason itself; that the more even our lights are superior, the more do they point out the necessity of our submission; and that unbelief, far from being the

party

party of strength of mind, and of reason, is, on the contrary, that of error and weakness.

In faith, reason hath therefore its uses, as it hath its limits: and as the law, good and holy in itself, served however only to conduct to Jesus Christ, and there stopped as at its term; in the same way reason, good and just in itself, since it is the gift of God, and a participation of the sovereign reason, ought only to serve, and is given to us for the sole purpose of preparing the way for faith. It is forward, and quits the bounds of its first institution, when it attempts to go beyond these sacred limits.

This taken for granted, let us see which of the two, viz. the believer or the unbeliever, makes the most prudent use of his reason. Submission to things held out to our belief, perhaps suspected of credulity, either on the side of the authority which proposes them; if it be light, it is weakness to give credit to them; or on the side of the things of which they wish to persuade us; if they be in opposition to the principles of equity, of honour, of society, and of conscience, it is ignorance to receive them as true; or, lastly, on the side of the motives which are employed to persuade us; if they be vain, frivolous, and incapable of determining a wise mind, it is imprudence to give way to them. Now, it is easy to prove that the authority which exacts the submission of the believer, is the greatest, the most respectable, and the best established, which can possibly be upon the earth; that the truths proposed to his belief are the only ones conformable to the principles of equity, of honour, of society, and of conscience; and, lastly, that the motives employed to persuade him are the most decisive, the most triumphant, and the most proper to gain submission from the least credulous minds.

When I speak of the authority of the Christian religion, I do not pretend to confine the extent of that term to the single authority of its holy assemblies, in which, through the mouths of its pastors, the church makes decisions, and holds out to all believers the infallible rules of worship and of doctrine. As it is not heresy, but unbelief, which this discourse concerns, I do not here so much consider religion as opposed to the sects which the spirit of error hath separated from the unity, that is to say, as confined to the sole catholic church, but as forming, since the beginning of the world, a society apart, sole depositary of the knowledge of a God, and of the promise of a Mediator; always opposed to all the religions which have since arisen in the universe; always contradicted, and always the same; and I say that its authority bears along with it such shining characters of truth, that it is impossible, without folly, to refuse submission to it.

In the first place, in matter of religion, antiquity is a character which reason respects; and we may say, that a prepossession is already formed in favour of that belief, consecrated by the religion of the first men, and by the simplicity of the primitive

times

times. Not but what falsehood is often decked out with the same titles, and that old errors exist among men, which seem to contest the antiquity of their origin with the truth; but it is not difficult, to whoever wishes to trace their history, to go back even to their origin. Novelty is always the constant and most inseparable character of error: and the reproach of the prophet may alike be made to them all: " They sacrifice to new gods " that come newly up, whom their fathers feared " not."

In effect, if there be a true religion upon the earth, it must be the most ancient of all; for, if there be a true religion upon the earth, it must be the first and the most essential duty of man towards the God who wishes to be honoured by it. This duty must therefore be equally ancient as man; and, as it is attached to his nature, it must, as I may say, be born with him. And this, my brethren, is the first character by which the religion of Christians is at once distinguished from superstitions and sects. It is the most ancient religion in the world. The first men, before that an impious worship was carved out of divinities of wood and of stone, worshipped the same God whom we adore, raised up altars and offered sacrifices to him, expected from his liberality the reward of their virtue, and from his justice the punishment of their disobedience. The history of the birth of this religion, is the history of the birth of the world itself.

The

The divine books which have preferved it down to us; contain the firft monuments of the origin of things. They are themfelves more ancient than all thofe fabulous productions of the human mind, which afterwards fo miferably amufed the credulity of the following ages; and as error ever fprings from the truth, and is only a faulty imitation of it, all the fables of paganifm are founded on fome of the principal features of that divine hiftory; in fo much that it may be affirmed that every thing, even to error itfelf, renders homage to the antiquity and to the authority of our holy fcriptures.

Now, my brethren, is there not already fomething refpectable in this character alone? The other religions, which have vaunted a more ancient origin, have produced nothing, in fupport of their antiquity, but fabulous legends, which funk into nothing of themfelves. They have disfigured the hiftory of the world by a chaos of innumerable and imaginary ages, of which no event hath been left to pofterity, and which the hiftory of the world hath never known. The authors of thefe grofs fictions did not write till many ages after the actions which they relate, and it is faying every thing to add, that that theology was the fruit of poefy; and the inventions of that art, the moft folid foundations of their religion.

Here, it is a train of facts, reafonable, natural, and in agreement with itfelf. It is the hiftory of a family continued from its firft head down to

him

him who writes it, and authenticated in all its circumſtances. It is a genealogy in which every chief is characteriſed by his own actions, by events which ſtill ſubſiſted then, by marks which were ſtill known in the places where they had dwelt. It is a living tradition, the moſt authenticated upon the earth, ſince Moſes hath written only what he had heard from the children of the patriarchs, and they related only what their fathers had ſeen. Every part of it is coherent, hangs properly together, and tends to clear up the whole. The features are not copied, nor the adventures drawn from elſewhere, and accommodated to the ſubject. Before Moſes, the people of God had nothing in writing. He hath left nothing to poſterity but what he had verbally collected from his anceſtors, that is to ſay, the whole tradition of mankind; and the firſt, he hath compriſed in one volume, the hiſtory of God's wonders and of his manifeſtations to men, the remembrance of which had till then compoſed the whole religion, the whole knowledge, and the whole conſolation of the family of Abraham. The candour and ſincerity of this author appear in the ſimplicity of his hiſtory. He takes no precaution to ſecure belief, becauſe he ſuppoſes that thoſe for whom he writes require none to believe; and all the facts which he relates being well-known among them, it is more for the purpoſe of preſerving them to their poſterity, than for any inſtruction in them to themſelves.

Vol. III.   C   Behold,

Behold, my brethren, which way the Christian religion begins to acquire influence over the mind of men. Turn on all sides, read the history of every people and of every nation, and you will find nothing so well established upon the earth: What do I say? You will find nothing more worthy the attention of a rational mind. If men be born for a religion, they are born for this one alone. If there be a Supreme Being who hath manifested the truth to men, this alone is worthy of men and of him. Every where else the origin is fabulous; here it is equally certain as all the rest; and the latter ages, which cannot be disputed, are, however, only the proofs of the certitude of the first. Therefore, if there be an authority upon the earth to which reason ought to yield, it is to that of the Christian religion.

To the character of its antiquity must be added that of its perpetuity. Figure to yourselves here that endless variety of sects and of religions which have successively reigned upon the earth: Follow the history of the superstitions of every people and of every country; they have flourished a few years, and afterwards sunk into oblivion along with the power of their followers. Where are the gods of Emath, of Arphad, and of Sepharvaim? Recollect the history of those first conquerors: In conquering the people, they conquered the gods of the people; and, in overturning their power, they overturned their worship. How beautiful, my
brethren,

brethren, to fee the religion of our fathers alone maintaining itfelf from the firft, furviving all fects; and, notwithftanding the diverfe fortunes of thofe who have profeffed it, alone paffing from father to fon, and braving every exertion to efface it from the heart of men! It is not the arm of flefh which hath preferved it. Ah! The people of God hath, almoft always, been weak, oppreffed, and perfecuted. No; it is not, fays the prophet, by their own fword that our fathers got the land in poffeffion; but thy right hand, O Lord, and thine arm, and the light of thy countenance, becaufe thou hadft a favour unto them. One while flaves, another fugitives, and another tributaries of various nations; they a thoufand times faw Chaldea, Affyria, Babylon, the moft formidable powers of the earth, the whole univerfe confpire their ruin, and the total extinction of their worfhip; but this people, fo weak, oppreffed in Egypt, wandering in the defert, and afterwards carried in captivity into a foreign land, no power hath ever been able to exterminate, while fo many others, more powerful, have followed the deftiny of human things; and its worfhip hath always fubfifted with itfelf, in fpite of all the efforts made by almoft every age to deftroy it.

Now, whence comes it, that a worfhip fo contradicted, fo arduous in its obfervances, fo rigorous in its punifhments upon tranfgreffors, and even fo liable to be eftablifhed or to be overthrown, through the mere inconftancy and ignorance of
the

the people who was its firſt depoſitary; whence comes it that it alone hath been perpetuated amid ſo many revolutions, while the ſuperſtitions ſupported by all the power of empires and of kingdoms, have ſunk into their original oblivion? Ah! is it not God, and not man, who hath done all theſe things? Is it not the arm of the Almighty which hath preſerved his work? And ſince every thing invented by the human mind has periſhed, is it not to be inferred, that what hath always endured was alone the work of the divine wiſdom?

Laſtly, If to its antiquity and to its perpetuity, you add its uniformity, no pretext for reſiſtance will be left to reaſon. For, my brethren, every thing changes upon the earth, becauſe every thing follows the mutability of its origin. Occaſions, the differences of ages, the diverſe humours of climates, and the neceſſity of the times, have introduced a thouſand changes in all the human laws. Faith alone hath never changed. Such as our fathers received it, ſuch have we it at preſent, and ſuch ſhall our deſcendants one day receive it. It hath been unfolded through the courſe of ages, and likewiſe, I confeſs, through the neceſſity of ſecuring it from the errors which have been attempted to be introduced into it; but every thing which once appeared to belong to it, hath always appeared as appertaining to it. There is little wonder in the duration of a religion, when accommodations are made to times and to conjunctures,

tures, and when they may add or diminish according to the fancy of the ages, and of those who govern; but never to relax, in spite of the change of manners and of times; to see every thing change around, and yet be always the same, is the grand privilege of the Christian religion. And by these three characters, of antiquity, of perpetuity, and of uniformity, which exclusively belong to it, its authority is the only one upon the earth capable of determining a wise mind.

But if the submission of the believer be reasonable on the part of the authority which exacts it, it is not less so on the part of the things which are proposed to his belief. And here, my brethren, let us enter into the foundation of the Christian worship. It is not afraid of investigation, like those abominable mysteries of idolatry, the infamy and horror of which were concealed by the darkest obscurity. A religion, says Tertullian, which would shun examination, and would dread being searched into, should ever be suspected. The more the Christian worship is investigated, the more are beauties and hidden wonders found in it. Idolatry inspired man with foolish sentiments of the Divinity: philosophy, with very unreasonable ones of himself: cupidity, with iniquitous ones towards the rest of men. Now, admire the wisdom of religion, which remedies all these three evils, which the reason of all ages had never been able either to eradicate or even to find out.

And,

And, 1*stly*, what other legislator hath spoken of the divinity, like that of the Christians? Find elsewhere if you can, more sublime ideas of his power, of his immensity, of his wisdom, of his grandeur, and of his justice, than those which are given us in our scriptures. If there be over us a supreme and eternal Being, in whom all things live, he must be such as the Christian religion represents him. We alone compare him not to the likeness of man. We alone worship him seated above the cherubims, filling every where with his presence, regulating all by his wisdom, creating light and darkness, author of good, and punisher of vice. We alone honour him as he wishes to be honoured; that it is to say, we make not the worship due to him, to consist in the multitude of victims, nor in the external pomp of our homages; but in adoration, in love, in praise, and in thanksgiving. We refer to him the good which is in us, as to its principle; and we always attribute vice to ourselves, which takes its rise only in our corruption. We hope to find in him the reward of a fidelity, which is the gift of his grace, and the punishment of transgressions, which are always the consequence of the bad use which we make of our liberty. Now, what can be more worthy of the supreme Being than all these ideas!

2*dly*, A vain philosophy either had degraded man to the level of the beast, by centering his felicity in the senses; or had foolishly exalted him

even

even to the likeness of God, by persuading him that he might find his own happiness in his own wisdom. Now, the Christian morality avoids these two extremes: it withdraws man from carnal pleasures, by discovering to him the excellency of his nature, and the holiness of his destination; it corrects his pride, by making him sensible of his own wretchedness and meanness.

Lastly, cupidity rendered man unjust towards the rest of men. Now, what other doctrine than that of Christians, hath ever so well regulated our duties on this head. It instructs us to yield obedience to the powers established by God, not only through fear of their authority, but through an obligation of conscience; to respect our superiors, to bear with our equals, to be affable towards our inferiors, to love all men as ourselves. It alone is capable of forming good citizens, faithful subjects, patient servants, humble masters, incorruptible magistrates, clement princes, and zealous friends. It alone renders the honour of marriage inviolable, secures the peace of families, and maintains the tranquility of states. It not only checks usurpations, but it prohibits even the desire of others property; it not only requires us, not to view with an envious eye the prosperity of our brother, but it commands us to share our own riches with him, if need require; it not only forbids us to attempt his life, but it requires us to do good, even to those who injure us; to bless those who curse us, and to

be

be all only of one heart and of one mind. Give me, said formerly St Augustin to the heathens of his time, a kingdom all composed of people of this kind: Good God, what peace! what felicity! What a representation of heaven upon the earth! Have all the ideas of philosophy ever come near to the plan of this heavenly republic? And is it not true, that if a God hath spoken to men, to lay open to them the ways of salvation, he could never have held any other language?

To all these maxims, so worthy of reason, it is true, that religion adds mysteries which exceed our comprehension. But, besides that good sense should induce us to yield thereon to a religion so venerable through its antiquity, so divine in its morality, so superior to every thing on the earth in its authority, and alone worthy of being believed, the motives it employs for our persuasion are sufficient to conquer unbelief.

1*stly*, These mysteries were foretold many ages before their accomplishment, and foretold with every circumstance of times and places; nor are they vague prophecies, referred to the credulity of the vulgar alone, uttered in a corner of the earth, of the same age as the events, and unknown to the rest of the universe. They are prophecies which, from the beginning of the world, have constituted the religion of an entire people; which fathers transmitted to their children as their most precious inheritance; which were preserved in the holy
temple

temple as the moſt ſacred pledge of the divine promiſes; and, laſtly, to the truth of which the nation moſt inveterate againſt Jeſus Chriſt, and their firſt depoſitory, ſtill at preſent bears witneſs in the face of the whole univerſe: prophecies, which were not myſteriouſly hidden from the people, left their falſehood ſhould be betrayed; like thoſe vain oracles of the Sybils, carefully ſhut up in the capitol, fabricated to ſupport the Roman pride, expoſed to the view of the pontiffs alone, and produced, piece-meal, from time to time, to authoriſe, in the mind of the people, either a dangerous enterpriſe, or an unjuſt war. On the contrary, our prophetical books were the daily ſtudy of a whole people. The young and the old, women and children, prieſts and men of all ranks, princes and ſubjects, were indiſpenſibly obliged to have them continually in their hands; every one was entitled to ſtudy his duties there, and to diſcover his hopes. Far from flattering their pride, they held forth only the ingratitude of their fathers; in every page they announced misfortunes to them as the juſt puniſhment of their crimes; to kings they reproached their diſſipations, to the pontiffs their profuſion, to the people their inconſtancy and unbelief; and, neverthelefs, theſe holy books were dear to them; and, from the oracles which they ſaw continually accompliſhing in them, they awaited with confidence the fulfilment of thoſe which the whole univerſe hath now witneſſed. Now, the knowledge of what is to come is the least suspicious character of the divinity.

2*dly*, These mysteries are founded upon facts so evidently miraculous, so well-known in Judea, so agreed to then, even by those whose interest it was to reject them, so signalized by events which interested the whole nation, so often repeated in the cities, in the country, in the temple, and in the public places, that the eyes must be shut against the light to call them in question. The apostles have preached them, have written them, even in Judea, a very short time after their fulfilment; that is to say, in a time when the pontiffs, who had condemned Jesus Christ, still living, might so easily have controverted and proclaimed their imposture, had they really been a deception upon mankind. Jesus Christ, by fulfilling his promise of rising again, confirmed his gospel, and it is not to be supposed either, that the apostles could be deceived on a fact so decisive and so essential for them; on that fact so often foretold, and looked forward to, as the principal point on which all the rest was to turn; that fact so often confirmed, and that before so many witnesses; nor that they themselves wished to deceive us, and to preach a falsehood to men at the expence of their own ease, honour, and life, the only return which they had to expect for their imposture. Would these men, who have left to us only such pious and wise precepts, have given to the earth an example of folly hitherto unknown to every

every people, and without view, intereſt, or motive, have coolly devoted themſelves to the moſt excruciating tortures, and to a death ſuffered with the moſt heroical piety, merely to maintain the truth of a thing, of which they themſelves knew the falſehood? Would theſe men have all tranquilly ſubmitted to death for the ſake of another man who had deceived them, and who, having failed in his promiſe of riſing again from the grave, had only impoſed, during life, upon their credulity and weakneſs: Let the impious man no longer reproach to us, as a credulity, the incomprehenſible myſteries of faith. He muſt be very credulous himſelf, to be able to perſuade himſelf of the poſſibility of ſuppoſitions ſo abſurd.

Laſtly, The whole univerſe hath been docile to the faith of theſe myſteries; the Ceſars, whom it degraded from the rank of gods; the philoſophers, whom it convicted of ignorance and vanity; the voluptuous, to whom it preached ſelf-denial and ſufferance; the rich, whom it obliged to poverty and humility; the poor, whom it commanded to love even their abjection and indigence; all men, of whom it combatted all the paſſions. This faith, preached by twelve poor men without learning, talents, or ſupport, hath ſubjected emperors, the learned equally as the illiterate, cities and empires; myſteries apparently ſo abſurd, have overthrown all the ſects, and all the monuments of a proud reaſon, and the folly of the croſs hath been wiſer

than

than all the wifdom of the age. The whole univerfe hath confpired againft it, and every effort of its enemies, hath only added frefh confirmation to it. To be a believer, and to be deftined to death, were two things infeparable; yet the danger was only an additional charm; the more the perfecutions were violent, the more progrefs did faith make; and the blood of the martyrs was the feed of believers. O God! who doth not feel thy finger here? Who, in thefe traits, would not acknowledge the character of thy work? Where is the reafon which doth not feel the vanity of its doubts to fink into nothing here, and which ftill blufhes to fubmit to a doctrine, to which the whole univerfe hath yielded? But not only is this fubmiffion reafonable, it is likewife glorious to men.

PART II. Pride is the fecret fource of unbelief. In that oftentation of reafon, which induces the unbeliever to contemn the common belief, there is a deplorable fingularity which flatters him, and occafions him to fuppofe in himfelf more vigour of mind and more light than in the reft of men, becaufe he boldly ventures to caft off a yoke to which they have all fubmitted, and to ftand up againft what all the reft had hitherto been contented to worfhip.

Now, in order to deprive the unbeliever of fo wretched a confolation, it is only neceffary to demonftrate, in the firft place, that nothing is more glorious to reafon than faith; glorious on the fide

of

of its promises for the future; glorious from the situation in which it places the believer for the present; lastly, glorious from the grand models which it holds out to his imitation.

Glorious on the side of the promises contained in it. What are the promises of faith, my brethren? The adoption of God, an immortal society with him, the complete redemption of our bodies, the eternal felicity of our souls, freedom from the passions, our hearts fixed by the possession of the true riches, our minds penetrated with the ineffable light of the sovereign reason, and happy in the clear and always durable view of the truth. Such are the promises of faith; it informs us that our origin is divine, and our hopes eternal.

Now, I ask, is it disgraceful to reason to believe truths which do such honour to the immortality of its nature? What, my brethren, would it then be more glorious to man to believe himself of the same nature as the beasts, and to look forward to the same end? What, the unbeliever would think himself more honoured by the conviction that he is only a vile clay, put together by chance, and which chance shall dissolve, without end, destination, hope, or any other use of his reason and of his body, than that of brutally plunging himself, like the brutes, into carnal gratifications! What, he would have a higher opinion of himself, when viewed in the light of an unfortunate wretch, accidentally placed upon the earth, who looks for-

ward

ward to nothing beyond life, whose sweetest hope is that of sinking back to nonentity, who relates to nothing but himself, and is reduced to find his felicity in himself, though he can there find only anxieties and secret terrors! Is this then that miserable distinction by which the pride of unbelief is so much flattered? Great God! How glorious to thy truth, to have no enemies but men of this character! For my part, as St Ambrose formerly said to the unbelievers of his time, I glory in believing truths so honourable to man, and in expecting the fulfilment of promises so consolotary. To refuse belief to them, is sorrily to punish one's self. Ah! if I be deceived, in prefering the hope of one day enjoying the eternal society of the righteous in the bosom of God to the humbling belief of being of the same nature as the beasts, it is an error dear to me, which I delight in, and upon which I wish never to be undeceived.

But, if faith be glorious on the side of its promises for the future, it is not less so from the situation in which it places the believer for the present. And here, my brethren, figure to yourselves a truly righteous man, who lives by faith, and you will acknowledge that there is nothing on the earth more sublime. Master of his desires and of all the movements of his heart; exercising a glorious empire over himself; in patience and in equanimity enjoying his soul, and regulating all his passions by the bridle of temperance; humble in prosperity, firm

firm under misfortunes, cheerful in tribulations, peaceful with those who hate peace, callous to injuries, feeling for the afflictions of those who trespass against him, faithful in his promises, religious in his friendships, and unshaken in his duties; little affected with riches, which he contemns; fatigued with honours, which he dreads; greater than the whole world, which he considers only as a mass of earth: what dignity!

Philosophy conquered one vice only by another. It pompously taught contempt of the world, merely to attract the applauses of the world; it sought more the glory of wisdom, than wisdom itself. In destroying the other passions, it continually, upon their ruins, raised up one much more dangerous; I mean to say pride: Like that prince of Babylon who overthrew the altars of the national gods, merely to exalt upon their wrecks his own impious statue, and that monstrous colossus of pride which he wanted the whole earth to worship.

But faith exalts the just man above even his virtue. Through it he is still greater in the secrecy of his heart, and in the eyes of God, than before men. He forgives without pride; he is disinterested without shew; he suffers without wishing it to be known; he moderates his passions without perceiving it himself; he alone is ignorant of the glory and of the merit of his actions; far from graciously looking upon himself, he is ashamed of his virtues much more than the sinner is of his vices;

vices; far from courting applaufe, he hides his works from the light, as if they were deeds of darknefs; love of duty is the fole fpring of his virtue; he acts under the eyes of God alone, and as if there were no longer men upon the earth; what dignity! Find, if you can, any thing greater in the univerfe. Review all the various kinds of glory with which the world gratifies the vanity of men; and fee, if, all together, they can beftow that degree of dignity to which the godly are raifed by faith.

Now, my dear hearer, what more honourable to man than this fituation? Do you confider him as more glorious, more refpectable, more grand, when he follows the impulfes of a brutal inftinct; when he is the flave of hatred, revenge, voluptuoufnefs, ambition, envy, and all thofe other monfters which alternately reign in his heart?

For, are you who make a boaft of unbelief thoroughly acquainted with what is an unbeliever? He is a man without morals, probity, faith, or character, who owns no rule but his paffions, no law but his iniquitous thoughts, no mafter but his defires, no check but the dread of authority, no God but himfelf; an unnatural child, feeing he believes that chance alone hath given him fathers; a faithlefs friend, feeing he looks upon men merely as the wretched fruits of a wild and fortuitous concurrence, to whom he is connected only by tranfitory ties; a cruel mafter, feeing he is convinced

that

that the strongest and the most fortunate have always reason on their side. For, who could henceforth place any dependence upon you? You no longer fear a God; you no longer respect men; you look forward to nothing after this life; virtue and vice are merely prejudices of education in your eyes, and the consequences of popular credulity. Adulteries, revenge, blasphemies, the blackest treacheries, abominations which we dare not even to name, are no longer, in your opinion, but human prohibitions, and regulations established through the policy of legislators. According to you, the most horrible crimes, or the purest virtues, are all equally the same, since an eternal annihilation shall soon equalise the just and the impious, and for ever confound them both in the dreary mansion of the tomb. What a monster must you then be upon the earth? Does this representation of you highly gratify your pride, or can you support even its idea?

Besides, you pride yourself upon irreligion, as springing from your superiority of mind; but trace it to its source. What hath led you to free-thinking? Is it not the corruption of your heart? Would you have ever thought of impiety had you been able to ally religion with your pleasures? You began to hesitate upon a doctrine which incommoded your passions; and you have marked it down as false from the moment that you found it irksome. You have anxiously sought to persuade yourself

yourself what you had such an interest to believe; that all died with us; that eternal punishments were merely the terrors of education; that inclinations born with us could never be crimes; what know I? And all those maxims of free thinking originating from hell. We are easily persuaded of what we wish. Solomon worshipped the gods of foreign women only to quiet himself in his debaucheries. If men had never had passions, or if religion had countenanced them, unbelief would never have appeared upon the earth. And a proof that what I say is true, is that, in the moments when you are disgusted with guilt, you imperceptibly turn towards religion; in the moments when your passions are more cool, your doubts diminish; you render, as if in spite of yourself, a secret homage in the bottom of your heart to the truth of faith; in vain you try to weaken it, you cannot succeed in extinguishing it; at the first signal of death, you raise your eyes towards heaven, you acknowledge the God whose finger is upon you, you cast yourself upon the bosom of your Father, and the Author of your being; you tremble over a futurity which you had vaunted not to believe; and, humbled under the hand of the Almighty, on the point of falling upon and crushing you like a worm of the earth, you confess that he is alone great, alone wise, alone immortal, and that man is only vanity and lies.

Lastly,

Lastly, If fresh proofs were necessary to my subject, I could prove to you how glorious faith is to man on the side of the grand models which it holds out for our imitation. Consider Abraham, Isaac, and Jacob, said formerly the Jews to their children. Consider the holy men who have gone before you, to whom their faith hath merited so honourable a testimony, said formerly St Paul to the faithful, after having related to them, in that beautiful chapter of his epistle to the Hebrews, their names, and the most wonderful circumstances of their history, from age to age.

Behold the excellency of the Christian faith. Recollect all the great men which, in all ages, have submitted to it; such magnanimous princes, such religious conquerors, such venerable pastors, such enlightened philosophers, such estimable learned men, wits so vaunted in their age, such noble martyrs, such penitent anchorites, such pure and constant virgins, heroes in every description of virtue. Philosophy preached a pompous wisdom; but its sage was no where to be found. Here what a cloud of witnesses! What an uninterrupted tradition of Christian heroes from the blood of Abel down to us!

Now, I ask, shall you blush to tread in the steps of so many illustrious names? Place on the one side all the great men whom, in all ages, religion hath given to the world, and on the other, that small number of black and desperate minds whom unbelief

unbelief hath produced. Doth it appear more honourable for you to rank yourself among the latter party? To adopt for guides, and for your models, those men whose names are only recollected with horror, those monsters whom it hath pleased providence to permit, that nature should, from time to time, bring forth; or the Abrahams, the Josephs, the Moseses, the Davids, the apostolic men, the righteous of ancient and of modern times? Support, if you can, this comparison. Ah! said formerly St Jerome on a different occasion, if you believe me in error, it is glorious for me to be deceived with such guides.

And here, my brethren, leaving unbelievers for a moment, allow me to address myself to you. Avowed unbelief is a vice perhaps rare among us; but the simplicity of faith is not perhaps less so. We would feel a horror at quitting the belief of our fathers; but we wish to refine upon our sincerity. We do not permit ourselves to doubt upon the main part of the mysteries; but obedience is philosophically given, by imposing our own yoke, by weighing the holy truths, receiving some as reasonable, reasoning upon others, and measuring them by our own feeble lights; and our age, more than any other, is full of these half believers, who, under the pretext of taking away from religion all that credulity or prejudice may have added to it, deprive faith of the whole merit of submission.

Now,

Now, my brethren, fanctity ought only to be
spoken of with a religious circumspection. Faith
is a virtue almost equally delicate as modesty: a
single doubt, a single word injures it; a breath,
as I may say, tarnishes it. Yet, neverthelefs, what
licence do they not allow themselves in modern
converfations upon all that is most respectable in
the faith of our fathers? Alas! the terrible name
of the Lord could not be even pronounced under
the law by the mouth of man; and, at present, all
that is most sacred and most august in religion, is
become a common subject of worldly converfations:
there every thing is talked over, and freely decided
upon. Vain and superficial men, whose only knowledge of religion confifts of a little more temerity
than the illiterate and the common people; produ-
cing, as their whole stock of learning, some com-
mon-place and hackneyed doubts, which they have
picked up, but never had formed themfelves; doubts
which have fo often been cleared up, that they seem
now to exist no longer but to glorify the truth;
men who, amid the most dissolute manners, have
never devoted an hour of serious attention to the
truth of religion, act the philosopher, and boldly
decide upon points which a whole life of study, accompanied with learning and piety, could scarcely
clear up.

Even persons of a sex, in whom ignorance on
certain points would be meritorious, and who,
though knowing, good-breeding and decency require

quire that they should affect to be ignorant; persons who are better acquainted with the world than with Jesus Christ; who even know not of religion what is necessary to regulate their manners, pretend doubts, wish to have them explained, are afraid of believing too much, have suspicions upon the whole, yet have none upon their own miserable situation, and the visible impropriety of their life. O God! it is thus that thou deliverest up sinners to the vanity of their own fancies, and permittest that those who pretend to penetrate into thine adorable secrecies know not themselves. Faith is therefore glorious to man; this has just been shewn to you: it now remains for me to prove that it is necessary to him.

Part III. Of all the characters of faith, the necessity of it is the one which renders the unbeliever most inexcusable. All the other motives which are employed to lead him to the truth are foreign, as I may say, to him; this one is drawn from his own ground-work, I mean to say, from the nature itself of his reason.

Now, I say that faith is absolutely necessary to man, in the gloomy and obscure paths of this life; for his reason is weak, and it requires to be assisted; because it is corrupted, and it requires to be cured; because it is changeable, and it requires to be fixed. Now, faith alone is the aid which assists and enlightens it, the remedy which cures it, the bridle

bridle and the rule which retains and fixes it. Yet a moment of attention; I shall not misemploy it.

I say, 1*stly*, that reason is weak, and that an aid is necessary to it. Alas! my brethren, we know not, neither ourselves, nor what is external to us. We are totally ignorant how we have been formed, by what imperceptible progressions our bodies have received arrangement and life, and what are the infinite springs, and the divine skill, which give motion to the whole machine. " I cannot " tell," said that illustrious mother, mentioned in the Maccabees, to her children, " how ye came " into my womb; for I neither gave you breath " nor life, neither was it I that formed the mem- " bers of every one of you: but doubtless the " Creator of the world, who formed the genera- " tion of man, and found out the beginning of " all things, will also, of his own mercy, give you " breath and life again, as ye now regard not your " own selves for his law's sake." Our body is itself a mystery, in which the human mind is lost and overwhelmed, and of which the secrets shall never be fathomed; for there is none but him alone who hath presided at its formation, who is capable of comprehending them.

That breath of the divinity which animates us, that portion of ourselves which renders us capable of loving and of knowing, is not less unknown to us: we are entirely ignorant how its desires, its fears, its hopes, are formed, and how it can give to itself

self its ideas and images. No one hath hitherto been able to comprehend how that spiritual being, so different in its nature from matter, hath possibly been united in us with it by such indissoluble ties, that the two substances no longer form but one whole, and the good and evil of the one become the good and evil of the other. We are a mystery therefore to ourselves, as St Augustin formerly said; and we would be difficulted to say, what is even that vain curiosity which pries into every thing, or how it hath been formed in our soul.

In all around us we still find nothing but enigmas; we live as strangers upon the earth, and amid objects which we know not. To man, nature is a closed book; and the Creator, to confound, it would appear, human pride, hath been pleased to overspread the face of this abyss with an impenetrable obscurity.

Lift up thine eyes, O man! Consider those grand luminaries suspended over your head, and which swim, as I may say, through those immense spaces in which thy reason is lost. Who, says Job, hath formed the sun, and given a name to the infinite multitude of stars? Comprehend, if thou can, their nature, their use, their properties, their situation, their distance, their revolutions, the equality or the inequality of their movements. Our age hath penetrated a little into their obscurity, that is to say, it hath a little better conjectured upon them than the

the preceding ages; but what are its difcoveries, when compared to what we are ftill ignorant of?

Defcend upon the earth, and tell us, if thou know, what it is that keeps the winds bound up; what regulates the courfe of the thunders and of the tempefts; what is the fatal boundary which places its mark, and fays to the rufhing waves, "Here you fhall go, and no farther;" and how the prodigy fo regular of its movements is formed; explain to us the furprifing effects of plants, of metals, of the elements; find out in what manner gold is purified in the bowels of the earth; unravel, if thou can, the infinite fkill employed in the formation of the very infects which crawl before us; give us an explanation of the various inftincts of animals; turn on every fide; nature in all her parts offers nothing to thee but enigmas. O man! thou knoweft nothing of the objects, even under thine eyes, and thou wouldft pretend to fathom the eternal depths of faith? Nature is a myftery to thee, and thou wouldft have a religion which had none? Thou art ignorant of the fecrets of man, and thou wouldft pretend to know the fecrets of God? Thou knoweft not thyfelf, and thou wouldft pretend to fathom what is fo much above thee? The univerfe, which God hath yielded up to thy curiofity and to thy difputes, is an abyfs in which thou art loft; and thou wouldft that the myfteries of faith, which he hath folely expofed to thy docility and to thy refpect, fhould have nothing which surpasses thy feeble lights? O blindness! were every thing, excepting religion, clear and evident, thou then, with some shew of reason, mightst mistrust its obscurities; but since every thing around thee is a labyrinth in which thou art bewildered, ought not the secret of God, as St Augustin formerly said, to render thee more respectful and more attentive, far from being more incredulous?

The necessity of faith is, therefore, founded, in the first place, upon the weakness of reason; but it is likewise founded upon its profound depravity. And, in effect, what was more natural to man, than to confess his God the author of his being and of his felicity, his end and his principle; than to adore his wisdom, his power, his goodness, and all those divine perfections of which he hath engraven upon his work such profound and evident marks? These lights were born with us. Nevertheless, review all those ages of darkness and of superstition which preceded the gospel, and see how far man had degraded his Creator, and to what he had likened his God. There was nothing so vile in the created world but his impiety erected into gods, and man was the noblest divinity which was worshipped by man.

If, from religion, you pass to the morality, all the principles of natural equity were effaced, and man no longer bore, written in his heart, the work of that law which nature has engraven on it. Plato, even that man so wise, and who, according to St Auguſtin, had ſo nearly approached to the truth, neverthelefs aboliſhes the holy inſtitution of marriage; and, permitting a brutal confuſion among men, he for ever does away all paternal names and rights, which, even in animals, nature hath ſo evidently refpeſted; and gives to the earth men all uncertain of their origin, all coming into the world without parents, as I may ſay; and confequently without ties, tenderneſs, affection, or humanity; all in a ſituation to become inceſtuous or parricides, without even knowing it.

Others came to announce to men that voluptuoufneſs was the ſovereign good; and whatever might have been the intention of the firſt author of this ſect, it is certain that his difciples fought no other felicity than that of the brutes : the moſt ſhameful debaucheries became philofophical maxims. Rome, Athens, Corinth beheld exceſſes, where, it may be ſaid, that man was no longer man. Even this is nothing; the moſt abominable vices were confecrated there: temples and altars were erected to them: lafcivioufneſs, inceſt, cruelty, treachery, and other ſtill more abandoned crimes, were made divinities of: the worſhip became a public debauch and proſtitution; and gods, ſo criminal, were no longer honoured but by crimes; and the apoſtle, who relates them to us, takes care to inform us that ſuch was not merely the licentioufneſs of the people, but of ſages and philofophers who had erred in the vanity ty of their own thoughts, and whom God had delivered up to the corruption of their heart. O God! in permitting human reason to fall into such horrible errors, thou intended to let man know, that reason, when delivered up to its own darkness, is capable of every thing, and that it can never take upon itself to be its own guide, without plunging into abysses from which thy law and thy light are alone capable of withdrawing him.

Lastly, If the depravity of reason so evidently expose the necessity of a remedy to cure it, its eternal inconstancies and fluctuations yet more instruct man, that a check and a rule are absolutely requisite to fix it.

And here, my brethren, if the brevity of a discourse would permit all to be said, what vain disputes, what endless questions, what different opinions have formerly engrossed all the schools of the heathen philosophy! And think not that it was upon matters which God seems to have yielded up to the contestation of men; it was upon the nature even of God, upon his existence, upon the immortality of the soul, upon the true felicity.

Some doubted the whole; others believed that they knew every thing. Some denied a God; others gave us one of their own fashioning; that is to say, some of them slothful, an indolent spectator of human things, and tranquilly leaving to chance the management of his own work, as a care unworthy of his greatness, and incompatible
                                                                with

with his conveniency : fome others made him the flave of fates, and fubject to laws which he had no hand in impofing upon himfelf: others again incorporated, with the whole univerfe, the foul of that vaft body, and compofing, as it were, a part of that world which is entirely his work. Many others of which I know nothing, for I pretend not to recapitulate them all ; but as many fchools, .fo many were the fentiments upon fo effential a point. So many ages, fo many frefh abfurdities upon the immortality and the nature of the foul; here, it was an affemblage of atoms ; there, a fubtile fire ; in another place, a minnte and penetrating air ; in another fchool, a portion of the divinity. Some made it to die with the body ; others would have it to have exifted before the body : fome again made it to pafs from one body to another ; from man to the horfe, from the condition of a reafonable being to that of animals without reafon. There were fome who taught that the true happinefs of man is in the fenfes; a greater number placed it in the reafon ; others again found it only in fame and glory ; many in floth and indolence. And what is the moft deplorable here, is, that the exiftence of God, his nature, the immortality of the foul, the deftination and the happinefs of men, all points fo effential to his deftiny, fo decifive with regard to his eternal mifery or happinefs, were neverthelefs become problems, every where deftined merely to amufe the leifure of the fchools

and

and the vanity of the Sophists; idle questions, in which they were never interested for the principle of truth, but solely for the glory of coming off conqueror. Great God! It is in this manner that thou sportest with human wisdom.

If from thence we entered into the Christian ages, who could enumerate that endless variety of sects which, in all times, hath broken the unity, in order to follow strange doctrines? What were the abominations of the Gnosticks, the extravagant follies of the Valentinians, the fanaticism of Montanus, the contradictions of the Manicheans? Follow every age; as, in order to prove the just, it is necessary that there be heresies, You will find that in every age the church hath always been miserably rent with them.

Recall to your remembrance the sad dissentions of only the past age. Since the separation of our brethren, what a monstrous variety in their doctrine! What endless sects sprung from only one sect! What numberless particular assemblies in one same schism! O faith! O gift of God! O divine torch, which comes to clear up darkness, how necessary art thou to man! O infallible rule, sent from heaven, and given in trust to the church of Jesus Christ, always the same in all ages, always independant of places, of times, of nations, and of interests, how requisite it is that thou served as a check upon the eternal fluctuations of the human mind! O pillar of fire, at same time so obscure and

so

so luminous, of what importance it is that thou always conducted the camp of the Lord, the tabernacle and the tents of Israel, through all the perils of the desert, the rocks, the temptations, and the dark and unknown paths of this life!

For you, my brethren, what instruction should we draw from this discourse, and what should I say to you in concluding? You say that you have faith; shew your faith by your works. What shall it avail you to have believed, if your manners have belied your belief? The gospel is yet more the religion of the heart than of the mind. That faith which makes Christians is not a simple submission of the reason; it is a pious tenderness of the soul; it is a continual longing to become like unto Jesus Christ; it is an indefatigable application in rooting out from ourselves whatever may be inimical to a life of faith. There is an unbelief of the heart, equally dangerous to salvation as that of the mind. A man who obstinately refuses belief, after all the proofs of religion, is a monster, whom we contemplate with horror; but a Christian who believes, yet lives as though he believed not, is a madman, whose folly compasseth comprehension: the one procures his own condemnation, like a man desperate; the other, like an indolent one, who tranquilly allows himself to be carried down by the waves, and thinks that he is thereby saving himself. Make your faith then certain, my brethren, by your good works; and if you shudder at the sole name

name of an impious perfon, have the fame horror at yourfelves, feeing we are taught by faith, that the deftiny of the wicked Chriftian fhall not be different from his, and that his lot fhall be the fame as that of the unbeliever. Live conformably to what you believe. Such is the faith of the righteous, and the only one to which the eternal promifes have been made.

SERMON II.

DOUBTS UPON RELIGION.

JOHN vii. 27.

Howbeit we know this man, whence he is; but when Chrift cometh, no man knoweth whence he is.

SUCH is the grand pretext oppofed by the unbelief of the Jews to the doctrine and to the miniftry of Jefus Chrift; doubts upon the truth of his miffion. We know who thou art, and whence thou comeft, faid they to him; but the Chrift whom we expect, when he cometh, no man knoweth whence he is. It is far from clear, then, that thou art the Meffiah promifed to our fathers; perhaps it is an evil fpirit which, through thee, operates thefe wonders before our eyes, and impofes upon the credulity of the vulgar; fo many deceivers have already appeared in Judea, who, giving themfelves out for the Great Prophet who is to come, have seduced the people, and at last drawn down upon themselves the punishment due to their imposture. Keep us no longer in doubt: if thou be the Christ, tell us plainly, and in such a way as that room shall no longer be left either for doubt or for mistake.

I would not dare to say this here, my brethren, were the language of doubts upon faith not become so common now among us, that precaution is needless in undertaking to confute it: behold the almost universal pretext employed in the world to authorise a life altogether criminal. We every where meet with sinners who coolly tell us, that they would be converted were they well assured that all we tell them of religion were true; that perhaps there is nothing after this life; that they have doubts and difficulties upon our mysteries, to which they can find no satisfactory answer; that, after all, the whole appears very uncertain; and that, before engaging to follow all the rigid maxims of the gospel, it would be proper to be well assured that our toils shall not be lost.

Now, my intention at present is not to overthrow unbelief, by the grand proofs which establish the truth of the Christian faith: setting aside that elsewhere we have already established them, it is a subject far too extensive for a discourse, and often beyond even the capacity of the majority of those who listen to us; it is frequently paying too much deference to the frivolous objections of those who

who give themselves out as freethinkers in the world, to employ the gravity of our miniſtry in refuting and overthrowing them.

We muſt take a ſhorter and more eaſy way, therefore, at preſent. My deſign is not to enter into the foundation of the proofs which render teſtimony to the truth of faith; I mean only to expoſe the falſity of unbelief: I mean to prove that the greateſt part of thoſe who call themſelves unbelievers, are not ſo; that almoſt all thoſe ſinners who vaunt, and are continually alleging to us their doubts, as the only obſtacle to their converſion, have actually none; and that, of all the pretexts employed as an excuſe for not changing their life, that of doubts upon religion, now the moſt common, is the leaſt true and the leaſt ſincere.

It appears ſurpriſing at firſt that I ſhould undertake to prove to thoſe who believe to have doubts upon religion, and are continually objecting them to us, that they have actually none: neverthelefs, with a proper knowledge of men, and, above all, with a proper attention to the character of thoſe who make a boaſt of doubting, nothing is more eaſy than this conviction. I ſay to their character, in which are always to be found licentiouſneſs, ignorance, and vanity; and ſuch are the three uſual ſources of their doubts: they give the credit of them to unbelief, which has ſcarcely a ſhare in them.

1ſtly,

1stly, It is licentiousness which proposes, without daring to believe them. First reflection.

2dly, It is ignorance which adopts, without comprehending them. Second reflection.

Lastly, It is vanity which boasts, without being able to succeed in drawing any resource from them. Last reflection.

That is to say, that the greatest part of those who call themselves unbelievers, are licentious enough to wish to be so; too ignorant to be so in reality; and, nevertheless, sufficiently vain to wish to appear so. Let us unfold these three reflections, now become so important among us; and let us overthrow licentiousness rather than unbelief, by laying it open to itself.

PART I. It must at once be admitted, my brethren, and it is melancholy for us that we owe this confession to the truth: it must be admitted, I say, that our age and those of our fathers have seen real unbelievers. In that depravity of manners in which we live, and amid all the scandals which have so long afflicted the church, it is not surprising that men have sometimes been found who have denied the existence of a God; and that faith so weakened in all, should, in some, be at last wholly extinguished. As chosen and extraordinary souls appear in every age, whom the Lord filleth with his grace, his lights, and his most shining gifts, and upon whom he delighteth in liberally pouring forth all the riches of his mercy; so,

likewise,

likewife, are feen others in whom iniquity is, as I may fay, confummate; and whom the Lord feems to have marked out, to difplay in them the moſt terrible judgments of his juſtice, and the moſt fatal effects of his neglect and wrath.

The church, where all thefe fcandals are to increafe even to the end, cannot, therefore, boaſt of being entirely purged from the fcandal of unbelief: ſhe hath, from time to time, her ſtars which enlighten, and her monſters who disfigure her; and, along with thofe great men, celebrated for their lights and for their fanctity, who in every age have ferved as her fupport and ornament, ſhe hath alfo witneſſed a liſt of impious men, whofe names are ſtill at prefent the horror of the univerfe, who have dared, in writings full of blafphemy and impiety, to attack the myſteries of God, to deny falvation and the promifes made to our fathers, to overturn the foundation of faith, and to preach free-thinking among believers.

I do not pretend, therefore, to fay, that, among fo many wretches who fpeak the language of unbelief among us, there may not perhaps be found fome one fufficiently corrupted in mind and in heart, and fo far abandoned by God, as actually and in effect to be an unbeliever: I mean only to eſtabliſh, that thefe men grounded in impiety are rare; and that, among all thofe who are continually vaunting their doubts and their unbelief, and make a deplorable oſtentation of them, there is

not

not perhaps a single one upon whose heart faith doth not still preserve its rights, and who doth not inwardly dread that God whom he apparently refuses to acknowledge. To overthrow, it is not always necessary to combat our pretended unbelievers; it would often be combating only phantoms: they require only to be displayed such as they are: the wretched decoration of unbelief quickly tumbles down, and nothing remains but their passions and their debaucheries.

And behold the first reason upon which I have established the general proposition, that the majority of those who make a boast of their doubts have actually none; it is, that their doubts are those of licentiousness, and not of unbelief. Why, my brethren? Because it is licentiousness which hath formed their doubts, and not their doubts licentiousness; because that, in fact, it is to their passions and not to their doubts that they hold; lastly, because that, in general, they attack in religion only those truths inimical to their passions. Behold reflections which in my opinion are worthy of your attention; I shall lay them before you without ornament, and in the same order in which they presented themselves to my mind.

I say, in the first place; because their doubts have sprung from licentiousness, and not licentiousness from their doubts. Yes, my brethren, not one of all those who affect to profess themselves unbelievers has ever been seen to begin by
doubts

doubts upon the truths of faith, and afterwards from doubts to fall into licentiousness: they begin with the passions; doubts come afterwards: they first give way to the irregularities of the age, and to the excesses of debauchery; and when attained to a certain length, and they find it no longer possible to return upon their steps, they then say, in order to quiet themselves, that there is nothing after this life, or, at least, they are well pleased to find people who say so. It is not, therefore, the little certainty they find in religion which authorises their conclusion that we ought to yield ourselves up to pleasure, and that self-denial is needless, since every thing dies with us: it is the yielding of themselves up to pleasure which creates doubts upon religion, and, by rendering self-denial next to impossible, leads them to conclude that, consequently, it is needless. Faith becomes suspected only when it begins to be troublesome; and, to this day, unbelief hath never made a voluptuary; but voluptuousness hath made almost all the unbelievers.

And a proof of what I say, you whom this discourse regards, is that, while you have lived with modesty and innocence, you never doubted. Recollect those happy times when the passions had not yet corrupted your heart; the faith of your fathers had then nothing but what was august and respectable; reason bent without pain to the yoke of authority; you never thought of doubts or difficulties:

ficulties: from the moment your manners changed, your views upon religion have no longer been the same. It is not faith, therefore, which hath found new difficulties in your reason; it is the practice of duties which hath encountered new obstacles in your heart. And should you tell us, that your first impressions, so favourable to faith, sprung solely from the prejudices of education and of childhood, we shall answer, that the second, so favourable to impiety, have sprung solely from the prejudices of the passions and of debauchery; and that, prejudices for prejudices, it appears to us, that it is still better to keep by those which are formed in innocence and lead us to virtue, than to those which are born in the infamy of the passions, and preach up only freethinking and guilt.

Thus nothing is more humiliating for unbelief than recalling it to its origin: it bears a false name of learning and of light: and it is a child of iniquity and of darkness. It is not the strength of reason which has led our pretended unbelievers to skepticism; it is the weakness of a corrupted heart which has been unable to surmount its infamous passions; it is even a mean cowardliness which, unable to support and to view with a steady eye the terrors and the threatenings of religion, endeavours to shake off their thoughts by continually repeating that they are childish terrors; it is a man who, afraid of the night, sings as he goes along

along to prevent himself from thinking: debauchery always makes us cowardly and fearful; and it is nothing but an excess of fear of eternal punishments which occasions a sinner to be continually preaching up and singing to us that they are doubtful; he trembles, and wishes to strengthen himself against himself; he cannot support, at the same time, the view of his crimes, and that of the punishment which awaits them; that faith, so venerable, and of which he speaks with such contempt, nevertheless terrifies and disquiets him still more than those other sinners who, without doubting its punishments, yet are frequently not less unfaithful to its precepts: it is a coward who hides his fear under a false ostentation of bravery. No, my brethren, our pretended free-thinkers give themselves out as men of courage and firmness; examine them narrowly, and they are the weakest and most cowardly of men.

Besides, it is not surprising that licentiousness lead us to doubt of religion: the passions require the aid of unbelief; for they are too feeble and too unreasonable to maintain their own cause. Our lights, our feelings, our conscience, all struggle within us against them: we are under the necessity, therefore, of seeking a support for them, and of defending them against ourselves: for, it is a matter of satisfaction, to justify to one's self whatever is pleasing. We would neither wish that passions which are dear to us should be criminal, nor that we should continually to have to support the interests of our pleasures against those of our conscience: we wish tranquilly to enjoy our crimes, and to free ourselves from that troublesome monitor which continually espouses the cause of virtue against ourselves: while remorses contest the pleasure of our enjoyments, they must be very imperfectly tasted: it is paying too great a price for guilt, to purchase it at the expence of that quiet which is sought in it: we must either terminate our debaucheries, or try to quiet ourselves in them; and as it is impossible to enjoy peace of mind in them, and next to impossible to terminate them, the only refuge seems that of doubting the truths which disquiet us; and, in order to attain to tranquility, every effort is used to inculcate the persuasion of unbelief.

That is to say, that the great effort of licentiousness is that of leading us to the desire of unbelief: the horrible security of the unbeliever is coveted; total hardness of heart is considered as a happy state; it is unpleasant to have been born with a weaker and more fearful conscience; the lot of those, apparently firm and unshaken in impiety, is envied; while they, in their turn, perhaps a prey to the most gloomy remorses, and vaunting a courage they are far from having, view our lot with envy; for, judging of us from the language we hold upon free-thinking, they take us for what we take them, that is to say, for what we are not,

and

and for what both they and we would wish to be.
And it is thus, O my God! that these false heroes
of impiety live in a perpetual illusion, continually
deceive themselves, and appear what they are not,
only because they would wish to be it: they would
willingly have religion to be but a dream: they
say in their heart " There is no God;" that is to
say, this impious language is the desire of their
heart: they would ardently wish no God; that
that Being, so grand and so necessary, were a chimera; that they were the sole masters of their own
destiny; that they were accountable only to themselves for the horrors of their life and the infamy
of their passions; that all finished with them; and
that, beyond the grave, there were no supreme and
eternal Judge, the punisher of vice and the re-
warder of virtue: they wish it; they destroy as
much as they can through the impious wishes of
their heart, but they cannot efface, from the foundation of their being, the idea of his power and
the dread of his punishments.

In effect, it would be too vulgar for a man,
vain and plunged in debauchery, inwardly to say
to himself: I am still too weak, and too much
abandoned to pleasure, to quit it, or to lead a
more regular and Christian life. That pretext
would still leave all his remorses: it is much sooner done to say to himself, It is needless to live
otherwise, for there is nothing after this life. This
pretext is far more convenient, for it puts an end

to every thing; it is the moſt favourable to indolence, for it eſtranges us from the ſacraments, and from all the other ſlaveries of religion. It is much ſhorter to ſay to himſelf, "There is nothing," and to live as if he were in effect perſuaded of it; it is at once throwing off every yoke and all reſtraint; it puts an end to all the irkſome meaſures which ſinners of another deſcription ſtill guard with religion and with the conſcience. This pretext of unbelief, by perſuading us that we actually doubt, leaves us in a certain ſtate of indolence on every thing regarding religion, which prevents us from ſearching into ourſelves, and from making too melancholy reflections on our paſſions: we meanly allow ourſelves to be ſwept away by the fatal courſe, upon the general prepoſſeſſion that we believe nothing; we have few remorſes, for we think ourſelves unbelievers, and becauſe that ſuppoſition leaves us almoſt the ſame ſecurity as impiety: at leaſt, it is a diverſion which dulls and ſuſpends the ſenſibility of the conſcience; and, by operating ſo as to make us always take ourſelves for what we are not, it induces us to live as if we actually were what we wiſh to be.

That is to ſay, that the greateſt part of theſe pretended free-thinkers, and of theſe debauched and licentious unbelievers, ought to be conſidered as weak and diſſolute men, who, not having the force to live chriſtianly, nor even the hardineſs to be atheiſts, remain in that ſtate of eſtrangement from religion,

religion, as the moſt convenient to indolence; and, as they never try to quit it, they fancy that they actually hold to it: it is a kind of neutrality betwixt faith and irreligion, contrived by indolence for its own eaſe; for it requires exertion to adopt a party; and, in order to remain neuter, nothing more is required than not to think, and to live by habit; thus they never fathom, nor take any reſolution upon themſelves. Hardened and avowed impiety hath ſomething, I know not what, which ſtrikes with horror: religion, on the other hand, preſents objects which alarm, and are by no means convenient to the paſſions. What is to be done in theſe two extremities, of which the one ſhocks reaſon, and the other ſenſes? They reſt wavering and undecided; in the mean time they enjoy the calm which is left by that ſtate of indeciſion and indifference: they live without wiſhing to know what they are; for it is much more convenient to be nothing, and to live without thinking, or any knowledge of themſelves. No, my brethren, I repeat it; theſe are not unbelievers, they are cowards, who have not the courage to eſpouſe a party; who know only to live voluptuouſly, without rule, without morality, and often without decency; and who, without being atheiſts, live however without religion, for religion requires conſiſtency, reaſon, elevation of mind, firmneſs, noble ſentiments, and of all theſe they are incapable. Such, however, are the heroes of whom impiety boaſts; behold the

ſuffrages

suffrages upon which it grounds its defence, and opposes to religion, by insulting us; behold the partisans with whom it thinks itself invincible; and weak and wretched must its resources indeed be, since it is reduced to seek them in men of this description.

First reason which proves that licentiousness springs not from doubts, but doubts from licentiousness. The second reason is only a fresh proof of the first; it is that actually, if they do not change their life, it is not to their doubts, but solely to their passions that they hold.

For I ask nothing of you here but candour, you who continually allege your doubts upon our mysteries. When you sometimes think of quitting that sink of vice and debauchery in which you live, and when the passions, more tranquil, allow you to reflect, do you then oppose your uncertainties upon religion? Do you say to yourselves, " But " if I return it will be necessary to believe things " which seem incredible?" Is this the grand difficulty? Ah! you inwardly say, but if I return it will be necessary to break off this connection, to deny myself these excesses, to terminate these societies, to shun these places, to proceed to things which I shall never support, and to adopt a manner of life to which all my inclinations are repugnant. These are what check you; these are the wall of separation which removes you from God. You speak so much to others of your doubts; how

comes

comes it that you never speak of them to yourselves? This is not a matter, therefore, of reason and of belief; it is a matter of the heart and of licentiousness; and the delay of your conversion springs not from your uncertainties upon faith, but from the sole doubt in which the violence and the empire of your passions leave you of ever being able to free yourselves from their subjection and infamy. Such, my brethren, are the true chains which bind our pretended unbelievers to their own wretchedness.

And this truth is more evident from this, that the majority of those who profess themselves unbelievers, live, nevertheless, in perpetual variations upon the point even of unbelief. In certain moments they are affected with the truths of religion: they feel themselves torn with the keenest remorses; they even apply to the servants of God most distinguished for their learning and piety, to hold converse with, and receive instructions from them: in others, they make game of these truths; they treat the servants of God with derision, and piety itself as a chimera: there is scarcely one of these sinners, even of those who make the greatest ostentation of their unbelief, whom the spectacle of an unexpected death, a fatal accident, a grievous loss, or a reverse of fortune hath not cast into gloomy reflections on his situation, and excited desires of a more Christian life; there is hardly one who, in these trying situations, seeks not consolation in the
support

support of the godly, and take not some step which leaves hopes of amendment. It is not to their companions in impiety and licentiousness that they then have recourse for consolation; it is not by those impious railleries upon our mysteries, and by that horrible philosophy that they try to alleviate their sufferings: these are discourses of festivity and dissipation, and not of affliction and sorrow: it is the religion of the table, of pleasures, of riotings; it is not that of solemn adversity and sadness: the relish of impiety vanishes with that of pleasures. Now, if their unbelief were founded in real uncertainties upon religion, so long as these uncertainties existed, unbelief should be the same; but as their doubts spring only from their passions, and as their passions are not always the same, nor equally violent and masters of their heart, so their doubts continually fluctuate like their passions; they increase, they diminish, they are eclipsed, they reappear, they are mutable, exactly in the same degree as their passions; in a word, they share the lot of the passions, for they are nothing but the passions themselves.

In effect, to leave nothing unsaid on this subject, and to make you thoroughly feel how much this vaunted profession of unbelief is despicable, observe that, reply to every difficulty of the boasting sinner, reduce him to have nothing more to say, and yet still he does not yield; you have not thereby by gained him; he retires within himself, as if he had still more overpowering reasons which he disdains to bring forward: he keeps firm, and opposes a mysterious and decisive air to all those proofs which he cannot resolve. You then pity his madness and obstinacy: you are mistaken; be touched only for his libertine life, and his want of candour; for, let a mortal disease strike him on quitting you; approach his bed of anguish, ah! you will find this pretended unbeliever convinced; his doubts cease, his uncertainties end, all that deplorable display of unbelief vanishes and tumbles in pieces; there is no longer even question of it; he has recourse to the God of his fathers, and trembles at the judgments he made a shew of not believing. The minister of Jesus Christ, called in, has no occasion to enter into controversy to undeceive him on his impiety: the dying sinner anticipates his cares and his ministry: he is ashamed of his past blasphemies, and repents of them; he acknowledges their falsity and deception; he makes a public reparation of them to the majesty and to the truth of religion; he no longer demands proofs, he asks only consolations. Nevertheless, this disease hath not brought new lights upon faith; the blow which strikes his flesh has not cleared up the doubts of his mind; ah! it is because it touches his heart, and terminates his riots; in a word, it is that his doubts were in his passions, and that whatever tends to extinguish his passions, tends, at the same time, to extinguish his doubts.

It happens, I confess, that sinners are sometimes found, who push their madness and impiety even to that last moment: who expire in vomiting forth with their impious soul, blasphemies against the God who is to judge them, and whom they refuse to acknowledge. For, O my God! thou art terrible in thy judgments, and sometimes permittest that the atheist die in his impiety. But such examples are rare; and you well know, my brethren, that an entire age scarcely furnishes one of these shocking spectacles. But view, in that last moment, all the others who vaunted their unbelief; see a sinner on the bed of death, who had hitherto appeared the firmest in impiety, and the most resolute in denying all belief; he even anticipates the proposal of having recourse to the church remedies: he lifts up his hands to heaven, and gives striking and sincere marks of a religion which was never effaced from the bottom of his heart; he no longer rejects, as childish bugbears, the threatenings and chastisements of a future life; what do I say? this sinner, formerly so firm, so stately in his pretended unbelief, so much above the vulgar fears, then becomes weaker, more fearful, and more credulous than the lowest of the people; his fears are more excessive, his very religion more superstitious, his practices of worship more silly, and more extravagant than those of the
vulgar;

vulgar; and as one excefs borders on its oppofite excefs, he is feen to pafs in a moment from impiety to fuperftition; from the firmnefs of the philofopher, to all the weaknefs of the ignorant and fimple.

And here it is that, with Tertullian, I would appeal to this dying finner, and let him hold forth, in my ftead, againft unbelief; it is here that, to the honour of the religion of our fathers, I would wifh no other teftimony of the weaknefs and of the infincerity of the pretended 'atheift, than this expiring foul, who, furely now, can fpeak only the language of truth; it is here that I would affemble all unbelievers around his bed of death; and, to overthrow them by a teftimony which could not be fufpicious, would fay to him, with Tertullian: " O foul! before thou quitteft this
" earthly body, which thou art fo foon to be freed
" from, fuffer me to call upon thy teftimony:
" fpeak, in this laft moment, when vanity is no
" more, and thou oweft all to the truth; fay, if
" thou confidereft the terrible God, into whofe
" hands thou goeft, as a chimerical being with
" whom weak and credulous minds are alarmed?
" Say, if, all now difappearing from thine eyes,
" if, for thee, all creatures returning to nothing,
" God alone doth not appear to thee immortal,
" unchangeable, the being of all ages and of eter-
" nity, and who filleth the heavens and the earth?
" We now confent, we, whom thou haft always
" confidered

"considered as superstitious and vulgar minds,
"we consent that thou judge betwixt us and un-
"belief, to which thou hast ever been so partial.
"Though, with regard to faith, thou hast hither-
"to been as a stranger and the enemy of religion,
"religion refers its cause to thee, against those
"with whom the shocking tie of impiety had so
"closely united thee. If all die with thee, why
"does death appear so dreadful? Why these up-
"lifted hands to heaven, if there be no God who
"may listen to thy prayers, and be touched by
"thy groanings? If nothing thyself, why belie
"the nothingness of thy being, and why tremble
"upon the sequel of thy destiny? Whence come,
"in this last moment, these feelings of dread and
"of respect for the supreme Being? Is it not, that
"they have ever been in thee, that thou hast im-
"posed upon the public by a false ostentation of
"impiety, and that death only unfolds those dis-
"positions of faith and of religion, which, though
"dormant, have never ceased during life."

Yes, my brethren, could the passions be destroyed, all unbelievers would soon be recalled; and a
final reason, which fully proves it, is that, if they
seem to rise up against the incomprehensibility of
our mysteries, it is solely for the purpose of combating what touches them, and of attacking the
truths which interest the passions; that is to say,
the truth of a future state, and the eternity of future

ture punishments; this is always the favourite conclusion and fruit of their doubts.

In effect, if religion, without adding maxims and truths which restrain the passions, proposed only mysteries which exceed reason, we may boldly say, that unbelievers would be rare; almost no one is interested in those abstruse truths or errors, which it is indifferent to believe or to deny. You will find few real votaries of truth who become partisans and zealots in support of merely speculative and unimportant points, because they believe them to be true. The abstruse truths of mathematics have found, in our days, some zealous and estimable followers who have devoted themselves to the elucidation of what is held as most impenetrable in the infinite secrets and profound obscurities of that science; but these are rare and singular men: the infection was little to be dreaded, nor, in truth, has it spread; they are admired, but few would wish to follow their example. If religion proposed only truths equally abstruse, equally indifferent to the felicity of the senses, equally uninteresting to the passions and to self-love, the atheists would be still more rare than the mathematicians. The truths of religion are objected to, merely because they threaten us: no objections are made to the others, because their truth or their falsity is alike indifferent.

And tell us not that it is not through self-interest, but the sole love of truth, that the unbeliever rejects

rejects mysteries which reason rejects. This, I well know, is the boast of the pretended unbeliever, and he would wish us to think so; but of what consequence is the truth to men, who, so far from either seeking, loving, or knowing it, wish even to conceal it from themselves? What matters to them a truth beyond their reach, and to which they have never devoted a single serious moment; which, having nothing flattering to the passions, can never be interesting to these men of flesh and blood, plunged in a voluptuous life? Their object is to gratify their irregular desires, and yet have nothing to dread after this life; this is the only truth which interests them: give up that point, and the obscurity of all the other mysteries will not occupy even a thought; let them but tranquilly enjoy their crimes, and they will agree to every thing.

Thus the majority of atheists, who have left in writing the wretched fruits of their impiety, have always strove to prove that there was nothing above us; that all died with the body, and that future punishments or rewards were fables; to attract followers it was necessary to secure the suffrage of the passions. If ever they attacked the other points of religion, it was only to come to the main conclusion, that there is nothing after this life; that vices or virtues are names invented by policy to restrain the people; and that the passions are only natural and innocent inclinations, which every one

may

may follow, becaufe every one finds them in himfelf.

Behold why the impious, in the book of Wifdom, the Sadducees themfelves, in the gofpel, who may be confidered as the fathers and predeceffors of our unbelievers, never took any pains to refute the truth of the miracles related in the books of Mofes, and which God formerly wrought in favour of his people, nor the promife of the Mediator made to their fathers: they attacked only the refurrection of the dead, and the immortality of the foul: that point decided every thing for them. "Man dies like the beaft," faid they in the book of Wifdom; "we know not if their nature be "different, but their end and their lot are the "fame: trouble us no more, therefore, with a fu- "turity which is not; let us enjoy life; let us re- "fufe ourfelves no gratification: time is fhort; let "us haften to live, for we fhall die to-morrow, "and becaufe all fhall die with us." No, my brethren, unbelief hath always originated in the paffions: the yoke of faith is never rejected but in order to fhake off the yoke of duties; and religion would never have an enemy, were it not the enemy of licentioufnefs and vice.

But if the doubts of our unbelievers are not real, in confequence of being formed folely by licentioufnefs, they are alfo falfe, becaufe it is ignorance which adopts without comprehending them, and vanity which makes a boaft without being able to

make

make a resource of them: this is what now remains to me to unfold.

Part II. The same answer might be made to the majority of those who are continually vaunting their doubts upon religion, and find nothing but contradictions in what faith obliges us to believe, that Tertullian formerly made to the heathens upon all the reproaches they invented against the mysteries and the doctrine of Jesus Christ. They condemn, said he, what they do not understand; they blame what they have never examined, and what they know only by hearsay; they blaspheme what they are ignorant of, and they are ignorant of it, because they hate it too much to give themselves the trouble of searching into and knowing it. Now, continues this father, nothing is more indecent and foolish than boldly to decide upon what they know not; and all that religion would require of these frivolous and dissolute men, who so warmly rise up against it, is not to condemn before they are well acquainted with it.

Such, my brethren, is the situation of almost all who give themselves out in the world as unbelievers; they have investigated neither the difficulties nor the respectable proofs of religion; they know not even enough to doubt of them. They hate it; for how is it possible to love our condemnation? and upon that hatred are founded their doubts and their only arguments to oppose it.

In

In effect, when I glance my eye over all that the Chriftian ages have had of great men, elevated geniufes, profound and enlightened fcholars, who, after an entire life of ftudy and indefatigable application, have, with an humble docility, fubmitted to the myfteries of faith; have found the proofs of religion fo ftrong, that the proudeft and moft untractable reafon might, in their opinion, without derogation, comply; have defended it againft the blafphemies of the pagans; have filenced the vain philofophy of the fages of the age, and made the folly of the crofs to triumph over all the wifdom and erudition of Rome and Athens; it ftrikes me, that, in order to renew the attack againft myfteries fo long and fo univerfally eftablifhed; that, in order to be heard in appeal, if I may venture to fay fo, from the fubmiffion of fo many ages, from the writings of fo many great men, from fo many victories atchieved by faith, from the confent of the univerfe; in a word, from a prefcription fo long and fo well ftrengthened, it would require either new proofs that had never yet been controverted, or new difficulties that had never yet been ftarted, or new methods which difcovered a weak fide in religion as yet never found out. It feems to me, that, fingly to rife up againft fo many teftimonies, fo many prodigies, fo many ages, fo many divine monuments, fo many famous perfonages, fo many works which time hath confecrated, and which, like pure gold, have quitted the ordeal of unbelief only more refplendid and immortal; in a word, fo many furprifing, and till then unheard of, events, which eftablifh the faith of Chriftians, it would require very decifive and very evident reafons, very rare and new lights, to pretend even to doubt, much lefs to oppofe it. Would not that man be defervedly confidered as out of his fenfes, who fhould go to defy an whole army, merely to make an oftentation of a vain defiance, and to pride himfelf upon a burlefque bravery?

Neverthelefs, when you examine the majority of thofe who call themfelves unbelievers, who are continually clamouring againft the popular prejudices, who vaunt their doubts, and defy us to fatisfy or to anfwer them; you find that their only knowledge confifts of fome hackneyed and vulgar doubts, which, in all times, have been, and ftill continue to be, argued in the world; that they know nothing but a certain jargon of licentioufnefs which goes from hand to hand, which they receive without examination and repeat without underftanding: you find that their whole fkill and ftudy of religion are reduced to fome licentious fayings, which, if I may defcend fo low, are the proper language of the ftreets; to certain maxims which, through mere repetition, begin to relifh of proverbial meannefs. You will find no foundation, no principle, no fequence of doctrine, no knowledge even of the religion which they attack: they are men immerfed in pleafure, and who

who would be very forry to have a fpare moment
to devote to the inveftigation of wearifome truths
which they are indifferent whether they know or
not ; men of a light and fuperficial character, and
wholly unfitted for a moment's ferious meditation
or inveftigation ; let me again repeat, men drowned in voluptuoufnefs, and in whom even that portion of penetration and underftanding, accorded
by nature, hath been debafed and extinguifhed by
debauchery.

Such are the formidable fupports of unbelief
againft the knowledge of God : behold the frivolous, diffipated, and ignorant characters who dare
to tax, with credulity and ignorance, all that the
Chriftian ages have had, and ftill have of learned,
able, and celebrated perfonages: they know the language of doubts ; but they have learned it by rote,
for they never formed them ; they only repeat
what they have heard : it is a tradition of ignorance and impiety : they have no doubts : they
only preferve, for thofe to come, the language of
irreligion and doubts ; they are not unbelievers,
they are only the echoes of unbelief; in a word,
they know how to exprefs a doubt, but they are
too ignorant to doubt themfelves.

And a proof of what I advance is, that, in all
other doubts, we hefitate only in order to be inftructed ; every thing is examined which can elucidate the concealed truth. But here the doubt is
merely for doubting's fake ; a proof that we are
equally

equally uninterested in the doubt, as in the truth
which it conceals from us; they would be very
sorry were they under the necessity of clearing up
either the falsity, or the truth of the uncertainties
which they pretend to have upon our mysteries.
Yes, my brethren, were the punishment of doubt-
ers to be that of an indispensible obligation to seek
the truth, no one would doubt; no one would
purchase, at such a price, the pleasure of calling
himself an unbeliever; few indeed would be capable of it: decisive proof that they do not doubt,
and that they are as little attached to their doubts
as to religion (for their knowledge in both is
much about the same); but only that they have
lost those first feelings of discretion and of faith
which left us still some vestige of respect for the
religion of our fathers. Thus, it is doing too
much honour to men, so worthy both of pity and
contempt, to suppose that they have taken a side,
that they have embraced a system; you honour
them too much by ranking them among the impious followers of a Socinus, by ennobling them
with the shocking titles of deists or atheists: alas!
they are nothing; they are of no system; at least,
they neither know themselves what they are, nor
can they tell us what that system is; and, strange
as it may appear, they have found out the secret
of forming a state more despicable, more mean,
and more unworthy of reason, than even that of
impiety; and it is even doing them credit to call

them

them by the shocking title of unbeliever, which had hitherto been considered as the shame of humanity, and the highest reproach of man.

And, to conclude this article with a reflection which confirms the same truth, and is very humiliating for our pretended unbelievers, I observe that they, who affect to treat us as weak and credulous minds, who vaunt their reason, who accuse us of grounding a religion upon the popular prejudices, and of believing, solely because our predecessors have believed; they, I say, are unbelievers, and doubt upon the sole and deplorable authority of a debauchee, whom they have often heard to say, that futurity is a bug-bear, and made use of as a scarecrow to frighten only children and the common people: such is their only knowlege, and their only use of reason. They are impious, as they accuse us of being believers without examination, and through credulousness; but through a credulity which can find no excuse but in madness and folly; the authority of a single impious discourse, pronounced in a bold and decisive tone, hath subjugated their reason, and ranked them in the lists of impiety. They call us credulous, in yielding to the authority of the prophets, of the apostles, of men inspired by God, of the shining miracles wrought to establish the truth of our mysteries, and to that venerable tradition of holy pastors, who, from age to age, have transmitted to us the charge of doctrine and of truth; that is

to

to say, to the greatest authority that hath ever been on the earth ; and they think themselves less credulous, and it appears to them more worthy of reason, to submit to the authority of a free-thinker, who, in a moment of debauchery, pronounces, with a firm tone, that there is no God, yet, most likely, inwardly belies his own words. Ah! my brethren, how much does man degrade and render himself contemptible when he arrrogates a false glory from being no longer in the belief of a God!

Thus, why is it, think you, that our pretended unbelievers are so desirous of seeing real atheists confirmed in impiety; that they seek and entice them even from foreign countries, like a Spinosa, if the fact be, that he was called into France to be heard and consulted? It is because our unbelievers are not firm in unbelief, nor can they find any who are so; and, in order to harden themselves, they would gladly see some one actually confirmed in that detestable cause : they seek, in precedent, resources and defences against their own conscience; and, not daring of themselves to become impious, they expect from an example what their reason and even their heart refuses; and, in so doing, they surely fall into a credulity much more childish and absurd than that with which they reproach believers. A Spinosa, that monster, who, after embracing various religions, ended with none, was not anxious to find out some professed free-
thinker

thinker who might confirm him in the caufe of irreligion and atheifm: he formed to himfelf that
impenetrable chaos of impiety, that work of confufion and darknefs in which the fole defire of not
believing in God can fupport the wearinefs and
difguft of thofe who read it; in which, excepting
the impiety, all is unintelligible; and which would,
from its birth, have funk into oblivion, had it not,
to the fhame of humanity, attacked the fupreme
Being: that impious wretch, I fay, lived concealed, retired, tranquil: his dark productions were
his only occupation, and, to harden himfelf, he
needed only himfelf. But thofe who fo eagerly
fought him, who longed to fee and confult him,
thofe frivolous and diffolute men were fools who
wifhed to become impious; and who, not finding
fufficient authority to remain believers in the teftimony of all ages, of all nations, and of all the
great men who have honoured religion, fought, in
the fingle teftimony of an obfcure individual, of a
deferter from every religion, of a monfter obliged
to hide himfelf from the eyes of men, a deplorable
and monftrous authority which might confirm them
in impiety, and defend them from their own confcience. Great God! let the impious here hide
their faces; let them ceafe to make an oftentation
of an unbelief which is the fruit of their depravity
and ignorance, and no longer fpeak, but with blufhes, of the fubmiffion of believers: it is all a language
of deceit; they give to vanity what we give to truth.

I fay

I say vanity; and this is the grand and final reason which more clearly exposes all the falsity and weakness of unbelief. Yes, my brethren, all our pretended unbelievers are bullies, who give themselves out for what they are not; they consider unbelief as conveying the idea of something above the common; they are continually boasting that they believe nothing, and, by dint of boasting, they at last persuade themselves of it: like certain mushroom characters among us, who, though touching the obscurity and vulgarity of their ancestors, have the deplorable vanity of wishing to be thought of an illustrious birth, and descended from the greatest names; by dint of blazoning and repeating it, they attain almost to the belief of it themselves. It is the same with our pretended unbelievers; they still touch, as I may say, that faith which they have received at their birth, which still flows with their blood, and is not yet effaced from their heart; but they think it a vulgarity and meanness, at which they blush; by dint of saying and boasting that they believe nothing, they are convinced that they really do not believe, and have consequently a much higher opinion of themselves.

1*stly*, Because that deplorable profession of unbelief supposes an uncommon understanding, strength and superiority of mind, and a singularity which is pleasing and flattering; on the contrary, that the passions infer only licentiousness and debauchery, of which all men are capable, though they are not so of that wonderful superiority attributed to itself by impiety.

2*dly,* Because faith is so weakened in our age, that we find few in the world, who pique themselves upon wit and a little more knowledge or erudition than others, who do not allow themselves doubts and difficulties upon the most august and most sacred parts of religion. It would be a disgrace, therefore, in their company to appear religious and believers: they are men high in the public esteem, and any resemblance to them is flattering; in adopting their language, their talents and reputation are thought likewise to be adopted; and not to dare to follow or to copy them would, it seems, be making a public avowal of weakness and mediocrity: miserable and childish vanity! Besides, because they have heard say that certain characters distinguished in their age did not believe; and as the memory of their talents and great actions has been preserved only with that of their irreligion, they vaunt these grand examples: after such illustrious models, it appears dignified to believe nothing; their names are constantly in their mouths: it is a false embroidery, where a laughable vanity and littleness of mind alone are conspicuous, since nothing can be more miserable or mean than to give ourselves out for what we are not, or to assume the personage of another.

3*dly,* and *lastly,* Because the language of impiety is, in general, the consequence of licentious society: we wish to appear the same as our companions in debauchery; for it would be a shame to be dissolute, and yet seem to believe, in the very presence of our accomplices in riot. It is a sorry cause that of a debauchee who still believes; impiety and licentiousness are the only colour for debauchery; without these he would be only a novice in profligacy: the dread of punishments and of an hell is left to those yet unexercised in guilt; that remain of religion seems to favour still too much of childhood and the college. But when attained to a certain length in debauchery, ah! these vulgar weaknesses must all be soared above; their opinion of themselves is raised in proportion as they can persuade others that they are now above all these fears; they even mock those who appear still to dread: like the wife of Job, they say, with a tone of irony and impiety, "Dost thou still retain thine "integrity? Art thou so simple as to believe all "these tales with which thy childhood hath been "alarmed? Thou seest not that all these are mere- "ly the visions of weak minds, and that the more "knowing, who preach them up so much, believe "not a word of them themselves?"

O my God! How mean and despicable is the impious man, who seems so proudly to contemn thee? He is a coward, who outwardly insults, yet inwardly fears thee; he is a vain boaster, who makes a shew of unbelief, but tells not what passes within; he is an impostor, who, wishing to deceive

ceive us, cannot succeed in deceiving himself; he is a fool, who, without a single inducement, adopts all the horrors of impiety; he is a madman, who, unable to attain irreligion, or to extinguish the terrors of his conscience, extinguishes in himself all modesty and decency, and endeavours to make an impious merit of it in the eyes of men; who madly sacrifices, to the deplorable vanity of being thought an unbeliever, his religion which he still preserves, his God whom he dreads, his conscience which he feels, his eternal salvation which he hopes. What a desertion of God, and what a sink of madness and folly!

And could you, my brethren, (and in this wish I comprise the whole fruit of this discourse) who still feel a reverence for the religion of our fathers, but be sensible of the contemptability of those men who give themselves out as free-thinkers, and whom you often so much esteem; you would then comprehend how much the profession of unbelief, now so fashionable among us, is, of all other characters, the most frivolous, cowardly, and worthy of laughter; you would then know that every thing mean and shameful, even according to the world, is concealed under this ostentation of impiety, which the corruption of our manners hath now rendered so common even to both sexes.

1*stly*, Of licentiousness. They reach the avowal of impiety only when the heart is profoundly corrupted;

corrupted; when they actually live in private in the moſt ſhameful debauchery; and, were they known for what they are, they would for ever be diſhonoured even in the eyes of men.

2*dly*, Of meanneſs. They act the philoſopher and the wit, while, in ſecret, they are the moſt ſneaking, the moſt diſſolute, the moſt abandoned, and weakeſt of ſinners, the verieſt ſlaves of every paſſion unworthy of modeſty, and even of reaſon.

3*dly*, Of deceit and impoſition. They act a borrowed character; they give themſelves out for what they are not; and, while ſo loudly exclaiming againſt the godly, and treating them as impoſtors and hypocrites, they are themſelves the very cheat they decry, and the hypocrite of impiety and free-thinking.

4*thly*, Of oſtentation and wretched vanity. They act the hero, while inwardly trembling; for, on the firſt ſignal of death, they betray more cowardice than even the commoneſt of the people: they make a ſhew of openly inſulting that God whom they ſtill inwardly dread, and even hope to render favourable one day to themſelves: a character of childiſhneſs and buffoonery, which the world itſelf hath always conſidered as the loweſt, the vileſt, and the moſt riſible of all characters.

5*thly*, Of temerity. Without erudition or knowledge, they dare to ſet up as deciders upon what they are totally ignorant; to condemn the greateſt characters of every age; and to decide upon important

important points to which they have never given, and, indeed, to which they are incapable of giving, a single moment of serious attention : an indecency of character which can accord only with men who have nothing more to lose on the side of honour.

6thly, Of folly. They pride themselves in appearing without religion; that is to say, without character, morals, probity, fear of God and of man, and capable of every thing excepting virtue and innocence.

7thly, Of superstition. We have seen these pretended free-thinkers, who refuse to consult the oracles of the holy prophets, consulting conjurors; admitting in men that knowledge of futurity which they refuse to God; giving into every childish credulity, while rising up against the majesty of faith; expecting their aggrandisement and fortune from a deceitful oracle, and unwilling to hope their salvation from the oracles of our holy books; and, in a word, ridiculously believing in demons, while they make a boast of disbelieving a God.

Lastly, What, in my opinion, is most deplorable in these characters is, that they are in a situation which precludes almost every hope of salvation. For an actual unbeliever, if such there be, may, in a moment, be stricken of God, and overwhelmed, as it were, under the weight of that glory and majesty which he unknowingly had blasphemed: the eyes of this unfortunate wretch may still be
opened

opened by the Lord in his mercy; he may make his light to shine through his darkness, and reveal that truth which he resists only because he knows it not: he has still resources, such as perhaps rectitude, consistency, principles, (of error and illusion I confess, but still they are principles): he will be equally warm for his God when known, as he was his enemy when unknown. But the unbelievers, of whom I speak, have scarcely a way left of returning to God; they insult the Lord whom they know; they blaspheme that religion which they still preserve in their heart; they resist the impressions of conscience which still inwardly espouses the cause of faith against themselves; in vain does the light of God shine upon their heart, it serves only to render more inexcusable the treachery of their impiety. Were they, saith Jesus Christ, absolutely blind, they would be worthy of pity, and their sin would be less: but at present they see; and consequently the guilt of their irreligion is blasphemy against the Holy Ghost, which dwelleth for ever upon their head.

Let us repair then, my brethren, by our respect for the religion of our fathers; by a continual gratitude towards the Lord, who hath permitted us to be born in the way of salvation, into which so many nations have not as yet been deemed worthy to enter: let us repair, I say, the scandal of unbelief so common in this age, so countenanced among us, and which, become more bold through the

the number and quality of its partifans, no longer hides its head, but openly fhews itfelf, and braves, as it were, the religion of the prince, and the zeal of the paftors. Let us have in horror thofe impious and defpicable men, who pride themfelves in turning into ridicule the majefty of the religion they profefs : let us fly them as monfters unworthy to live, not only among believers, but even among thofe connected together by honour, probity, and reafon ; far from applauding their impious difcourfes, let us cover them with fhame by that contempt which they merit. It is fo low and fo mean, even according to the world, to difhonour that religion in which one lives ; it is fo beautiful, and there is fo much real dignity in making a pride of refpecting and of defending it, even with an air of authority and of indignation, againft the filly fpeeches which attack it. By defpifing unbelief, let us deprive it of the deplorable glory it feeks : from the moment they are defpifed unbelievers will be rare among us ; and the fame vanity which forms their doubts will foon annihilate or conceal them, when it fhall be a difgrace among us to appear impious, and a glory to be a believer. It is thus that this fcandal fhall be done away, and that altogether we fhall glorify the Lord in the fame faith, and in the expectation of the eternal promifes. Amen.

SER-

SERMON III.

EVIDENCE OF THE LAW OF GOD.

John viii. 46.

And if I say the truth, why do ye not believe me?

Jesus Chrift had hitherto confuted the incredulity of the Jews by his works and his miracles; at prefent, he recalls them to the judgment of their own confcience and to the evidence of the truth, which, in fpite of themfelves, rendered teftimony to his doctrine and to his miniftry. Neverthelefs, as they fhut their eyes againft the evidence of his miracles, in accufing him of operating them through the miniftry of devils, fo they likewife harden themfelves againft the evidence of his doctrine and of his miffion, fo clearly foretold in the fcriptures, by alleging pretended obfcurities, which rendered them, in their eyes, ftill doubtful and fufpicious.

For,

For, my brethren, however evident may be the truth, that is to say, the law of God, whether in our heart, where it is written in shining and ineffaceable characters, or in the rules which Jesus Christ hath left to us; we would always, either that our conscience see nothing in it but what our passions see, or that these rules be not so explicit but what we may always be able to find out some favourable interpretation and mollification of them.

In effect, two pretexts are commonly opposed by the sinners of the world against the evidence of truths, the most terrible of the law of God. 1*stly*, In order to calm themselves on a thousand abuses, authorised by the world, they tell us that they believe themselves to be in safety in that state; that their conscience reproaches them with nothing on that head; and that, could they be persuaded that they were in the path of error, they would instantly quit it. First pretext which is opposed to the evidence of the law of God: candour and tranquility of conscience.

2*dly*, They oppose that the gospel is not so clear and so explicit on certain points as we maintain it to be; that each interprets it in his own way, and makes it to say whatever he wishes; that what appears so positive to us, appears not so to all the world. Second pretext: the obscurity and uncertainty of the rules.

Now, I say that the law of God hath a two-fold mark of evidence, which shall overthrow these two pretexts,

pretexts, and shall condemn, at the day of judgment, all the vain excuses of finners.

1*stly*, It is evident in the confcience of the finner: firſt reflection. 2*dly*, It is evident in the fimplicity of the rules : fecond reflection. The evidence of the law of God in the confcience of men: firſt character of the law of God, which shall judge the falfe fecurity and the pretended candour of worldly fouls. The evidence of the law of God in the fimplicity of its rules: fecond character of the law of God, which shall judge the affected uncertainties, and the falfe interpretations of finners. And thus it is, O my God! that thy holy law shall judge the world, and that the criminal confcience shall one day be confounded before thy tribunal, both by the lights of his own confcience, and by the perfpicuity of thy heavenly maxims.

PART I. It is rather furprifing that the greateſt part of worldly fouls, in juſtification of the abufes of the world and the danger of its maxims, allege to us the candour and the tranquility of their confcience. Befides, that peace and fecurity, in the falfe paths of iniquity, are rather their punifhment than their excufe; and that, were it even true that the confcience should reproach them with nothing in manners regulated folely according to the falfe judgments of the world, that ſtate would ſtill be only fo much the worfe, and more hopelefs of falvation : it appears that, of all tribunals, that of confcience is the laſt to which an unbelieving fou
should

should appeal; and that nothing is lefs favourable to the errors of a finner than the finner himfelf.

I know that there are hardened fouls, to whom no ray of grace or of light can carry conviction; who live without remorfe and without anxiety in the horrors of an infamous licentioufnefs; in whom all confcience feems extinguifhed, and who carry the excefs of their blindnefs, fays St Auguftin, fo far, as even to glory in their very blindnefs. But thefe are only rare and dreadful examples of God's juftice upon men; and if fuch have appeared upon the earth, they only prove how far his neglect and the power of his wrath may fometimes go.

Yes, my brethren, whether we affect boldly and openly to caft off the authority of the law, like the impious and the licentious; whether we endeavour to mollify and artificially to reconcile it with our paffions, by favourable interpretations, like the greateft part of worldly fouls and common finners; our confcience renders a two-fold teftimony within us to this divine law: a teftimony of truth to the equity and to the neceffity of its maxims, and a teftimony of feverity to the exactitude of its rules.

I fay, in the firft place, a teftimony of truth to the equity of its maxims. For, my brethren, God is too wife not to love order; and he is, at the fame time, too good not to wifh our welfare. His law muft confequently bear thefe two characters; a character of equity, and a character of goodnefs: a character of equity, which regulates all the duties;

ties; a character of goodness, which makes us to find our peace and our happiness here below, in duty and in regularity.

Thus we feel, in the bottom of our hearts, that these rules are just and reasonable; that the law of God commands nothing but what is consistent with the real interests of man; that nothing is more consonant to the reasonable creature than gentleness, humanity, temperance, modesty, and all the virtues recommended in the gospel; that the passions prohibited by the law are the sole source of all our troubles; that the more we deviate from the precept, and from the law, the more do we remove ourselves from peace and tranquility of heart; and that the Lord, in forbidding us to yield ourselves up to impetuous and iniquitous passions, hath only forbidden us to yield ourselves up to our own tyrants, and that his only intention hath been to render us happy in rendering us believers.

Behold a testimony which the law of God finds in the bottom of our hearts. Hurried away by the delusion of the senses, we vainly cast off the yoke of the holy rules; we can never succeed in justifying, even to ourselves, our own irregularities; we always internally adopt the interests of the law against ourselves; we always find within us a justification of the rules against the passions. We cannot corrupt this internal witness of the truth, which pleads within us for virtue; we always feel a secret misunderstanding between our inclinations

and

and our lights: the law of God, born in our heart, inceffantly ftruggles there againft the law of the flefh foreign to man; it maintains its truths there in fpite of ourfelves, if it cannot maintain its authority; it officiates as a cenfurer, if it cannot ferve as a director; in a word, it renders us unhappy if it cannot render us believers.

Thus, in vain do we fometimes give way to all the bitternefs of hatred and of revenge; we immediately feel that this cruel pleafure is not made for the heart of man; that to hate, is, in fact, to punifh ourfelves; and, in returning to ourfelves after the tranfports of paffion, we find within us a principle of humanity which difavows their violence, and clearly points out to us, that gentlenefs and kindnefs were our firft inclinations; and that, in commanding us to love our brethren, the law of God hath only done fo, as to confult the right and moft reafonable feelings of our heart, and to reconcile us with ourfelves. Thou art more righteous than I, faid Saul to David, in the time of his ftrongeft hatred againft him. That goodnefs, born in the heart of all men, forced from him that confeffion, and inwardly difavowed the injuftice and the cruelty of his revenge.

In vain do we plunge ourfelves into brutal and fenfual gratifications, and madly range after whatever may fatisfy the infatiable defires of pleafure; we quickly feel, that debauchery leads us too far to be agreeable to nature: that whatever enflaves

and

and tyrannifes over us, overturns the order of our firft inftitution; and that the gofpel, in prohibiting the voluptuous paffions, hath provided for the tranquility of our heart, and for reftoring to us all its elevation and nobility. How many hired fervants of my father's, faid the prodigal ftill bound in the chains of vice, have bread enough, and to fpare! and I confume my days in wearinefs, and in fhame. It was a remain of reafon and of nobility which ftill fpake in the bottom of his heart.

Laftly, inveftigate all the precepts of the law of God, and you will feel that they have a neceffary connection with the heart of man; that they are rules founded upon a profound knowledge of what takes place within us; that they folely contain the remedies of our moft fecret evils, and the fuccours of our moft righteous inclinations; and that none but Him alone, who knoweth the bottom of hearts, could be capable of laying down fuch maxims to men. The heathens themfelves, in whom all truth was not yet extinguifhed, rendered this glory to the Chriftian morality; they were forced to admire the wifdom of its precepts, the neceffity of its reftraints, the fanctity of its counfels, the good fenfe and fublimity of all its rules; they were aftonifhed to find, in the difcourfes of Jefus Chrift, a more fublime philofophy than in the Roman or Grecian fchools; and they could not comprehend how the fon of Mary fhould be better acquainted with the duties, the defires, and all the fecret folds

of

of the human heart, than Plato and all his disciples.

Will you tell us, after this, that nature is our firſt law, and that tendencies to pleaſures, inherent in our being, can never be crimes; I have often ſaid it; it is an impiety only of converſation; it is an oſtentation of free-thinking, of which vanity makes a boaſt, but which truth inwardly belies. Auguſtin in his errors had ſpared no pains to efface from the bottom of his heart, thoſe remains of faith and of conſcience which ſtill recalled him to the truth; he had eagerly ſought, in the moſt impious opinions, and in the moſt ſhocking errors, wherewithal to comfort himſelf againſt his crimes; his mind flying the light which purſued him, wandered from impiety to impiety, and from error to error; nevertheleſs, in ſpite of all his efforts and flights, the truth, always victorious in the bottom of his ſoul, proclaimed its triumph in ſpite of himſelf; he could ſucceed neither in ſeducing nor in quieting himſelf in his diſorders: " I bore, O my God, ſays he, a conſcience racked, and ſtill bleeding as it were, from the grievous wounds which my paſſions inceſſantly made there; I was a burden to myſelf; I could no longer ſuſtain my own heart; I turned myſelf on every ſide, and no where could it find caſe; I knew not where to lay it, that I might be delivered from it, and that mine anxiety might be comforted."

Behold

Behold the testimony which a sinner, who, to all the keenness of the passions, added the impiety of opinions, and the abuse of lights, renders of himself. And these examples are of every age; our own has beheld famous and avowed sinners, who made an infamous boast of not believing in God, and who were looked upon as heroes in impiety and free-thinking; we have seen them, touched at last with repentance like Augustin, and recalled from their errors, we have seen them, I say, make an open avowal, that they had never been able to succeed in effacing the rules and truth from their soul; that, amidst all their most shocking impieties and excesses, their heart, still Christian, inwardly belied their derisions and blasphemies; that, before men, they vaunted a strength of mind which forsook them in private; that that apparent unbelief concealed the most cruel remorses, and the most gloomy fears; and that they had never been firm and tranquil in guilt.

Yes, my brethren, guilt, always timorous, every where bears a witness of condemnation against itself. Every where you render homage, by your inward anxieties and remorses, to the sanctity of that law which you violate; every where a fund of weariness and of sorrow, inseparable from guilt, makes you to feel that regularity and innocence are the only happiness which was intended for you on the earth: you vainly display an affected intrepidity; the guilty conscience always betrays itself. Cruel terrors march every where before you; folitude difquiets, darknefs alarms you; you fancy to fee phantoms coming from every quarter to reproach you with the fecret errors of your foul; unlucky dreams fill you with black and gloomy fancies; and guilt, after which you run with fo much relifh, purfues you afterwards like a cruel vulture, and fixes itfelf upon you, to tear your heart, and to punifh you for the pleafure which it had formerly given you. O my God! what refources haft thou not left in our heart to recal us to thee! And how powerful is the protection which the goodnefs and the righteoufnefs of thy law finds in the bottom of our being! Firft teftimony which the confcience renders to the law of God, a teftimony of truth to the fanctity of its maxims.

But it alfo renders a teftimony of feverity to the exactitude of its rules. For a fecond illufion of the greateft part of worldly fouls, who live exempted from great irregularities, but who otherwife live amidft all the pleafures, all the abufes, all the fenfualities, and all the diffipations authorifed by the world, is, that of wifhing to perfuade themfelves that the gofpel requires no more, and to perfuade us, that their confcience reproaches them with nothing, and that they believe themfelves fafe in that ftate. Now, I fay that here the worldly confcience is again not candid, and is deceived; and that, in fpite of all thofe mollifications which they endeavour to juftify to themfelves, it renders, in the bottom of our hearts, a testimony of severity to the law of God.

In effect, order requires that all our passions be regulated by the bridle of the law; all our inclinations, corrupted in their source, have occasion for a rule to rectify and correct them: we confess this ourselves; we feel that our corruption pervades the smallest as well as the greatest things; that self-love infects all our proceedings; and that we every where find ourselves weak, and in continual opposition to order and duty: we feel, then, that the rule ought, in no instance, to be favourable to our inclinations; that we ought every where to find it severe, because it ought every where to be in opposition to us; that the law cannot be in unity with us; that whatever favours our inclinations, can never be the remedy intended to cure them; that whatever flatters our desires, can never be the bridle which is to restrain them; in a word, that whatever nourishes self-love, is not the law which is established for the sole purpose of destroying and annihilating it. Thus, by an inward feeling, inseparable from our being, we always discriminate ourselves from the law; our inclinations from its rules; our pleasures from its duties; and, in all dubious actions where we decide in favour of our inclinations, we perfectly feel that we are deviating from the law of God, always more rigid than ourselves.

And

And allow me here, my brethren, to appeal to your confcience itfelf, which you always allege, and to which you continually refer us. Are you, honeftly fpeaking, at your eafe, as you wifh to perfuade us, in this life, altogether of pleafures, of diffipation, of indolence, and of fenfuality ; in a word, in this worldly life, of which you conftantly maintain the innocence? Have you hitherto been able to fucceed in per uading yourfelves, that it is the path which leads to falvation ? Do you not feel that fomething more is required of you by the gofpel than you perform ? Would you wifh to appear before God with nothing to offer to him but thefe pleafures, thefe amufements which you call innocent, and of which the principal groundwork of your life is compofed ? I put the queftion to you. In thofe moments when, more warmly affected perhaps by grace, you propofe ferioufly to think upon eternity, do you not place, in the plan which you then form of a new life, the privation of almoft all the very things in which you are continually telling us that you fee no harm ? Do you not begin by promifing to yourfelves, that, folely occupied then with your falvation, you will renounce the exceffes of gaming, the theatres, the vanities and indecencies of drefs, the diffipation of public affemblies and pleafures ; that you will devote more time to prayer, to retirement, to holy reading, and to the duties of religion ? Now, what is it that you hereby acknowledge,

ledge, unless it be, that, while you renounce not all these abuses; that you devote not more time to all these pious duties, you think not seriously upon your salvation; you ought to have no pretension to it; you are in the path of death and perdition.

But, besides, you who carry so far the severity of your censures against the godly, recollect all the rigour of your maxims, and of your derisions upon their conduct; do you not blame, do you not continually censure those persons who wish to connect, with a public profession of piety, those abuses, those amusements, of which you are the daily apologist, and who wish to enjoy the reputation of virtue without losing any of the pleasures of the world? Do you not mock their piety as a piece of mere grimace? Here it is that you emphatically display all the austerity of the Christian life. Do you not say that it is necessary either -totally to renounce the world, or to continue to live as the world lives; and that all these ambiguous virtues serve only to decry the true virtue? I agree with you in this; but I reply to you: Your conscience dictates to you that it is not safe to give yourself partially to God, and your conscience reproaches you nothing, as you say, in a life in which God enters not at all? You condemn those mistaken souls whom, at least, an apparent division between the world and Jesus Christ may comfort? And you justify to us your conduct, you who have nothing in its justification

but

but the abuses of the world and the danger of its habits? Do you then believe that the path of salvation is more rugged for those who profess piety than for you? That the world hath privileges thereon, which are forfeited from the moment that we mean to serve God? Be consistent then with yourselves; and either condemn no more a worldly virtue, or no longer justify the world itself; since whatever you blame in that virtue is only that portion of it which the world supplies.

And, in order to make you more sensibly feel how far you are from being candid on this head, you continually take a pride in repeating that we despair of human weakness; that, in order to act up to all that we say in these Christian pulpits, it would be necessary to withdraw to the deserts, or to be angels rather than men: nevertheless, render glory to the force of truth. If a minister of the gospel were to deliver to you from this place a doctrine quite opposite to that which we teach; were he to announce to you the same maxims which you daily hold forth in the world; were he to preach to you in this place of the truth, that the gospel is not so severe as it is published; that we may love the world and yet serve God; that there is no harm in gaming, in pleasures, in theatres, except what we ourselves occasion; that we must live like the world while we live in the world; that all that language of the cross, of penitence, of mortification, and of self-denial, is more calculated

for

for cloisters than for the court, and for persons of a certain rank; and, lastly, that God is too good to consider as crimes, a thousand things which are become habitual, and of which we wish you to make a matter of conscience; were he, I say, to preach these maxims to you in this holy place, what would you think of him? What would you say to his new doctrine? What idea would you have of this new apostle? Would you consider him as a man come down from heaven to announce to you this new gospel? Would you believe him to be better instructed than we in the holy truths of salvation, and in the rules of the Christian life? You would laugh at his ignorance, or his folly; you would perhaps be struck with horror at the profanation which he would make of his ministry.

And what, my brethren, these maxims announced before the altars would appear to you as blasphemy or madness; and, promulgated in your daily conversations, they would become rules of reason and of wisdom? In the mouth of a minister of the gospel, you would look upon them as the speeches of a madman; and, in your mouth, they should appear more solid and more weighty? You would laugh, or rather you would be struck with horror, at a preacher who should announce them to you; and you wish to persuade us that you speak seriously, and that you are consistent with yourselves when, with so much confidence, you hold them forth to us.

Ah!

Ah! my brethren, how treacherous we are to God! and how terrible will he be when he shall come to avenge, upon the lights of our own heart, the honour of his holy law! Our apparent obstinacy for the abuses of the world, of which we maintain the innocence, is a secret persuasion that the world and its abuses are a path of perdition; we publicly justify what we condemn in private; we are the hypocrites of the world and of its pleasures; and, through a most deplorable destiny, our life passes away in dissembling with ourselves, and in obstinately determining to perish in spite of ourselves. And surely, says the apostle John, if our heart, notwithstanding all our self-blindness, cannot help already condemning us in secret, have we more indulgence to expect from the terrible and sovereign Judge of hearts than from our heart itself?

Thus, my brethren, study the law of God in your own conscience, and you will see that it is not more favourable than we to your passions; consult the lights of your heart, and you will feel that they perfectly accord with our maxims; listen to the voice of truth, which speaks within you, and you will admit, that we only repeat what it is continually whispering to your heart? You have no occasion, says St Augustin, to apply to able men, in order to have the greatest part of your doubts cleared up; go no farther than yourselves for explanations and answers; apply to yourselves

for

for what you have to do; liften to the decifions of your heart; follow the firft impulfe of your confcience, and, you will always determine for that party moft conformable to the law of God: the firft impreffion of the heart is always for the ftrictnefs of the law againft the foftenings of felf-love: your confcience will always go farther, and will be more ftrict than ourfelves; and, if you have occafion for our decifions, it will rather be in order to moderate the feverity, than to expofe the falfe indulgence of it.

Behold the firft manner in which the law of God fhall one day judge us: that law, manifefted in the confcience of the finner, and as if born with him, fhall rife up againft him; our heart, marked with the feal of truth, fhall be the witnefs to depofe for our condemnation: our lights fhall be oppofed to our actions, our remorfes to our manners, our fpeeches to our thoughts, our inward fentiments to our public proceedings, and ourfelves to ourfelves. Thus we bear, each of us, our condemnation in our own heart. The Lord will not bring other proof than ourfelves, to determine the decifion of our eternal reprobation; and the foul before the tribunal of God, fays Tertullian, fhall appear at the fame time, both the criminal condemned, and the witnefs which fhall teftify againft his crimes. He will have nothing to reply, continues this father. You knew the truth will be faid to him, and you iniquitoufly withheld

it;

it; you admitted of the happiness of the souls who seek only God, and you sought him not yourselves: you drew shocking pictures of the world, of its wearinesses, of its perfidies, and of its wickednesses, and you were always its slave and blinded worshipper: you inwardly respected the religion of your fathers, and you made a deplorable vaunt of impiety: you secretly dreaded the judgments of God, and you affected not to believe in him. In the bottom of your heart you rendered justice to the piety of the godly: you proposed to resemble them at some future period; and you tore and persecuted them with your derisions and censures: in a word, your lights have ever been for God, and your actions for the world.

O my God! to what do men not carry their ingratitude and folly! Thou hast placed in us lights inseparable from our being, which, by disturbing the false peace of our passions and errors, continually recall us to order and to the truth; and, through an imposition of vanity, we make a boast of being tranquil in our errors; we glory in a peace which thy mercy is still willing to disturb; and, far from publishing the riches of thy grace upon our soul, which leaves us still open to the truth, we vaunt an obstinacy and a blindness which sooner or latter shall be realised, and shall, at last, be the just punishment of an ingratitude and of a deceit so injurious to thy grace. First character of the evidence of the law of God; it is evident in the confcience of the finner; but it is likewife fo in the fimplicity of its rules.

Part II. Since man is the work of God, man can no longer live but conformably to the will of his author; and fince God hath of man made his work, and his moft perfect work, he could never leave him to live by chance upon the earth without manifefting to him his will, that is to fay, without pointing out to him what he owed to his Creator, to his fellow-creatures, and to himfelf. Therefore, in creating him, he imprinted in his being a living light, inceffantly vifible to his heart, which regulated all his duties. But all flefh having perverted its way, and the abundance of iniquity, which had prevailed over the earth, (unable, it is true, to efface that light entirely from the heart of men), no longer permitting them to reflect, or to confult it, and apparently no longer even maintaining itfelf in them, unlefs to render them more inexcufable; God, whofe mercies feem to become more abundant in proportion as the wickednefs of men increafes, caufed to be engraven, on tables of ftone, that law which nature, that is to fay, which himfelf had engraven on our hearts: he placed before our eyes the law which we bear within us, in order to recall us to ourfelves. Neverthelefs, the people, who were its firft depofitaries, having again disfigured it by interpretations which adulterated its purity, Jefus Chrift, the wifdom and the light of God, came

at laft

last upon the earth to restore to it its original beauty; to purge it from the alterations of the synagogue; to dissipate the obscurities which a false learning and human traditions had spread through it; to lay open all its sublimity; to apply its rules to our wants; and, in leaving to us his gospel, no longer to leave an excuse, either to the ignorance or to the wickedness of those who violate its precepts.

Nevertheless, the second pretext which is opposed in the world to the evidence of the law of God, is the pretended ambiguity of its rules: they accuse us of making the gospel to say whatever we wish; they contest, they find answers, they spread obscurities through all; and they darken the law in such a manner, that the world itself insists on having the gospel on its side.

Now, I say that, besides the evidence of the conscience, the law of God is also evident in the simplicity of its rules; and, consequently, that the sinners, who wish thus to justify their iniquitous ways, shall one day be overthrown, both by the testimony of their own heart, and by the evidence of the holy rules.

Yes, my brethren, the law of God, says the prophet, is pure, enlightening the eyes even of those who would wish to conceal it from themselves. In effect, Jesus Christ, in coming himself to give to us a law of life and of truth for the regulation of our manners and our duties, and in which the evidence could not be too great, could

never

never undoubtedly have meant to leave obscurities in it capable of deluding us, and of favouring passions which he expresly came to overthrow. Human laws may be liable to these inconveniences: the mind of man, which hath invented them, being unable to foresee all, it hath also been unable to obviate all the difficulties which might one day arise in the minds of other men, on the strength of its expressions, and even on the nature of its rules. But the spirit of God, author of the holy rules held out in the gospel, hath foreseen all the doubts which the human mind could oppose to his law: he hath read, in the hearts of all men to come, the obscurities which their corruption might shed over the nature of his rules: consequently, he hath concerted them in a manner so divine and so intelligible, so simple and so sublime, that the most ignorant, equally as the most learned, can never misconstrue his intentions, and be ignorant of the ways of eternal life.

It is true, that sacred obscurities conceal in it the incomprehensible mysteries of faith; but the rules of the manners are explicit and precise; the duties are there evident; and nothing can be more clear, or less equivocal, than the precepts of Jesus Christ. Not but that doubts and difficulties may spring up in the detail of the obligations; that the assemblage of a thousand different circumstances may not, in such a manner, darken the rule, that it may sometimes escape the most learned; and that,

that, upon all the infinite duties of ſtations and conditions, all be ſo decided in the goſpel, that miſtakes cannot often take place.

But I ſay, (and I intreat of you to purſue theſe reflections which to me appear of the utmoſt conſequence, and to compriſe all the rules of the manners,) in the firſt place, that if, upon the detail of duties, the letter of the law be ſometimes dubious, the ſpirit of it is almoſt never ſo: that it is eaſily ſeen to which ſide the goſpel inclines, and to what the analogy and ruling ſpirit of its maxims lead us: I ſay, that they mutually clear up each other; that they all go to the ſame end; that they are like ſo many rays, which, uniting in one centre, form ſo grand a luſtre that it is impoſſible longer to miſtake them; that there are principal rules which ſerve to elucidate every particular difficulty; and, laſtly, that, if the law appear ſometimes equivocal to us, the intention of the legiſlator, by which we ought to interpret it, never leaves room for either doubt or miſtake.

Thus, you would wiſh to know, you who live at the court, where ambition is, as it were, the virtue of perſons of your rank; you would wiſh to know if it be a crime ardently to long for the honours and the proſperities of the earth, to be never ſatisfied with your ſtation, continually to wiſh advancement, and to connect, with that ſingle deſire, all your views, all your proceedings, all your cares, the whole foundation of your life. In an-
ſwer

fwer to this, you are there told, that your heart ought to be where your treasure is; that is to say, in the desire and in the hope of eternal riches; and that the Christian is not of this world. Decide thereupon the difficulty yourselves.

You demand if continual gaming, amusements, theatres, and so many other pleasures, so innocent in the eyes of the world, ought to be banished from the Christian life. You are there told, that blessed are they who weep; and that evil to those who laugh, and who receive their consolation in this world. Follow the spirit of this rule, and see to what it leads.

You enquire if, having to live in the world, you ought to live like the world; if we would wish to condemn almost all men who live like you; and if, in order to serve God, it be necessary to affect singularities which excite the ridicule of other men. You are there told, that we are not to conform to this corrupted age; that it is impossible to please men and to be the servant of Jesus Christ; and that the multitude is always the party of the reprobate. You have now to say whether the answer be explicit.

You doubt, if, having pardoned your enemy, you be also obliged to see him, to serve him, to assist him with your wealth and credit; and if it be not more equitable to reserve your favours and preferences for your friends. You are there told: do good to those who have wished evil to you;

speak

speak well of thofe who calumniate you; love thofe who hate you. Enter into the fpirit of this precept, and fay if it doth not fhed a light over your doubt, which inftantly clears it up and diffipates it.

Laftly, propofe as many doubts as you pleafe upon duties, and it will be eafy for you to decide them by the fpirit of the law, if the letter fay nothing of them; for the letter kills me, fays the apoftle: that is to fay, to ftop there, to look upon as duty only what is literally marked, to ftop at the rude limits, and to enter no farther into the principle and into the fpirit which vivifies, is to be a Jew, and to be willing to be felf-deceived. No longer tell us then, my brethren, when we condemn fo many abufes which you, without fcruple, allow yourfelves: " But the gofpel fays nothing of " them." Ah! the gofpel fays every thing to thofe who wifh to underftand it: the gofpel leaves nothing undecided to whoever loves the law of God: the gofpel is competent to all, to whoever fearches it, only for inftruction; and it goes fo much the farther, and fays fo much the more, as that, without ftopping to regulate a particular detail, it regulates the paffions themfelves; that, without detailing all the actions, it goes to reprefs thofe inclinations which are the fources of them; and that, without confining itfelf to certain external circumftances of the manners, it propofes to us, as rules of duty, only felf denial, hatred of the

world,

world, love of fufferance, contempt for whatever takes place, and the whole extent of its crucifying maxims : firſt reflection.

I ſay, in the ſecond place, that it is not the obſcurity of the law, but our paſſions, ſtill dear, which give riſe to all our doubts upon the duties; that the worldly ſouls are thoſe who find moſt difficulty and moſt obſcurity in the rules of the manners; that nothing appears clear to thoſe who would wiſh that nothing were ſo; that every thing appears doubtful to thoſe who have an intereſt in its being ſo: I ſay, with St Auguſtin, that it is a willing ſpirit alone which gives underſtanding of the precepts; that, unleſs the rules and duties are loved, they can never be thoroughly known; that we enter into the truth only through charity; and that the ſincere deſire of ſalvation is the grand ſolver of all difficulties: I ſay that faithful and fervent ſouls have almoſt never any thing to oppoſe to the law of God; and that their doubts are rather pious alarms upon holy actions, than pretexts and difficulties to authoriſe profane ones.

Men have learned to doubt upon the rules of the manners, only ſince they have wiſhed to connect them with their iniquitous paſſions. Alas! all was almoſt decided for the firſt believers: in theſe happy ages, we ſee not that the firſt paſtors of the church had many difficulties to reſolve upon the detail of the duties: thoſe immenſe volumes, which decide their doubts by endleſs reſolutions,

have

have appeared only with the corruption of manners: in proportion as believers have had more paſſions to ſatisfy, they have had more doubts to propoſe; it hath been neceſſary to multiply volumes upon volumes, in order to reſolve difficulties which cupidity alone formed; difficulties already all reſolved in the goſpel, and upon which the firſt ages of faith would have been ſcandaliſed, that they had dared to form even a doubt. Our ages, ſtill more diſſolute than thoſe which preceded us, have ſtill beheld theſe enormous collections of caſes and reſolutions increaſing and multiplying to infinity: all the moſt inconteſtible rules of the morality of Jeſus Chriſt are there become almoſt problems; there is no duty upon which corruption hath not had difficulties to propoſe, and to which a falſe learning hath not found mollifications: every thing has there been agitated, conteſted, and put in doubt: the mind of man hath there been ſeen quibbling with the ſpirit of God, and ſubſtituting human doctrines in place of that doctrine which Jeſus Chriſt hath brought to us from heaven; and although we pretend not univerſally to blame all thoſe pious and able men, who have left to us theſe laborious maſſes of deciſions, it had been to be wiſhed that the church had never called in ſuch aids; and we cannot help looking upon them as remedies which are themſelves become diſeaſes, and as the ſad fruits of the neceſſity of the times,

times, of the depravity of manners, and of the decay of truth among men.

Doubts upon the duties arife, therefore, from the corruption of our hearts, much more than from the obfcurities of the rules. The light of the law, fays St Auguftin, refembles that of the fun; but vainly doth it fhine, glitter, enlighten; the blind are unaffected by it: now, every finner is that blind perfon; the light is near to him, furrounds him, penetrates him, enters from every quarter into his foul; but he is always himfelf far from the light. Purify your heart, continues that holy father; remove from it the fatal bandage of the paffions; then fhall you clearly fee all your duties, and all your doubts fhall vanifh. Thus we continually fee that, when touched with grace, a foul begins to adopt folid meafures for eternity, his eyes are opened upon a thoufand truths which, till then, he had concealed from himfelf: in proportion as his paffions diminifh, his lights increafe; he is aftonifhed by what means he could fo long have fhut his eyes upon truths which now appear to him fo evident and fo inconteftible; and, far from a facred guide having then occafion to conteft, and to maintain againft him the interefts of the law of God, his prudence is required to conceal, as I may fay, from that contrite foul, the whole extent and all the terrors of the holy truths; to quiet him on the horror of paft irregularities, and to moderate the fears into which he is thrown by the novelty

and

and the furprife of his lights. It is not then the rules which are cleared up, it is the foul which frees itfelf from, and quits its blindnefs; it is not the law of God which becomes more evident, it is the eyes of the heart which are opened to its luftre; in a word, it is not the gofpel, but the finner who is changed.

And a frefh proof of what I advance is, that, upon thofe points of the law where no particular paffion or intereft blinds us, we are equitable and clear-fighted. A mifer, who hides from himfelf the rules of faith, upon the infatiable love of riches, clearly fees the maxims which condemn ambition or luxury. A voluptuary, who tries to juftify to himfelf the weaknefs of his inclinations, gives no quarter to the mean defires, and to the fordid attachments of avarice. A man, mad for exaltation and fortune, and who confiders the eternal exertions which he is under the neceffity of making, in order to fucceed, as weighty and ferious cares, and alone worthy his birth and his name, fees all the unworthinefs of a life of amufement and pleafure, and clearly comprehends that a man, born with a name, degrades and difhonours himfelf by lazinefs and indolence. A woman, feized with the rage of gaming, yet otherwife regular, is inveterate against the flighteft faults which attack the conduct, and continually juftifies the innocence of exceffive gaming, by contrafting it with irregularities of another defcription, from which fhe finds herfelf free.

Another,

Another, on the contrary, intoxicated with her perfon and with her beauty, totally engroffed by her deplorable paffions, confiders that obftinate perfeverance in an eternal gaming as a kind of difeafe and derangement of the mind, and, in the fhame of her own engagements, fees nothing but an innocent weaknefs and involuntary inclinations, the deftiny of which we find in our hearts.

Review all the paffions, and you will fee that, in proportion as we are exempted from fome one, we fee, we condemn it in others; we know the rules which forbid it; we go even to the rigour againft others, upon the obfervance of duties which intereft not our own weakneffes, and we carry our feverity beyond even the rule itfelf. The Pharifees, fo inftructed in, and fo fevere upon the guilt of the adulterefs, and upon the punifhments attached by the law to the infamy of that infidelity, faw not their own pride, their hypocrify, their implacable hatred, and their fecret envy againft Jefus Chrift. Obfcurities are only in our own heart; and we never begin to doubt upon our duties, but when we begin to love thofe maxims which oppofe them. Second reflection.

In effect, I tell you, in the third place, you believe that the gofpel is not fo exprefs as we pretend, upon the greater part of the rules which we wifh to prefcribe to you; that we carry its feverity to excefs, and that we make it to fay whatever we pleafe. Hear it then itfelf, my brethren; we
confent

consent that, of all the duties prescribed to you by it, you shall think yourselves obliged to observe only those which are marked there in terms so precise and clear that it is impossible to mistake or misconstrue them: more is not required of you, and we free you from all the rest. Hear it then: " And whosoever doth not bear his cross, and " come after me, cannot be my disciple. Who- " soever he be of you, that forsaketh not all that " he hath, he cannot be my disciple. The king- " dom of heaven suffereth violence, and the vio- " lent take it by force. Except ye repent, ye " shall all likewise perish. Ye cannot serve God " and mammon. Wo unto you that are full; " for ye shall hunger. Wo unto you that laugh " now; for ye shall mourn and weep. Blessed " are they that weep now; for ye shall laugh. He " that loveth his father, his wife, his children, " yea, and his life also, better than me, is not " worthy of me. I say unto you that ye shall " weep and lament, but the world shall rejoice; " and ye shall be sorrowful, but your sorrow shall " be turned into joy."

Do I speak here my brethren? Do I come to deceive you by an excess of severity, to add to the gospel, and to bring you only my own thoughts? Weak creature that I am, I have occasion myself for indulgence; and if I took in the weakness of my own heart, the doctrine which I announce to you, alas! I would speak to you only the language

of

of man: I would tell you that God is too good
to punish inclinations which are born, it would
appear, with us; that, to love God, it is not necessary to hate one's self: that, when rich, we ought
to enjoy our wealth, and allow ourselves every
gratification. Behold the language which I would
hold; for man, delivered up to himself, can speak
only this language of flesh and blood. But would
you believe me, as I have already demanded;
would you respect my ministry; would you look
upon me as an angel from heaven, who should
come to announce to you this new gospel.

That of Jesus Christ speaks another language to
you; I have related to you only his own divine
words; these are the duties which he prescribes to
you in clear and express terms. We consent that
you confine your whole piety to these limits, and
that you leave all the rest as doubtful, or, at least,
commanded in terms less clear, and more susceptible of favourable interpretations. Reckon not among your duties, but these holy and incontestible
rules; we exact nothing more; limit yourselves to
performing what they prescribe to you; and you
will see that you shall do more than we even demand of you; and that the most common and
most familiar maxims of the gospel go infinitely
farther than all our discourses. Third reflection.

I also say to you, in the fourth place, that, if
almost all be contested in the world, upon the most
incontestible duties of Christian piety, it is because
the

the gospel is a book unknown to the greatest part of believers; it is that, through a deplorable abuse, a whole life is passed in acquiring vain learning, equally useless to man, to his happiness, and to his eternity; and the book of the law is never read, in which is contained the knowledge of salvation, the truth which is to deliver us, the light which is to conduct us, the titles of our hopes, the testimony of our immortality, the consolations of our exilement, and the aids of our pilgrimage: it is that, on entering into the world, care is taken to present to us those books, in which are explained the rules of that profession to which we are allotted; and that the book of the law, in which the rules of the profession of the Christian are contained, that profession which shall survive all others, alone necessary, and the only one which shall accompany us into eternity; that book, I say, is left in neglect, and enters not into the plan of studies which ought to occupy our earlier years; lastly, it is that fabulous and lascivious histories childishly amuse our leisure; and that the history of God's wonders and mercies upon men, filled with events so grand, so weighty, so interesting, which ought to be the sole occupation, and the whole consolation of our life, does not appear to us worthy even of our curiosity.

I am not surprised, after this, if we have continual occasion to maintain the gospel against the abuses and the prejudices of the world; if we are

listened

listened to with the same surprise, when we announce the commonest truths of the Christian morality, as though we announced the belief and the mysteries of those savage and far distant nations, whose countries and manners are hardly known; and if the doctrine of Jesus Christ find the same opposition at present in minds that it experienced at the birth of faith, it is, that there are Christians to whom the book of the gospel is almost equally unknown as it then was to the heathens; who scarcely know whether Jesus Christ be come to bring laws to men, and who cannot, for a single moment, support, without weariness, the reading of that divine book, the rules of which are so sublime, the promises so consoling, and of which the pagans themselves, who embraced faith, so much admired the beauty and the divine philosophy. Thus, my brethren, read the holy books, and read them with that spirit of faith, of submission, of trust, which the church exacts, and you will soon be as well acquainted with your duties, and with the rules of the manners, as the doctors themselves who teach you.

And indeed, my brethren, whence comes it, I beg of you, that the first believers carried so far the purity of manners, and the holiness of Christianity? Were other maxims announced to them than those which we announce to you? Was another gospel preached to them, more clear and more explicit than that which we preach to you? Nevertheless,

Neverthelefs, they were idolatrous and diffolute nations, who had brought, to the truths of faith, all the prejudices of the fuperftitions, and of the moft infamous voluptuoufneffes authorifed even by their worfhip. Did the gofpel contain the fmalleft obfcurities favourable to the paffions, it furely ought to have been thofe firft difciples of faith who fhould have made the miftake. Neverthelefs, whence comes it that they never propofed to the apoftles and to their fucceffors the fame difficulties which you continually oppofe to us, in fupport of the abufes of the world, and of the interefts of the paffions? Whence comes it, that, with more inclinations and more prejudices than we for pleafures, thofe bleffed believers at once comprehended how far, in order to obey the gofpel, it was neceffary to deny them to themfelves?

Ah! it was that, night and day, they had the book of the law in their hands: it was that patience, and the confolation of the fcriptures, were the fweeteft occupation of their faith; it was that the letters of the holy apoftles, and the relation of the life and of the maxims of Jefus Chrift, were the fole bond, and the daily converfations of thefe infant churches; in a word, it is that, to whoever reads the gofpel, whatever regards the duties is quickly decided. Fourth reflection.

Laftly, I fay, even admitting that fome obfcurities fhould be found there, doth not the law of God find all its evidence in inftruction and in the ministry? The Christian pulpits announce to you the purity of the holy maxims; the pastors publicly preach them; men, full of zeal and of knowledge, convey them down to posterity, in works worthy of the better times of the church; never had the piety of believers more aids; no age ever was more enlightened, or better knew the spirit of faith and the whole extent of duties. We no longer live in those ages of ignorance in which the rules subsisted only in the abuses which had adulterated them; in which the ministry was often an occasion of error and of scandal for believers; and in which the priest was considered as more enlightened, whenever he was more superstitious than his people.

It would seem, O my God! that, in order to render us more inexcusable, in proportion as the wickedness of men increases on the one side, the knowledge of the truth, which is to condemn them, augments on the other; in proportion as the manners become corrupted, the rules become more evident; in proportion as faith becomes languid, it is cleared up and purified; like those fires which, in expiring, give a momentary flash, and never display their lustre with such brilliancy as when on the eve of being extinguished.

Not that there are not still among us many blind guides and prophets who announce their own dreams. But the snare is to be dreaded only by those who are willing to be deceived: when
sincerely

sincerely inclined to seek the Lord, we soon find the hand which knows to lead us to him : it is not then, properly speaking, the false guides who lead us astray, it is ourselves who seek them, because we wish to err with them ; they are not the first authors of our ruin, they are only the encouragers of it ; they do not lead us into the path of perdition, they only leave us there ; and we are already determined to perish before we apply for their suffrage. In effect, we sensibly feel ourselves the danger and the imprudence of the choice we make; even the more we find the oracle complying, the more we mistrust his lights ; the more he respects our passions, the less we respect his ministry; he is frequently made the subject even of our derisions; we turn into ridicule that very indulgence which we have sought ; we vaunt the having found a protector so convenient for the human weaknesses ; and, through a blindness which cannot be mentioned without tears, the soul and eternal salvation are confided to a man who is believed unworthy, not only of respect, but even of attention and decency ; like those Israelites who, a moment after having bowed the knee to the golden calf, and expected from it their salvation and their deliverance, broke it in pieces with disgrace, and reduced it to ashes.

But, after all, when the ignorance or the weakening of ministers should even be an occasion of error, the examples of the holy undeceive you.

You

You see what, from the beginning, hath been the path of those who have obtained the promises, and whose memory and holy toils we still honour upon the earth : you see that none of them hath accomplished his salvation by that way which the world vaunts as being so safe and so innocent : you see that all the holy have repented, crucified their flesh, despised the world with its pleasures and maxims : you see that those ages, so opposite to each other for their manners and customs, have never made any change in the manners of the just; that the holy of the first times were the same as those of the last; that the countries, even the most dissimular for their disposition and behaviour, have produced holy, all resembling each other; that those of the most distant climates, and the most different from our own, resemble those of our nation; that, in every tongue and in every tribe, they have all been the same; lastly, that their situations have been different; that some have wrought out their salvation in obscurity, others in elevation; some in poverty, others in abundance; some in the dissipation of dignities and of public cares, others in silence and in the calm of solitude: in a word, some in the cottage, others on the throne; but that the cross, violence, and self-denial hath been the common path of all.

What then art thou, to pretend to reach heaven by other ways; and thou flatterest thyself that, in that crowd of illustrious servants of the living

God,

God, thou alone fhalt be privileged? My God! with what luftre haft thou not furrounded the truth, in order to render man inexcufable! His confcience fhews it to him; thy holy law guards it for him; the voice of the church makes it to refound in his ears; the example of thy holy inceffantly places it before his eyes; every thing rifes up againft guilt; all take the interefts of thy holy law againft his falfe peace; from every quarter proceed rays of light which go to bear the truth even to the bottom of his foul: no place, no fituation can protect him from thofe divine fparks emitted from thy bofom, which every where purfue him, and which, in enlightening, rack him: the truth, which ought to deliver him, renders him unhappy; and, unwilling to love its light, he is forced, before hand, to feel its juft feverity.

What then, my dear hearer, prevents the truth from triumphing in your heart? Wherefore do you change, into an inexhauftible fource of cruel remorfes, lights which ought to be, within you, the whole confolation of your forrows? Since, by a confequence of the riches of God's mercy upon your foul, you cannot fucceed, like fo many impious and hardened hearts, to ftifle that internal monitor which inceffantly recalls you to order and duty, why will you obftinately withftand the happinefs of your lot? Why fo many efforts to defend you from yourfelf? So many ftarts and flights to fhun yourfelf? At laft, reconcile your hearts

with

with your lights, your confcience with your manners, yourfelf with the law of God; behold the only fecret of attaining to that peace of heart which you feek. Turn yourfelf on every fide, you muft always come to that. Obfervance of the law is the true happinefs of man: it is deceiving himfelf to look upon it as a yoke: it alone places the heart at liberty. Whatever favours our paffions, fharpens our ills, increafes our troubles, multiplies our bonds, and aggravates our flavery; the law of God alone, in repreffing them, places us in order, quiets, cures, and delivers us. Such is the deftiny of finful man, to be incapable of happinefs here below, but by overcoming his paffions; to attain by violence alone to the true pleafures of the heart, and afterwards to that eternal peace prepared for thofe who fhall have loved the law of the Lord.

SERMON IV.

IMMUTABILITY OF THE LAW OF GOD.

JOHN viii. 46.

And if I say the truth, why do ye not believe me?

It is not enough to have defended the evidence of the law of God against the affected ignorance of the sinners who violate it; it is necessary likewise to establish its immutability against all the pretexts which seem to authorise the world to dispense itself from its holy rules.

Jesus Christ is not satisfied with announcing to the Pharisees that the truth which they know shall one day judge them; that in vain they concealed it from themselves; and that the guilt of the truth, known and contemned, would be for ever upon their head. It is through the evidence of the law that he at first recalls them to their own conscience;

science; he afterwards accuses them of having struck even at its immutability; of substituting human customs and traditions in place of the perpetuity of its rules; of accommodating them to times, to circumstances, and to interests; and declares to them that, even to the end of ages, a single jota shall not be changed in his law; that heaven and the earth shall pass away, but that his law and his holy word shall for ever be the same.

And Behold, my brethren, the abuses which still reign among us against the law of God. We have shewn to you that, in spite of the doubts and the obscurities which our lusts have spread over our duties, the light of the law, always superior to our passions, dissipated, in spite of ourselves, these obscurities, and that we were never hearty in the transgressions which we tried to justify to ourselves. But it is little to be willing, like the Pharisees, to darken the evidence of the law; like them, we likewise strike at its immutability; and, as if the law of God could change with the manners of the age, the differences of conditions, the necessity of situations, we believe that we can accommodate it to these three different circumstances, and in them find pretexts, either to mollify its severity, or altogether to violate its precepts.

1*stly*, In effect, the heart of men is changeable; every age sees new customs spring up among us; times and the customs always determine our manners: now, the law of God is immutable in its duration,

ration, always the fame in all times and in all places; and, by this firſt character of immutability, it alone ought to be the conſtant and perpetual rule of our manners: firſt reflection.

2*dly*, The heart of man is vain; whatever levels us with the reſt of men, wounds our pride; we love diſtinctions and preferences; we believe that, in the elevation of rank and of birth, we find privileges againſt the law: now, the law of God is immutable in its extent; it levels all ſtations and all conditions; it is the fame for the great and for the people, for the prince and for the ſubject; and, by this ſecond character of immutability, it ought to recall to the fame duties that variety of ſtations and conditions which ſpreads ſo much inequality over the detail of manners and of the rules: ſecond reflection.

Laſtly, The heart of man connects every thing with itſelf; he perſuades himſelf that his intereſts ought to be preferred to the law and to the intereſts of God himſelf; the ſlighteſt inconveniencies are reaſons, in his eyes, againſt the rule: now, the law of God is immutable in all ſituations of life; and, by this laſt character of immutability, there is neither perplexity, nor inconveniency, nor apparent neceſſity, which can diſpenſe us from its precepts: laſt reflection.

And behold the three pretexts, which the world oppoſes to the immutability of the law of God, overthrown: the pretext of manners and cuſtoms;

the pretext of rank and of birth; the pretext of situations and inconveniencies. The law of God is immutable in its duration; therefore, the manners and the customs can never change it: the law of God is immutable in its extent; therefore, the difference of ranks and of conditions leaves it every where the same: the law of God is immutable in all situations; therefore, inconveniencies, perplexities, never justify the smallest transgression of it.

Part I. One of the most urgent and most usual reproaches which the first supporters of religion formerly made to the heathens, was the instability of their moral system, and the continual fluctuations of their doctrine. As the fullness of truth was not in vain philosophy, and as they drew not their lights, said Tertullian, from that sovereign reason which enlightens all minds, and which is the immutable teacher of the truth; but from the corruption of their heart, and the vanity of their thoughts; they qualified good and evil according to their caprices, and, among them, vice and virtue were almost arbitrary names. Nevertheless, continues this father, the most inseparable character of truth, is that of being always the same: good and evil take their immutability from that of God himself, whom they glorify or insult; his wisdom, his holiness, his righteousness, are the only eternal rules of our manners; and it belongs not to men, at their pleasure, to change

what

what men have not eftablifhed, and what is more ancient than men themfelves.

Now, it was not furprifing that morality had nothing determinate, in the heathen fchools, delivered up to the pride, and to the variations of the human mind; it was vanity, and not the truth, which made philofophers; the rules changed with the ages; new times brought new laws: in a word, the tenets did not change the manners; it was the change of manners which drew after it that of the tenets.

But, what is aftonifhing, is, that Chriftians, who have received from heaven the eternal and immutable law which regulates their manners, believe it to be equally changeable as the morality of philofophers; that they perfuade themfelves that the rigorous duties, which the gofpel at firft prefcribed to the primitive ages of the church, are mollified with the relaxation of manners, and are no longer made for the weaknefs and the corruption of our ages.

In effect, the gofpel, the law of Jefus Chrift, is immutable in its duration: feeing every thing change around it, it alone changes not; the duties which it prefcribes to us, founded upon the wants and upon the nature of man, are, like it, of all times and of all places. Every thing changes upon the earth, becaufe every thing partakes of the mutability of its origin; empires and ftates have their rife and their fall; arts and fciences
fall

fall or fpring up with the ages; cuftoms continually change with the tafte of the people, and with climates; from on high, in his immutability, God feems to fport with human affairs, by leaving them in an eternal revolution: the ages to come will deftroy what we, with fo much anxiety, rear up; we deftroy what our fathers had thought worthy of an eternal duration; and, in order to teach us in what eftimation we ought to hold things here below, God permitteth that they have nothing determinate or folid, but that very inconftancy which inceffantly agitates them.

But, amid all the changes of manners and ages, the law of God remains always the immutable rule of ages and of manners. Heaven and the earth fhall pafs away; but the holy words of the law fhall never pafs away: fuch as the firft believers received them at the birth of faith, fuch have we them at prefent, fuch fhall our defcendants one day receive them; laftly, fuch fhall the bleffed in heaven eternally love and adore them. The fervour or the licentioufnefs of ages add or diminifh nothing to their indulgence, or from their feverity; the zeal or the complaifance of men, renders them neither more auftere, nor more accommodating. The intolerant rigour, or the exceffive relaxation of opinions and tenets, leaves them all the wife fobriety of their rules; and they form that eternal gofpel which the angel, in the Revelation,

lation, announces from on high in heaven, from the beginning, to every tongue and to every nation.

Neverthelefs, my brethren, when, in the manners of the primitive believers, we fometimes reprefent to you all the duties of the gofpel exactly fulfilled, their freedom from the world, their abfence from theatres and public pleafures, their affiduity in the temples, the modefty and the decency of their drefs, their charity for their brethren, their indifference for all perifhable things, their continual defire of going to be re-united to Jefus Chrift; in a word, that fimple, retired, and mortified life, fuftained by fervent prayer, and by the confolation of the holy books, and fuch, in effect, as the gofpel prefcribes to all the difciples of faith ; when we bring forward to you, I fay, thefe ancient models, in order to make you feel,. by the difference betwixt the primitive manners and yours, how diftant you are from the kingdom of God ; far from being alarmed at finding yourfelves diffimilar to fuch a degree, that hardly could it be believed that you were difciples of the fame Mafter, and followers of the fame law; you reproach us with continually recalling, even to wearinefs, thefe primitive times, of never fpeaking but of the primitive church, as if it were poffible to regulate our manners, upon manners of which every trace hath long been done away, impracticable at prefent among us, and which the times and cuftoms have univerfally abolifhed. You fay, that men muft be

taken

taken as they are; that it were to be wished that the primitive fervour had been kept up in the church; but that every thing becomes relaxed and weakened through time, and that, to pretend to bring us back to the life of the primitive ages, is not holding out means of salvation, but is merely preaching up that nobody can now pretend to it.

But I demand of you, in the first place, my brethren, if the times and the years, which have so much adulterated the purity of Christianity, have adulterated that of the gospel? Are the rules become more pliable and more favourable to the passions, because men are become more sensual and more voluptuous? And hath the relaxation of manners softened the maxims of Jesus Christ? When he hath foretold in the gospel, that, in the latter times, that is to say, in the ages in which we have the misfortune to live, faith should almost no longer be found upon the earth, that his name should hardly be known there, that his maxims should be destroyed, that the duties should be incompatible with the customs, and that the just themselves should allow themselves to be almost infected by the universal contagion, and to be dragged away by the torrent of example; hath he then added, that, in order to accommodate himself to the corruption of these latter times, he would relax something of the severity of his gospel; that he would consent that customs, established by the ignorance and the licentiousness of the ages, should succeed to

the

the rules and to the duties of his doctrine; that he would then exact of his difciples infinitely lefs than he exacted at the birth of faith; and that his kingdom, which, at firft, was promifed only to force, fhould then be granted to indolence and lazinefs? Hath he added this, I demand of you? On the contrary, he warns his difciples that then, in thefe latter times, it will, more than ever, be neceffary to pray, to faft, to retire to the mountains, in order to fhun the general corruption: he warns them, that wo unto thofe who fhall then remain expofed amid the world; that thofe alone fhall be fafe who fhall diveft themfelves of all, and who fhall fly from amid the cities; and he concludes, by exhorting them once more to watch and to pray without ceafing, in order not to be included in the general condemnation.

And, in effect, my brethren, the more diforders augment, the more ought piety to be fervent and watchful; the more we are furrounded with dangers, the more doth prayer, retreat, mortification, become neceffary to us. The licentioufnefs of the prefent manners adds ftill new obligations to thofe of our fathers; and, far from the path of falvation having become more eafy than in thofe former times, we fhall perifh with a moderate virtue, which, fupported then by the common example, would perhaps have been fufficient to fecure our falvation.

Befides,

Besides, my brethren, I demand of you, in the second place, do you really believe that the rigorous precepts of the gospel, those maxims of the cross, of violence, of self-denial, of contempt for the world, have been made only for the primitive ages of faith? Do you believe that Jesus Christ hath destined all the rigours of his doctrine for those chaste, innocent, charitable, and fervent men, who lived in these happy times of the church; those men who denied themselves every pleasure, those primitive heroes of religion, who, almost all, preserved, even to the end, the grace of regeneration which had made them Christians? What, my brethren, Jesus Christ would have rewarded their zeal and their fidelity only by aggravating their yoke, and he would have reserved all his indulgence for the corrupted men of our ages? Jesus Christ would have made strict laws of reserve, of modesty, of retirement, only for those primitive Christian women who renounced all to please him; who divided themselves only with the Lord and their husbands; who, shut up in the inclosure of their houses, brought up their children in faith and in piety? And he would exact less at present of those sensual, voluptuous, and worldly women, who continually wound our eyes by the indecency of their dress, and who corrupt the heart by the looseness of their manners, and by the snares which they lay for innocence? And where would here be that so much vaunted equity and wisdom of the

Christian

Chriftian morality? More fhould then be exacted of him who owes lefs? The tranfgreffions of the law fhould then difpenfe from its feverity thofe who violate it? It would fuffice to have paffions, to be entitled to gratify them? The way of heaven would be rendered eafy to finners, while all its roughnefs would be kept for the juft? And the more vices men fhould have, the lefs fhould they have occafion for virtues?

Again allow me, my brethren, to add, in the laft place, if the change of manners could change the rules, if cuftoms could juftify abufes, the eternal law of God fhould then accommodate itfelf to the inconftancy of the times, and to the ridiculous tafte of men: a gofpel would then be neceffary for every age and for every nation; for our cuftoms were not eftablifhed in the times of our fathers, and undoubtedly they fhall not pafs to our laft defcendants; they are not common to all the nations who, like us, worfhip Jefus Chrift. Therefore, thefe cuftoms cannot either become our rule or change it; for the rule is of all times and of all places; therefore, new manners do not form a new gofpel, feeing we fhould anathematife even an angel who fhould come to announce to us a new one; and that the gofpel would be no longer but a human, and little to be trufted law for men, if it could change with men: therefore, the rules and duties are not to be judged by manners and cuftoms, but the manners and cuftoms are to be judged ed by the duties and rules: therefore, it is the law of God which ought to be the conſtant rule of the times, and not the variation of times to become even the rule of the law of God.

No longer tell us then, my brethren, that the times are no longer the ſame; but the law of God, is it not? That you cannot reform manners univerſally eſtabliſhed; but you are not charged with the reformation of the univerſe: change yourſelf; ſave your own ſoul with which you are entruſted; behold all that is exacted of you: laſtly, that the Chriſtians of the primitive times had either more force or more grace than we: ah! they had more faith, more conſtancy, more love for Jeſus Chriſt, more contempt for the world: behold all that diſtinguiſhed them from us.

Have we not the ſame ſources of grace as they, the ſame miniſtry, the ſame altar, the ſame victim? Do the mercies of the Lord not flow with the ſame abundance upon his church? Have we not ſtill among us pure and holy ſouls, who renew the fervour and faith of the primitive times, and who are living proofs of the poſſibility of the duties, and of the mercies of the Lord upon his people? " Tell us no longer then," ſays the ſpirit of God, " that the former days were better than " theſe; for thou doſt not enquire wiſely con- " cerning this." To follow Jeſus Chriſt, ſufferance muſt always be required: in all ages, it hath been neceſſary to bear his croſs, not to conform to the corrupted age, and to live as strangers upon the earth: in all times, the holy have had the same passions as we to resist, the same abuses to shun, the same snares to dread, the same obstacles to surmount: and, if there be any difference here, it is, that, in former times, it was not merely arbitrary customs which they had to shun, nor the derisions of the world which they had only to dread, in declaring for Jesus Christ; it was the most cruel punishments to which they must expose themselves; it was the power of the Cesars, and the rage of tyrants, which they must despise; it was superstitions, become respectable through their antiquity, countenanced by the laws of the empire, and by the consent of almost all the people, which they had to shake off: it was, in a word, the whole universe which they had to arm against themselves. But the faith of these pious men was stronger than punishments, than the tyrants, than the Cesars, than the whole world, and our faith cannot hold out against the absurdity of customs, or the puerility of derision; and the gospel, which could formerly make martyrs, scarcely at present can it form a believer. The law of God is then immutable in its duration; always the same in all times and in all places; but it is likewise immutable in its extent, and the same for all stations and conditions: this is my second reflection.

PART II. The most essential character of the law of Jesus Christ, is that of uniting, under the

same

fame rules, the Jew and the Gentile, the Greek and the Barbarian, the great and the people, the prince and the fubject; in it there is no longer exception of perfons. The law of Mofes, at leaft in its cuftoms and in its ceremonies, was given only to a fingle people; but Jefus Chrift is an univerfal Legiflator; his law, as his death, is for all men. He came, of all people to make only one people; of all ftations and of all conditions to form only one body : it is the fame fpirit which animates it, the fame laws which govern it : different functions may there be exercifed, different places, more or lefs honourable, be occupied; but it is the fame fpring which rules all the members of it. All thefe hateful diftinctions, which formerly divided men, are deftroyed by the church: that holy law knows neither poor nor rich; neither noble nor bafe born; neither mafter nor flave; it fees in men only the title of believer, which equals them all: it diftinguifhes them not by their names, or by their offices, but by their virtues; and the greateft in its fight are thofe who are the moft holy.

Neverthelefs, a fecond illufion, pretty common againft the immutability of the law of God, is the perfuafion that it changes and becomes mollified in favour of rank and of birth; that its obligations are lefs rigid for perfons born to elevation; and that the obftacles, which high places and the manners attached to grandeur throw in the way of the observance of the strict duties of the gospel, and which render the practice of them almost impossible to the great, likewise render their transgression more innocent. They figure to themselves that the abuses, permitted, in all times, by custom to the great, are likewise accorded to them by the law of God, and that there is another path of salvation for them than for the people. Thence, all the laws of the church violated; the times and the days consecrated to abstinence, confounded with the rest of days, are looked upon as privileges refused to the vulgar, and reserved solely for rank and birth: thence, to live only for the senses, to be attentive only to satisfy them, to refuse nothing to taste, to vanity, to curiosity, to idleness, to ambition, to make a God of one's self; the same prosperity, which facilitates all these excesses, excuses and justifies them.

But, my brethren, I have already said it, the gospel is the law of all men: great, people, you have all promised, upon the sacred fonts, to observe it. The church, in receiving you into the number of her children, hath not proposed to the great other vows to make, and other rules to practise, than to the common people: you have all there made the same promises; all sworn, in the face of the altars, to observe the same gospel. The church hath not then demanded of you, if, by your birth according to the flesh, you were great, or of the common people; but if, by your

regeneration

regeneration in Jesus Christ, you meant to be faithful, and to engage yourself to follow his law: upon the vow which you have made of it, she hath placed the holy gospel upon your head, in order to mark that you submitted yourself to that sacred yoke.

Now, my brethren, all the duties of the gospel are reduced to two points. Some are proposed in order to resist and to weaken that fund of corruption which we bear from our birth; the others in order to perfect that first grace of the Christian which we have received in baptism; that is to say, the one in order to destroy in us the old Adam; the others in order to make Jesus Christ to grow there. Violence, self-denial, and mortification, regard the first: prayer, retirement, vigilance, contempt for the world, desire of invisible riches, are comprised in the second: behold the whole gospel. Now, I demand of you, what is there in these two descriptions of duties from which rank or birth can dispense you?

Ought you to pray less than the other believers? Have you fewer favours to ask than they, fewer obstacles to overcome, fewer snares to avoid, fewer desires to resist? Alas! the more you are exalted, the more do dangers augment, the more do occasions of sin spring up under your feet, the more is the world beloved, the more doth every thing favour your passions, the more doth every thing militate against your good desires; is it in a

situation

situation so terrible for salvation that you find privileges which render it more mild and more commodious. The more, therefore, that you are exalted, the more doth mortification become necessary to you; for, the more that pleasures corrupt your heart, the more is vigilance necessary, because the dangers are more frequent; the more ought faith to be lively, because every thing around you weakens and extinguishes it; the more ought prayer to be continual, because the grace, in order to support you, ought to be more powerful; humility of heart more heroical, because the attachments to things here below are more unavoidable: lastly, the more you are exalted, the more doth salvation become difficult to you; this is the only privilege you can expect from elevation. Also, thou often warnest us, great God, that thy kingdom is only for the poor and the lowly: thou speakest not of the difficulty of salvation for the great and the powerful, but in terms which would seem to deprive them of all hope of pretending to it, if we knew not that thou wishest the salvation of all men, and that thy grace is still more powerful for our sanctification, than prosperity for our corruption.

And surely, my brethren, if grandeur and elevation were to render our condition more fortunate and more favourable with regard to salvation, in vain would the doctrine of Jesus Christ teach us to dread grandeurs and human prosperities; in vain

vain would it be said to us: That blessed are they who weep, and who suffer here below; that wo unto those who laugh now, for they shall mourn and weep; and unto those who are rich, for they have received their consolation; and that, to receive our reward in this world, through the transitory riches and honours which we there receive, is almost a certain sign that we are not to receive it in the other. On the contrary, grandeur and prosperity would become a state worthy of envy, even according to the rules of faith; against the maxim of Jesus Christ, it would be necessary to call those happy who are immersed in pleasures and in opulence; since, besides the comforts of a smiling fortune, they would likewise find there a way of salvation more mild and more easy than in an obscure state; those who suffer, and who weep here below, would then be the most miserable of all men; since, to all the bitternesses of their condition, would likewise be added those of a gospel, more rigorous and more austere for them than for the persons born in abundance. What new gospel would it then be necessary to announce to you, if such were the rules of the morality of Jesus Christ?

But I say not even enough. Granting that prosperity should not exact more rigid precautions in consequence of the dangers which surround it, it would exact, at least, more rigorous reparations, through the crimes and excesses which are inseparable

rable from it. Alas! my brethren, is it not among you that the paſſions no longer know any bounds; that the jealouſies are more keen, the hatreds more laſting, revenge more honourable, evil-ſpeaking more cruel, ambition more boundleſs, and voluptuouſneſs more ſhameful? Is it not among the great that the moſt ſhocking debauchery even refines upon the common crimes; that diſſipations become an art; and that, in order to prevent thoſe diſguſts inſeparable from licentiouſneſs, reſources are ſought in guilt againſt guilt itſelf? What indulgence then can you promiſe yourſelves on the part of religion? If the moſt righteous be reſponſible for the whole law, ſhould the greateſt ſinners be diſcharged from it? Meaſure your duties upon your crimes, and not upon your rank; judge of yourſelves by the inſults which you have offered to God, and not by the vain homages which are paid to you by men; number the days and the years of your crimes which ſhall be the eternal titles of your condemnation, and not the years and the ages of the antiquity of your race, which are only vain titles written upon the aſhes of your tombs; examine what you owe to God, and not what men owe to you. If the world were to judge you, you might promiſe yourſelves diſtinctions and preferences; but the world ſhall itſelf be judged; and he, who will judge it and you alſo, ſhall diſtinguiſh men only by their vices or by their virtues. He will not demand the names, he will demand only the deeds: calculate thereupon the distinctions which you ought to expect.

Thus, we see not that Jesus Christ, in the gospel, proposed to the princes of the people, and to the grandees of Jerusalem, other maxims than to the citizens of Judea, and to his disciples, all taken from the lowest ranks of the people; he speaks in the capital of Judea, and before all that Palestine had the most illustrious, as he speaks upon the borders of the sea, or upon the mountains, to that obscure populace which followed him; his maxims are not changed with the rank of those who listen to him. The cross, violence, contempt of the world, self-denial, abstinence from pleasures: behold what he announces at Jerusalem, the seat of kings, as at Nazareth, the most obscure place of Judea; to that young man who was so rich, as to the children of Zebedee, whose only inheritance was their nets; to the sisters of Lazarus, of a distinguished rank in Palestine, as to the woman of Samaria of a more obscure condition; his enemies themselves confessed that this was his peculiar character, and were forced to render him this justice, that he taught the way of God in truth, and that he had no respect of rank or of persons.

What do I say? Even after his death the gospel seemed a doctrine sent down from heaven, only because that, announcing to the great and to the powerful sorrowful and crucifying maxims, apparently

rently so incompatible with their station, they, nevertheless, submitted to the yoke of Jesus Christ, and embraced a law which, amid all their prosperity and abundance, permitted to them no more pleasures and comforts here below, than to the common and simple people. And, in effect, why should the first defenders of faith have regarded the conversion of Cesars, and of the powerful of the age, as a proof of the truth and of the divinity of the gospel? What would there be so surprising, that the rich and the powerful had embraced a doctrine which would distinguish them from the people by a greater indulgence; which, while it would prescribe tears, fasting, self-denial to others, would relax in favour of the great, and would consent that profusions, pleasures, sensualities, gaming, public places, all so rigorously forbidden to common believers, became an innocent occupation for them; and, that what is a road of perdition for others, should, for them alone, be a road of salvation? It would then be the wisdom of the age which would have established the gospel, and not the folly of the cross; it would be the artifices and the deferences of men, and not the arm of the Almighty; it would be flesh and blood, and not the power of God; and the conversion of the universe would have nothing more wonderful, than the establishment of superstitions and of sects.

And candidly, my brethren, if the gospel had distinctions to make, and condescensions to grant,

if

if the law of God could relax something of its severity, would it be in favour of those who are born to rank and to abundance? What! It would preserve all its rigour for the poor and the unfortunate? It would condemn to tears, to fastings, to penitence, to poverty, those unfortunate souls whose days are mingled with almost nothing but sufferance and sorrow, and whose only comfort is that of eating with temperance the bread earned with the sweat of their brow? And it would discharge from these rigorous duties the grandees of the earth? And it would exact nothing painful of those whose days are only diversified by the variety of their pleasures? And it would reserve all its indulgence for those soft and voluptuous souls, who live only for the senses, who believe that they are upon the earth for the sole purpose of enjoying an iniquitous felicity, and who know no other god than themselves?

Great God! It is the blindness which thy justice sheds over human prosperities: after having corrupted the heart, they likewise extinguish all the lights of faith. It rarely happens but that the great, so enlightened upon the interests of the earth, upon the ways to fortune and to glory, upon the secret springs which give motion to courts and empires, live in a profound ignorance of the ways of salvation. They have been so much accustomed to preference by the world, that they are persuaded they ought likewise to find them in religion.

ligion. Because men do them credit for the smallest steps taken in their favour, they believe, O my God! that thou regardest them with the same eyes as men; and that, in fulfilling some weak duties of piety, in taking some small steps for thee, they go even beyond what they owe to thee: as if their smallest religious works acquired a new merit from their rank; in place of which, they acquire it, in thy sight, only from that faith and from that charity which animates them.

It is thus that the law of God, immutable in its extent, is the same for all stations, for the great and for the people. But it is likewise immutable in all the situations of life; and it is neither a difficult conjuncture, nor perplexity, nor apparent danger, nor pretext of public good, in which to violate, or even to soften it, becomes a legitimate and necessary modification: this was to have been my last reflection; but I abridge and go on.

Yes, my brethren, every thing becomes reason and necessity against our duties, that is to say, against the law of God; situations the least dangerous, conjunctures the least embarrassing, furnish us with pretexts to violate it with safety, and persuade us that the law of God would be unjust, and would exact too much of men, if, on these occasions, it were not to use indulgence with regard to us.

Thus, the law of God commands us to render to each that which is his due, to retrench, in order to pay thofe debts incurred through our exceffes, and not to permit that our unfortunate creditors fuffer by our fenfelefs profufions: neverthelefs, the general perfuafion is that, in a grand place, it is neceffary to fupport the eclat of a public dignity; that the honour of the mafter requires that mean and forry externals difgrace not the elevated poft which he hath confided to us; that we are refponfible to the fovereign, to the ftate, to ourfelves, before being fo to individuals: and that public propriety is then fuperior to the particular rule.

Thus, the law of God enjoins us to tear out the eye which giveth offence, and to caft it from us; to feparate ourfelves from an object which, in all times, hath been the rock of our innocence, and near to which we can never be in fafety: neverthelefs, the noife which a rupture would make, the fufpicions which it might awaken in the public mind, the ties of fociety, of relationfhip, of friendfhip, which feem to render the feparation impoffible without eclat, perfuade us that it is not then commanded, and that a danger, become as if neceffary, becomes a fecurity to us.

Thus, the law of God commands us to render glory to the truth; not to betray our confcience by iniquitoufly withholding it; that is to fay, not to diffemble it, through human interefts, from thofe to whom our duty obliges us to announce it: neverthelefs, we perfuade ourfelves that truths,
which

which would be unavailing, ought to be fuppreffed; and that a liberty, of which the only fruit would be that of rifking our fortune, and of rendering ourfelves hated, without rendering thofe better to whom we owe the truth, would rather be an indifcretion than a law of charity and of juftice.

Thus, the law of God prefcribes to us to have in view, in public cares, only the utility of the people, for whom alone the authority is entrufted to us; to confider ourfelves as charged with the interefts of the multitude, as the avengers of injuftice, the refuge againft oppreffion and poverty: neverthelefs, we believe ourfelves to be fituated in conjunctures, in which it is neceffary to fhut our eyes upon iniquity, to fupport abufes which we know to be untenable, to facrifice confcience and duty to the neceffity of the times, and, without fcruple, to violate the cleareft rules, becaufe the inconveniencies, which would arife from their obfervance, feem to render their tranfgreffion neceffary. Laftly, Human pretexts, interefts, and inconveniencies, always make the balance to turn to their fide; and duty, and the law of God, always yield to conjunctures and to the neceffity of the times.

Now, my brethren, I do not tell you, in the firft place, that the intereft of falvation is the greateft of all interefts; that fortune, life, reputation, the whole world itfelf, put in comparifon with your foul,

foul, ought to be reckoned as nothing; and that, though heaven and the earth should change, that the whole world should perish, and every evil burst upon our head, these inconveniencies would always be infinitely less than the transgression of the law of God.

Secondly, I do not tell you that the law hath always, at least, security in its favour against the pretext, because the obligation of the law is clear and precise, in place of which, the pretext, which introduces the exception, is always doubtful; and that, consequently, to prefer the pretext to the law, is to leave a safe way, and to make choice of another, for which no person can be answerable to you.

Lastly, I do not tell you that, the gospel having been only given to us in order to detach us from the world and from ourselves, and to make us die to all our terrestrial affections, it is deceiving ourselves to consider, as inconveniencies, certain consequences of that divine law, fatal either to our fortune, to our glory, or to our ease, and to persuade ourselves that it is then permitted to us to have recourse to expedients which mollify it, and conciliate its severity with the interests of our self-love. Jesus Christ hath never meant to prescribe to us easy and commodious duties, and which take nothing from the passions; he came to bring the sword and separation to hearts, to divide man from his relations, from his friends, from himself; to hold out to us a way rugged and difficult to keep.
Thus,

Thus, what we call inconveniencies and unheard-of extremities, are, at bottom, only the spirit of the law, the moſt natural conſequences of the rules, and the end that Jeſus Chriſt had intended in preſcribing them to us.

That young man of the goſpel regarded as an inconveniency, the being unable to go to pay the laſt duties to his father, and to gather in what he had ſucceeded to, if he followed Jeſus Chriſt; and it was preciſely that ſacrifice which Jeſus Chriſt exacted of him. Thoſe men invited to the feaſt looked upon as an inconveniency, the one to forſake his country-houſe, the other his trade, the laſt to delay his marriage; and it was in order to break aſunder all theſe ties, which bound them ſtill too much to the earth, that the father of the family invited them to come and ſeat themſelves at the feaſt. Eſther, at firſt, conſidered as an inconveniency to go to appear before Ahaſuerus, contrary to the law of the empire, and to declare herſelf a daughter of Abraham, and protectreſs of the children of Iſrael; and, nevertheleſs, as the wiſe Mordecai repreſented to her, the Lord had raiſed her to that point of glory and proſperity only for that important occaſion. Whatever is a conſtraint to us, appears a reaſon againſt the law; and we take for inconveniencies the obligations themſelves.

Beſides, my brethren, is it not certain that the principal merit of our duties is derived from the obſtacles which never fail to oppoſe their practice;

that the most essential character of the law of Jesus Christ is that of exciting against it all the reasons of flesh and blood; and virtue would resemble vice, if outwardly and inwardly it found in us only facilities and conveniencies? The righteous, my brethren, have never been peaceable observers of the holy rules: Abel found inconveniencies in the jealousy of his own brother; Noah in the unbelief of his own citizens; Abraham in the disputes of his servants; Joseph in the dangers to which he was exposed through his love of modesty and the rage of a faithless woman; Daniel in the customs of a profane court; the pious Esdras in the manners of his age; the noble Eleazar in the snares of a specious temperament: lastly, follow the history of the just, and you will see that, in all ages, all those who have walked in the precepts and in the ordinances of the law, have experienced inconveniencies, in which righteousness itself seemed to authorise the transgression of the rules; have encountered obstacles in their way, where the lights of an human reason seemed to decide in favour of the pretext against the law; in a word, where virtue seemed to condemn virtue itself: and that, consequently, it is not new for the law of God to meet with obstacles; but that it is new to pretend to find in these obstacles legitimate excuses for dispensing ourselves from the law of God.

And the decisive argument which confirms this truth is, that our passions alone form the inconveniencies

niencies which authorife us in feeking mollifications to our duties and to the law of God; and that views of fortune, of glory, of favour, engage us in certain proceedings, juftify them in our eyes, in fpite of the evidence of rules which condemn them, only becaufe we love our glory and our fortune more than the rules themfelves.

Let us die to the world and to ourfelves, my brethren; let us reftore to our heart the fentiments of love and of preference, which it owes to its Lord: then every thing fhall appear pofsible; difficulties fhall, in an inftant, be done away; and what we call inconveniencies either fhall no longer be reckoned as any thing, or we fhall confider them as infeparable proofs of virtue, and not as the excufes of vice. How eafy it is to find pretexts when we love them! Arguments are never wanting to the paffions. Self-love is always ready in placing, at leaft, appearances on its fide; it always changes our weakneffes into duties, and our inclinations foon become legitimate claims; and what in this is moft deplorable, fays St Auguftin, is that we call in even religion itfelf in aid of our paffions; that we draw motives from piety, in order to violate piety itfelf; and that we have recourfe to holy pretexts to authorife iniquitous defires.

It is thus, O my God! that almoft our whole life is paffed in feducing ourfelves; that we employ the lights of our reafon only in darkening thofe of faith; that we confume the few days we have to

pafs

pafs upon the earth only in feeking authorities for our paffions, in imagining fituations in which we believe ourfelves to be enabled to difobey thee with impunity; that is to fay, that all our cares, all our reflections, all the fuperiority of our views, of our lights, of our talents, all the wifdom of our meafures and of our counfels, are limited to the accomplifhment of our ruin, and to conceal from ourfelves our eternal deftruction.

Let us fhun this evil, my brethren; let us reckon no way fafe for us but that of the rules and of the law; and let us remember that there fhall be more finners condemned through the pretexts which feem to authorife the tranfgreffions of the law, than through the avowed crimes which violate it. It is thus that the law of God, after having been the rule of our manners upon the earth, fhall be their eternal confolation in heaven.

SER-

SERMON V.

FOR CHRISTMAS DAY.

Luke ii. 10.

For, behold, I bring you good tidings of great joy, which shall be to all people; for unto you is born, this day, in the city of David, a Saviour, which is Christ the Lord.

Behold, in effect, the grand tidings which, for four thousand years, the world had expected; behold the grand event which so many prophets had foretold; so many ceremonies had figured; so many righteous had awaited, and which all nature seemed to promise, and to hasten by the universal corruption spread through all flesh; behold the grand blessing which God's goodness prepared for men, after the infidelity of their first parent had rendered them all subject to sin and death.

The Saviour, the Chrift, the Lord, at laft appears this day on the earth. The over-fhadowed bring forth the righteous; the ftar of Jacob appears to the univerfe; the fceptre is departed from Judah, and he, who was to come, is arrived; the age of darknefs is accomplifhed; the promifed fign of the Lord to Judea hath appeared; a virgin has conceived and brought forth, and out of Bethlehem comes the leader who is to enlighten and govern all Ifrael.

What new bleffings, my brethren, doth this birth not announce to men? It would not, during fo many ages, have been announced, awaited, defired; it would not have formed the religion of a whole people, the object of all the prophecies; the unravelling of all the figures, the fole end of all the proceedings of God towards men, had it not been the grandeft mark of his love which he could give them. What a bleffed night is that which prefides at this divine bringing-forth! It hath feen the light of the world fhine forth in its darknefs; the heavens refound with joy and fongs of thankfgiving.

But, my brethren, we muft participate in the bleffings which this birth is meant to bring us, in order to enter into all the tranfports of delight which it fpreads through the heavens and the earth. The common joy is founded only on the common falvation which is offered to us; and if, in fpite of this aid, we ftill obftinately perfift in perifhing, perishing, the church weeps over us, and we mingle mourning and sorrow with that joy with which such blessed tidings inspire it.

Now, what are the inestimable blessings which this birth brings to men? The heavenly spirits come themselves to make it known to the shepherds; it comes to render glory to God, and peace to men; and behold the whole foundation of this grand mystery laid open. To God, that glory of which men had wished to deprive him; to men, that peace of which they had never ceased their struggles to deprive themselves.

PART I. Man had been placed upon the earth for the sole purpose of rendering, to the author of his being, that glory and that homage which were his due. All called him to these duties; and every thing, which ought to have called, removed him from them. To his supreme Majesty he owed his adoration and his homage; to his paternal goodness his love; to his infinite wisdom, the sacrifice of his reason and of his lights. These duties, engraven on his heart, and born with him, were still also incessantly proclaimed to him by all creatures; he could neither listen to himself, nor to all things around him, without finding them; nevertheless, he forgets, he effaces them from his heart. He no longer saw in the work, that honour and that worship which were due to the sovereign Architect; in the blessings with which he loaded him, that love which he owed to his benefactor;

factor; in the obscurity spread through even natural causes, that impossibility, much less, of fathoming the secrecies of God, and that mistrust, in which he ought to live, of his own lights. Idolatry, therefore, rendered to the creature that worship which the Creator had reserved for himself alone: the synagogue honoured him from the lips, and that love, which it owed to him, was confined to external homages totally unworthy of him: philosophy lost itself in its own ideas, measured the lights of God by those of men, and vainly believed that reason, which knew not itself, was able to know all truth: three sores, spread over the face of the whole earth. In a word, God was no longer either known or glorified, and man was no longer known to himself.

And, 1*stly*, To what excesses had idolatry not carried its profane worship? The death of a person loved, quickly exalted him to a divinity; and his vile ashes, on which his nothingness was stamped in characters so indelible, became themselves the title of his glory and of his immortality. Conjugal love made gods to itself; impure love followed the example, and determined to have its altars: the wife and the mistress, the husband and the lover, had temples, priests, and sacrifices. The folly, or the general corruption, adopted a worship so ridiculous and so abominable; the whole universe was infected with it; the majesty of the laws of the empire authorised it; and the magnificence of
the

the temples, the pomp of the facrifices, the immenfe riches of the images, rendered that folly refpectable. Every people was jealous in having its gods; in default of man they offered incenfe to the beaft; impure homages became the worfhip of thefe impure divinities; the towns, the mountains, the fields, the deferts, were ftained with them, and beheld fuperb edifices confecrated to pride, to lafcivioufnefs, to revenge. The number of the divinities equalled that of the paffions; the gods were almoft as numerous as the men; all became god with man; and the true God was the only one unknown to man.

The world was plunged, almoft from its creation, in the horror of this darknefs; every age had added to it frefh impieties. In proportion as the appointed time of the Deliverer drew near, the depravity of men feemed to increafe. Rome itfelf, miftrefs of the univerfe, gave way to all the different worfhips of the nations fhe had fubjugated; and beheld exalted, within her walls, the different idols of fo many conquered countries, that they became the public monuments of her folly and blindnefs, rather than of her victories.

But, after all, though all flefh had corrupted his way, God no longer wifhed to pour out his wrath upon men, nor to exterminate them by a frefh deluge; he wifhed to fave them. He had placed in the heavens the fign of his covenant with the world; and that fign was not the fhining, though vulgar

vulgar rainbow which appears in the clouds; it was Jesus Christ his only Son, the Word made flesh, the true seal of the eternal covenant, and the sole light which comes to enlighten the whole world.

He appears on the earth, and restores to his Father that glory of which the impiety of a public worship had wished to deprive him. The homage rendered to him, by his holy soul united to the world, at once makes amends to his supreme Majesty for all the honours which the universe had hitherto denied him, in order to prostitute them to a creature. A Man-God adorer renders more glory to the divinity than all idolatrous ages and nations had deprived him of; and such homage must indeed have been agreeable to the sovereign God, seeing it alone effaced idolatry from the earth; made the blood of impure victims cease to flow; overturned the profane altars; silenced the oracles of demons; reduced to dust the vain idols, and changed their superb temples, till then the receptacle of every abomination, into houses of adoration and prayer. Thus was the universe changed: the only God, unknown even in Athens, and in those cities most celebrated for knowledge and polished manners, was worshipped: the world acknowledged its Author: God entered into his rights; a worship worthy of him was established over the whole earth; and he had every where adorers, who worshipped him in spirit and in truth.

Behold

Behold the first blessing accruing from the birth of Jesus Christ, and the first glory which he renders to his Father. But, my brethren, is this grand blessing for us? We no longer worship vain idols; an incestuous Jupiter, a lascivious Venus, a cruel and revengeful Mars; but is God, therefore, more glorified among us? In their place do we not substitute fortune, voluptuousness, court favour, the world, with all its pleasures? For, whatever we love more than God, that we worship; whatever we prefer to God, that becomes our god; whatever becomes the sole object of our thoughts, of our desires, of our affections, of our fears and hopes, becomes likewise the object of our worship; and our gods are our passions, to which we sacrifice the true God.

Now, what idols of this kind still remain in the Christian world! You, that unfortunate creature, to whom you have prostituted your heart; to whom you sacrifice your wealth, your fortune, your glory, your peace; and from whom neither religious motives nor even those of the world can detach you, that is your idol: and what less is she than your divinity, since, in your madness, you do not refuse her even the name? You that court that fortune which engrosses you, to which you devote all your cares, all your exertions, all your movements, in short, your whole soul, mind, will, and life, that is your idol; and what criminal homage do you refuse from the moment that it is exacted

of

of you, and that it may become the price of its favour? You, that shameful intemperance, which debases your name and birth; which no longer accords even with our manners; which has drowned and besotted all your talents in the excesses of wine and debauchery; which, by rendering you callous to every thing else, leaves you neither relish nor feeling but for the brutal pleasures of the table, that is your idol: you think that you live only in those moments given to it; and your heart renders more homage to that infamous and abject god than your despicable and profane songs. The passions formerly made the gods; and Jesus Christ hath destroyed these idols only by destroying the passions which had raised them up: you exalt them again, by reviving all the passions which had rendered the whole world idolatrous. And what matters it to know a single god, if you elsewhere bestow your homages? Worship is in the heart; and if the true God be not the God of your heart, you place, like the pagans, vile creatures in his place, and you render not to him that glory which is his due.

Thus Jesus Christ doth not confine himself to manifesting the name of his Father to men, and to establishing, on the ruins of idols, the knowledge of the true God. He raiseth up worshippers, who reckon external homages as nothing, unless animated and sanctified by love; and who shall consider mercy, justice, and holiness, as the offerings

most

moſt worthy of God, and the moſt ſhining attendants of their worſhip: ſecond bleſſing from the birth of Jeſus Chriſt, and ſecond ſort of glory which he renders to his Father.

In effect, God was known, ſays the prophet, in Judea; Jeruſalem beheld no idols in the public places, uſurping the homages due to the God of Abraham; " there was neither iniquity in Jacob, " nor perverſeneſs in Iſrael:" that ſingle portion of the earth was free from the general contagion. But the magnificence of its temple, the pomp of its ſacrifices, the ſplendour of its ſolemnities, the exactitude of its lawful obſervances, conſtituted the whole merit of its worſhip; all religion was confined to theſe external duties. Its morals were not leſs criminal: Injuſtice, fraud, falſehood, adultery, every vice ſubſiſted, and were even countenanced by theſe vain appearances of worſhip: God was honoured from the lips; but the heart of that ungrateful people was ever diſtant from him.

Jeſus Chriſt comes to open the eyes of Judea on an error ſo groſs, ſo ancient, and ſo injurious to his Father. He comes to inform them, that man may be ſatisfied with externals alone, but that God regards only the heart; that every outward homage which withholds it from him, is an inſult and an hypocriſy, rather than a true worſhip; that it matters little to purify the external, if the internal be full of infection and putrefaction;

and

and that God is truly worshipped only by loving him.

But, alas! my brethren, is this mistake, so wretched and so often reproached to the synagogue by Jesus Christ, not still the error of the majority of us? To what, in fact, is the whole of our worship reduced? To some external ceremonies; to fulfilling certain public duties prescribed by the law; and even this is the religion of the most respectable. They come to assist in the holy mysteries; they do not, without scruple, depart from the laws of the church; they repeat some prayers which custom has consecrated; they go through the solemnities, and increase the crowd which runs to our temples: behold the whole. But are they, in consequence, more detached from the world, and from its criminal pleasures? Less occupied with the cares of a vain dress, or of fortune? More inclined to break off a criminal engagement, or to fly opportunities which have so often been a rock to their innocence? Do they bring to these external practices of religion, a pure heart, a lively faith, a guileless charity? All their passions submit amid all these religious works, which are given to custom rather than to religion.

And remark, I pray you, my brethren, that they would not dare to dispense themselves altogether from them; to live, like impious, without any profession of worship, and without fulfilling at least some of its public duties: They would consider
themselves

themselves as anathematised, and worthy of the thunder of heaven. And yet they dare to fully these holy duties by the most criminal manners! And yet they do not view themselves with horror, while rendering useless these superficial remains of religion, by a life which religion condemns and abhors! And they dread not the wrath of God, in continuing crimes which attract it on our heads, and in limiting all that is his due to vain homages which insult him!

Nevertheless, as I have already said, of all the worldly these are the most prudent, and, in the eyes of the world, the most regular. They have not yet thrown off the yoke, like so many others; they do not arrogate to themselves a shocking glory in not believing in God; they blaspheme not what they do not know; they do not consider religion as a mockery and a human invention; they still wish to hold to it by some externals; but they hold not to it by the heart; but they dishonour it by their irregularities; but they are not Christians but in name. Thus, even in a greater degree than formerly under the synagogue, the magnificent externals of religion subsist among us, along with a more profound and more general depravity of manners than ever the prophets reproached to the obstinacy and hypocrisy of the Jews: thus, that religion, in which we glory, is no longer, to the greatest number of believers, but a superficial worship: thus, that new covenant, which ought to be

written

written only in the heart; that law of spirit and life, which ought to render men wholly spiritual; that inward worship, which ought to have given to God worshippers in spirit and in truth, has given him only phantoms, only fictitious adorers; the mere appearances of worship; in a word, but a people still Jewish, which honours him from the lips, but whose corrupted heart, stained with a thousand crimes, chained by a thousand iniquitous passions, is always far distant from him.

Behold the second blessing, of the birth of Jesus Christ, in which we have no part. He comes to abolish a worship wholly external, which was confined to sacrifices of animals and lawful ceremonies, and which, in not rendering to God the homage of our love, alone capable of glorifying him, rendered not to him that glory which is his due: in place of these appearances of religion, he comes to substitute a law which ought to be fulfilled wholly in the heart; a worship, of which the love of his Father ought to be the first and the principal homage. Nevertheless, this holy worship, this new precept, this sacred trust, which he hath confided to us, has miserably degenerated in our hands; we have turned it into a worship wholly Pharisaical, in which the heart has no part; which has no influence in changing our irregular propensities; which has no effect upon our manners, and which only renders us so much the more criminal,

criminal, as we abuse the blessing which ought to wash out and purify all our crimes.

Lastly, Men had likewise wished to ravish from God the glory of his providence and of his eternal wisdom. Philosophers, struck with the absurdity of a worship which multiplied gods to infinity, and forced, by the sole lights of reason, to acknowledge one sole Supreme Being, disfigured the nature of that Being by a thousand absurd opinions. Some figured to themselves an indolent god; retired within himself; in full possession of his own happiness; disdaining to abase himself by paying attention to what passes on the earth; reckoning as nothing men whom he had created; equally insensible to their virtues as to their vices; and leaving wholly to chance the course of ages and seasons, the revolutions of empires, the lot of each individual, the whole machine of this vast universe, and the whole dispensation of human things. Others subjected him to a fatal chain of events; they made him a god without liberty and without power; and, while they regarded him as the master of men, they believed him to be the slave of destiny. The errors of reason were then the only rule of religion, and of the belief of those who were considered as even the wisest and most enlightened.

Jesus Christ comes to restore to his Father that glory of which the vain reasonings of philosophy had deprived him. He comes to teach to men that faith is the source of true lights; and that the sacrifices of reason is the first step of Christian philosophy. He comes to fix uncertainty, by instructing us in what we ought to know of the supreme Being, and what, with regard to him, we ought not to know.

It was not, in effect, sufficient that men, in order to render glory to God, should make a sacrifice to him of their life, as to the author of their being, and should, by that avowal, acknowledge the impiety of idolatry; that they should make a sacrifice to him of their love and of their heart, as to their sovereign felicity, and thereby proclaim the insufficiency and the inutility of the external and pharisaical worship of the synagogue; it was likewise required, that to him they should sacrifice their reason, as to their wisdom and to their eternal truth, and thus be undeceived with regard to the vain researches and the conceited knowledge of philosophers.

Now, the sole birth of a Man-God, the ineffable union of our nature with a divine person, disconcerts all human reason; and this incomprehensible mystery, held out to men as their whole knowledge, their whole truth, their whole philosophy, their whole religion, at once makes them feel, that the truth, which they hitherto had in vain sought, must be sought, not by vain efforts, but by the sacrifice of reason and of our feeble lights.

But,

But, alas! where among us are believers who make a thorough sacrifice of their reason to faith; and who, rejecting their own lights, humble their eyes, in a respectful and silent adoration, before the majestic impenetrability of religion? I speak not of those impious, still to be found among us, who deny a God. Ah! we must leave them to the horror and the indignation of the whole universe which knows a divinity, and which worships him; or rather leave them to the horror of their own conscience, which inwardly invokes and calls upon him in spite of themselves, while outwardly they are glorifying themselves in professing not to know him.

I speak of the majority of believers, who have an idea of the divinity, almost equally false and equally human, as had formerly the pagan philosophers; who consider him as nothing in all the accidents of life; who live as if chance or the caprice of men determined all things here below; and who acknowledge good-luck and bad-luck as the two sole divinities which govern the world, and which preside over every thing relative to the earth. I speak of those men of little faith who, far from adoring the secrecies of futurity in the profound and impenetrable councils of providence, go to search for them in ridiculous and childish prophecies; attribute to man a knowledge which God hath solely reserved to himself; with a senseless belief await, from the dreams of a false prophet,

phet, events and revolutions which are to decide the destiny of nations and empires: found thereupon vain hopes for themselves, and renew either the folly of pagan augurs and soothsayers, or the impiety of the pythoness of Saul, and of the oracles of Delphi and Dodona. I speak of those who wish to penetrate into the eternal ways of God on our lots; and who, being unable, by the sole powers of reason, to solve the insurmountable difficulties of the mysteries of grace with regard to the salvation of men, far from crying out with the apostle, "O the depth of the riches both of the "wisdom and knowledge of God!" are tempted to believe, either that God doth not interfere in our salvation; or, if he do, that it is needless for us to interfere in it ourselves. I speak of those dissolute characters in the world, who always find plausible and convincing, though, in fact, weak and foolish in the extreme, whatever unbelief opposes to faith; who are staggered by the first frivolous doubt proposed by the impious; who appear as if they would be delighted that religion were false; and who are less touched with that respectable load of proofs which overpower a conceited reason and its truth, than with a senseless discourse which opposes it, in which there is generally nothing important but the boldness of the impiety and of the blasphemy. Lastly, I speak of many believers who turn over to the people the belief of so many wonderful actions which the history

tory of religion has preserved to us; who seem to believe that, whatever is above the power of man, is likewise beyond the power of God; and who refuse credit to the miracles of a religion which is solely founded on them, and which is itself the greatest of all miracles.

Behold how we still snatched from God that glory which the birth of Jesus Christ had rendered to him. It had taught us to sacrifice our own lights to the incomprehensible mystery of his manifestation in our flesh, and no longer to live but by faith; it had fixed the uncertainties of the human mind, and recalled it from the errors and the abyss in which reason had plunged it, to the way of truth and life, and we abandon it: and even under the empire of faith, we wish still to walk as formerly, under the standards, if I may venture to speak in this manner, of a weak reason: the mysteries of religion, which we cannot comprehend, shock us; we suspect, we reform all; we would have God to think like man. Without altogether losing our faith, we suffer it to be inwardly weakened; we allow it to remain inactive: and it is this relaxation of faith which has corrupted our manners; multiplied vices; enflamed all hearts with a love of things present; extinguished the love of riches to come; placed trouble, hatred, and dissention among believers, and effaced those original marks of innocence, of sanctity, and of charity, which at first had rendered Christianity so respectable even

to

to thofe who refufed fubmiffion to it. But not only doth the birth of Jesus Chrift reftore to God that glory of which men had wifhed to deprive him; it likewife reftores to men that peace, of which they had never ceafed to deprive themfelves: "And on "earth peace, good will towards men."

PART II. An univerfal peace reigned throughout the univerfe when Jefus Chrift, the " Prince " of Peace," appeared on the earth: all the nations fubject to the Roman empire peaceably fupported the yoke of thofe haughty mafters of the world: Rome herfelf, after civil diffentions, which had almoft depopulated her walls, filled the iflands and deferts with her profcribed, and bathed Europe and Afia with the blood of her citizens, breathed from the horror of thefe troubles, and reunited under the authority of a Cefar, experienced, in flavery, a peace which fhe had never, during the enjoyment of her liberty, been able to accomplifh.

The univerfe was then at reft; but that was but a deceitful calm. Man, the prey of his own violent and iniquitous paffions, experienced within himfelf the moft cruel diffention and war: far from God, delivered up to the agitations and frenzies of his own heart; combatted by the multiplicity and the eternal contrariety of his irregular propenfities, he was unable to find peace, becaufe he never fought it but in the fource of all his troubles and difquiets. Philofophers made a boaft of being able to beftow it on their followers; but that universal verfal calm of the paffions which they gave hopes of to their fage, and which they fo emphatically announced, might fupprefs their fallies; but it left the whole venom in the heart. It was a peace of pride and oftentation; it mafked the outward man; but, under that mafk of ceremony, man always knew himfelf to be the fame.

Jefus Chrift comes to-day upon the earth, to bring that true peace to men which the world had never hitherto been able to give them. He comes radically to cure the evil; his divine philofophy is not confined to the promulgation of pompous precepts, which might be agreeable to reafon, but which cured not the wounds of the heart; and, as pride, voluptuoufnefs, hatred, and revenge, had been the fatal fources of all the agitations experienced by the heart of man, he comes to reftore peace to him, by draining them off, through his grace, his doctrine, and his example.

Yes, my brethren, I fay that pride had been the original fource of all the troubles which tore the heart of men. What wars, what frenzies, had that fatal paffion not lighted upon the earth? With what torrents of blood had it not inundated the univerfe? And what is the hiftory of nations and of empires, of princes and of conquerors, of every age and people, but the hiftory of thofe calamities with which pride from the beginning had afflicted men? The entire world was but a gloomy theatre, upon which that haughty and fenfelefs paffion

every

every day exhibited the moſt bloody ſcenes. But the external operations were but a faint image of the troubles which the proud man inwardly experienced. Ambition was a virtue: moderation was looked up as meanneſs: an individual overthrew his country, overturned the laws and cuſtoms, rendered millions miſerable, in order to uſurp the firſt place among his fellow-citizens; and the ſucceſs of his guilt enſured him every homage; and his name, ſtained with the blood of his brethren, acquired only additional luſtre in the public annals which preſerved its memory; and a proſperous villain became the grandeſt character of his age. That paſſion, deſcending among the crowd, became leſs ſtriking; but it was neither leſs animated nor furious: the obſcure was not more at his eaſe than the public man: each wiſhed to carry off the prize from his equals: the orator, the philoſopher, wrangled for, and tore from each other that glory, which, in fact, was the ſole end of all their toils and watchings; and, as the deſires of pride are inſatiable, man, to whom it was then honourable totally to yield himſelf up to it, being unable to reſt in any degree of elevation, was likewiſe incapable of peace and tranquility. Pride, become the ſole ſource of human honour and glory, was likewiſe become the fatal rock of the quiet and happineſs of men.

The birth of Jeſus Chriſt, by correcting the world of this error, re-eſtabliſhes on the earth that
peace

peace which pride had banished from it. He might have manifested himself to men, with all the marks of splendour which the prophets attributed to him: He might have assumed the pompous titles of conqueror of Judah, of legislator of the people, of deliverer of Israel; Jerusalem, in these glorious marks, would have recognised him whom she awaited: but Jerusalem, in these titles, saw only a human glory; and Jesus Christ comes to undeceive, and to teach her, that such glory is nothing; that such an expectation had been unworthy of the oracles of so many prophets who had announced him; that the Holy Spirit, which inspired them, could hold out only holiness and eternal riches to men; that all other riches, far from rendering them happy, only increased their evils and crimes; and that his visible ministry was to correspond with the splendid promises, which had, for so many ages, announced him, only by being wholly spiritual, and that he should intend only the salvation of men.

Thus, he is born at Bethlehem, in a poor and abject state; without external state or splendour, he whose birth the songs of all the armies of heaven then celebrated; without title which might distinguish him in the eyes of men, he who was exalted above all principality or power: he suffers his name to be written down among those of the obscurest subjects of Cesar; he whose name was above all other name, and who alone had the right of writing down the names of his chosen in the book of eternity: vulgar and simple shepherds alone came to pay him homage; he, before whom whatever is mighty on the earth, in heaven, and in hell, ought to bend the knee: lastly, whatever can confound human pride is assembled at the spectacle of his birth. If titles, rank, or prosperity had been able to render us happy here below, and to shed peace through our heart, Jesus Christ would have made his appearance clothed in them, and would have brought all these riches to his disciples; but he brings peace to us only by holding them in contempt, and by teaching us to hold them equally in contempt: he comes to render us happy, only by coming to suppress desires which hitherto had occasioned all our disquiets: he comes to point out to us more solid and more durable riches, alone capable of calming our hearts, of filling our desires, of easing our troubles: riches of which man cannot deprive us, and which require only to be loved and to be wished for, to be assured of possessing them.

Nevertheless, who tastes of this blessed peace? Wars, troubles, frenzies, are they more rare since his birth? Are those empires and states which worship him, in consequence more peaceful? Does that pride which he came to destroy occasion less commotion and confusion among men? Alas! Seek among Christians that peace which ought to be their inheritance, and where shall you find it? In cities?

cities? Pride sets every thing there in motion; every one wishes to soar above the rank of his anceftors: an individual, exalted by fortune, destroys the happiness of thousands who walk in his steps, without being able to attain the same point of prosperity. In the circle of domestic walls? They conceal only distresses and cares: and the father of the family, solely occupied with the advancement rather than the Christian education of his offspring, leaves to them, for inheritance, his agitations and disquiets, which they, in their turn, shall one day transmit to their descendants. In the palaces of kings? But, there it is that a lawless and boundless ambition gnaws, devours every heart; it is there that, under the specious mask of joy and tranquility, the most violent and the bittereft passions are nourished; it is there that happiness apparently resides, and yet where pride occasions the greatest number of discontented and miserable. In the sanctuary? Alas! there, ought surely to be found an asylum of peace; but ambition pervades even the holy place; the efforts there are more to raise themselves above their brethren, than to render themselves useful to them; the holy dignities of the church become, like those of the age, the reward of intrigue and caballing; the religious circumspection of the prince cannot put a stop to solicitations and private intrigues; we there see the same inveteracy in rivalships, the same sorrow in consequence of neglect, the same

jealousy

jealousy towards those who are preferred to us : a ministry is boldly canvassed for, which ought to be accepted only with fear and trembling : they seat themselves in the temple of God, though placed there by other hands than his : they head the flock without his consent to whom it belongs, and without his having said, as to Peter, " Feed my " sheep;" and, as they have taken the charge without call and without ability, the flock are led without edification and without fruit, alas! and often with shame. O peace of Jesus Christ! which surpasseth all sense, sole remedy against the troubles which pride incessantly excites in our hearts, who shall then be able to give thee to man?

But, secondly, if the disquiets of pride had banished peace from the earth, the impure desires of the flesh had not given rise to fewer troubles. M . forgetting the excellency of his nature, and the sanctity of his origin, gave himself up, like the beasts, without scruple, to the impetuosity of that brutal instinct. Finding it the most violent and the most universal of his propensities, he believed it to be also the most innocent and the most lawful. In order still more to authorise it, he made it part of his worship, and formed to himself impure gods, in whose temples that infamous vice became the only homage which did honour to their altars : even a philosopher, in other respects the wisest of pagans, dreading that marriage should put a kind of check on that deplorable passion,

had

had wiſhed to aboliſh that ſacred bond ; to permit among men, as among animals, a brutal confuſion, and only multiply the human race through crimes. The more that vice became general, the more it loſt the name of vice ; and, neverthelefs, what a deluge of miſeries had it not poured out upon the earth ? With what fury had it not been ſeen to arm people againſt people ; kings againſt kings ; blood againſt blood ; brethren againſt brethren ; every where carrying trouble and carnage, and ſhaking the whole univerſe ? Ruins of cities, wrecks of the moſt flouriſhing empires, ſceptres and crowns overthrown, became the public and gloomy monuments which every age reared up, in order, it would ſeem, to preſerve, to following ages, the remembrance and the fatal tradition of thoſe calamities with which that vice had afflicted the human race. It became itſelf an inexhauſtible ſource of troubles and anxieties to the man who then gave himſelf up to a bourdleſs gratification of it ; it held out peace and pleaſure ; but jealouſy, exceſs, frenzy, difguſt, inconſtancy, and black chagrin, continually walked in its ſteps : till then, that the laws, the religion, and the common example authoriſing it, the ſole love of eaſe, even in theſe ages of darkneſs and corruption, kept free from it a ſmall number of ſages.

But that motive was too feeble to check its impetuous courſe, and to extinguiſh its fires in the heart of men : a more powerful remedy was required :

quired: and that is, the birth of the Deliverer, who comes to draw men out of that abyss of corruption, in order to render them pure and without stain; to break asunder those shameful bonds, and to give peace to their hearts, by restoring to them that freedom and innocence of which the slavery and tyranny of that vice had deprived them. He is born of a virgin-mother, and the purest of all created beings: he thereby gives estimation and honour to a virtue unknown to the world, and which even his people considered as a reproach. Besides, in uniting himself with us, he becomes our head; incorporates us with himself; makes us to become members of his mystical body; of that body which no longer receives life and influence but from him; of that body whose every ministry is holy; which is to be seated at the right hand of the living God, and to glorify him for ever.

Behold, my brethren, to what height of honour Jesus Christ, in this mystery, exalts our flesh; he makes of it the temple of God; the sanctuary of the Holy Spirit; the portion of a body in which the fullness of the divinity resides; the object of the kindness and the love of his Father. But do we not still prophane this holy temple? Do we not still turn to shame the members of Jesus Christ? Do we, in a higher degree, respect our flesh, since it is become a holy portion of his mystical body? Does that shameful passion not still exercise the same fame tyranny over Christians, that is to say, over the children of sanctity and liberty? Does it not still disturb the peace of the universe, the tranquility of empires, the harmony of families, the order of society, the confidence of marriage, the innocence of social intercourse, the lot of every individual? Are not the most tragical spectacles still every day furnished to the world by it? Does it respect the most sacred ties and the most respectable character? Does it not reckon as nothing every duty? Does it pay attention even to decency? And does it not turn all society into a frightful confusion, where custom has effaced every rule? Even you, who listen to me, from whence have arisen all the miseries and unhappinesses of your life, is it not from that deplorable passion? Is it not that which has overturned your fortune; which has cast trouble and dissention through the heart of your family; which has swallowed up the patrimony of your fathers; which has dishonoured your name; which has ruined your health, and now makes you to drag on a gloomy and disgraceful life on the earth? Is it not, at least, that which actually rends your heart, at present filled with it? What goes on within you but a tumultuous revolution of fears, desires, jealousies, mistrusts, disgusts, and frenzies? And since that passion has stained your soul, have you enjoyed a single moment of peace? Let Jesus Christ again be born within your heart; he alone can be your true peace: chase from it the impure

spirits

spirits, and the mansion of your soul will be at rest: become once more a child of grace; innocence is the only source of tranquility.

Lastly, the birth of Jesus Christ reconciles men to his Father; it reunites the Gentile and the Jew; it destroys all those hateful distinctions of Greek and Barbarian, of Roman and Scythian; it extinguishes all animosities and hatreds; of all nations it makes only one people; of all his disciples, only one heart and one soul; last kind of peace which it brings to men. Formerly they were united together, neither by worship, a common hope, nor by the new covenant, which, in an enemy, holds out to us a friend. They considered each other almost as creatures of a different species: the diversity of religions, of manners, of countries, of languages, of interests, had, it would appear, as if diversified in them the same nature: scarcely did they recognise each other by that figure of humanity, which was the only sign of connection still remaining to them. Like wild beasts, they mutually exterminated each other; they centered their glory in depopulating the lands of their fellow-creatures, and in carrying in triumph their bloody heads as the splendid memorials of their victories: it might have been said that they held their existence from different irreconcilable creators, always watchful to destroy each other, and who had placed them here below only to revenge their quarrel, and to terminate their disagreement by the general extinction

extinction of one of the two parties; every difunited man, and nothing bound them together but intereſt and the paſſions, which were themſelves the ſole ſource of their diviſions and animoſities.

But Jeſus Chriſt is become our peace, our reconciliation, the corner-ſtone which binds and unites the whole fabric, the living head which unites all his members, and makes but one body of the whole. Every thing knits us to him; and whatever knits us to him unites us to each other. It is the ſame Spirit which animates us, the ſame hope which ſuſtains us, the ſame boſom which brings us forth, the ſame fold which aſſembles us, and the ſame Shepherd who conducts us; we are children of the ſame Father, inheritors of the ſame promiſes, citizens of the ſame eternal city, and members of one ſame body.

Now, my brethren, have ſo many ſacred ties been ſuccefsful in binding us together? Chriſtianity, which ought to be but the union of hearts, the tie to knit believers to each other, and Jeſus Chriſt to believers; and which ought to repreſent upon the earth an image of the peace of heaven; Chriſtianity itſelf is no longer but a horrible theatre of troubles and diſſentions: war and fury ſeem to have eſtabliſhed an eternal abode among Chriſtians; religion itſelf, which ought to unite, divides them. The unbeliever, the enemy of Jeſus Chriſt, the children of the falſe prophet, who came to ſpread war and devaſtation through men, are in peace;

and the children of peace, and disciples of him who, this day, comes to bring it to men, have their hands continually armed with fire and sword against each other! Kings rise up against kings; nations against nations; the seas which separate reunite them for their mutual destruction: a vile morsel of stone arms their fury and revenge; and whole nations go to perish and to bury themselves under its walls, in contesting to whom shall belong its ruins: the earth is not sufficiently vast to contain them, and to fix them, each one in the bounds which nature herself seems to have pointed out for states and empires; each wishes to usurp from his neighbour; and a miserable field of battle, which is scarcely sufficient to serve as a burial place to those who have disputed it, becomes the prize of those rivers of blood with which it is for ever stained. O divine Reconciliator of men! return then once more upon the earth, since the peace which thou broughtest to it at thy birth still leaves so many wars and so many calamities in the universe!

Nor is this all: that circle itself, which unites us under the same laws, unites not hearts and affections; hatreds and jealousies divide citizens equally as they divide nations; animosities are perpetuated in families, and fathers transmit them to their children, as an accursed inheritance. In vain may the authority of the prince disarm the hand, it disarms not the heart; in vain may the sword be wrested from them, with the sword of the tongue

they

they continue a thousand times more cruelly to pierce their enemy; hatred, under the necessity of confining itself within, becomes deeper and more rancorous, and to forgive is looked upon as a dishonourable weakness. Oh! my brethren, in vain then hath Jesus Christ descended upon the earth! He is come to bring peace to us; he hath left it to us as his inheritance; nothing hath he so strongly recommended to us as that of loving each other; yet fellowship and peace seem as if banished from among us, and hatred and animosity divide court, city, and families; and those whom the offices, the interests of the state, decency itself, and blood ought, at least, to unite, tear, defame, would wish to destroy, and to exalt themselves on the ruins of each other: and religion, which shews us our brethren even in our enemies, is no longer listened to; and that awful threatening, which gives us room to expect the same severity on the part of God which we shall have shewn to our brethren, no longer touches or affects us; and all these motives, so capable of softening the heart, still leave it filled with all the bitterness of hatred. We tranquilly live in this frightful state: the justice of our complaints with regard to our enemies, calms us on the injustice of our hatred and of our rooted aversion towards them; and if, on the approach of death, we apparently hold out to them the hand of reconciliation, it is not that we love them more, it is because the expiring heart hath no longer the

force

force to sustain its hatred, that almost all our feelings are extinguished, or, at least, that we are no longer capable of feeling any thing but our own weakness and our approaching dissolution. Let us then unite ourselves to the newly born Jesus Christ; let us enter into the spirit of that mystery; with him let us render to God that glory which is his due; it is the only mean of restoring to ourselves that peace, of which our passions have hitherto deprived us.

SERMON VI.

FOR THE DAY OF THE EPIPHANY.

MATTHEW ii. 2.

For we have seen his star in the east, and we are come to worship him.

Truth, that light of Heaven figured by the star which on this day appears to the magi, is the only thing here below worthy of the cares and the researches of man. It alone is the light of our mind, the rule of our heart, the source of solid joys, the foundation of our hopes, the consolation of our fears, the alleviation of our evils, the cure for all our afflictions: it alone is the refuge of the good conscience, and the terror of the bad; the inward punishment of vice, the internal recompense of virtue: it alone immortalifes those who have loved it, and renders illustrious the chains of those who suf-

fer

fer for it, attracts public honours to the afhes of its martyrs and defenders, and beftows refpectability on the abjection and the poverty of thofe who have quitted all to follow it: laftly, it alone infpires magnanimous thoughts, forms heroical men, fouls of whom the world is unworthy, fages alone worthy of that name. All our attentions ought therefore to be confined to know it; all our talents to manifeft it; all our zeal to defend it: in men we ought then to look only for truth, to have no wifh of pleafing them but by truth, to efteem in them only truth, and to be refolved that they never fhall pleafe us but by it: in a word, it would appear that it fhould have only to fhew itfelf, as on this day to the magi, to be loved; and that it fhews us to ourfelves in order to teach us to know ourfelves.

Neverthelefs, it is aftonifhing what different impreffions the fame truth makes upon men. To fome it is a light which directs their fteps, and, in pointing out their duty, renders it amiable to them: to others it is a troublefome light, and, as it were, a kind of dazzling, which vexes and fatigues them: laftly, to many it is a thick mift which irritates, inflames them with rage, and completes their blindnefs. It is the fame ftar which, on this day, appears in the firmament: the magi fee it; the priefts of Jerufalem know that it is foretold in the prophets; Herod can no longer doubt that it hath appeared, feeing wife men come from the extremities of the eaft, to feek, guided by its light,

the

the new King of the Jews. Nevertheless, how dissimilar are the dispositions with which they receive the same truth manifested to them.

In the magi it finds a docile and sincere heart: in the priests, a heart mean, deceitful, cowardly, and dissembling: in Herod, a corrupted and hardened heart. Consequently, it forms worshippers in the magi; dissemblers in the priests; and in Herod a persecutor. Now, my brethren, such is still at present among us the lot of truth: it is a celestial light which is shown to us, says St Augustin: but few receive it, many hide and dim it, and a still greater number contemn and persecute it: it shews itself to all; but how many indocile souls who reject it? How many mean and cowardly souls who dissemble it? How many black and hardened hearts who oppress and persecute it? Let us collect these three marked characters in our gospel, which are to instruct us in all our duties relative to truth: truth received, truth dissembled, truth persecuted. Holy Spirit, Spirit of Truth, destroy in us the spirit of the world, that spirit of error, of dissimulation, of hatred against the truth; and in this holy place destined to form ministers, who are to announce it even in the extremities of the earth, render us worthy of loving the truth, of manifesting it to those who know it not, and of suffering all for its sake.

PART I. I call truth that eternal rule, that internal light incessantly present within us, which, in

every

every action, points out to us what we ought, and what we ought not to do; which enlightens our doubts; which judges our judgments; which inwardly condemns or approves us, accordingly as our behaviour is agreeable or contrary to its light; and which, in certain moments more splendid and bright, more evidently points out to us the way in which we ought to walk, and is figured to us by that miraculous light which, on this day, conducts the magi to Jesus Christ.

Now, I say that, the first use which we ought to make of truth being for ourselves, the church, on this day, proposes to us, in the conduct of the magi, a model of those dispositions which alone can render the knowledge of truth beneficial and salutary to us. There are few souls, however they may be plunged in the senses and in the passions, whose eyes are not, at times, opened upon the vanity of the interests they pursue, upon the grandeur of the hopes which they sacrifice, and upon the ignominy of the life which they lead. But, alas! their eyes are opened to the light, only to be closed again in an instant; and the sole fruit which they reap; from the truth which is visible to, and enlightens them, is that of adding to the misfortune of having hitherto been ignorant of it, the guilt of having afterwards known it in vain.

Some confine themselves to vain reasonings upon the light which strikes them, and turn truth into a subject of controversy and vain philosophy;

others,

others, with minds yet unsettled, wish, it would appear, to know it; but they seek it not in an effectual way, because they would, at bottom, be heartily sorry to have found it: lastly, others, more tractable, allow themselves to be wrought upon by its evidence; but, discouraged by the difficulties and the self-denials which it presents to them, they receive it not with that delight and that gratitude which, when once known, it inspires. And behold the rocks, which the dispositions of the sages of the east towards that light of Heaven, which comes to shew new routes to them, teach us to shun.

Accustomed, in consequence of a public profession of wisdom and philosophy, to investigate every thing, and reduce it to the judgment of a vain reason, and to be far above all popular prejudices, they stop not, however, before commencing their journey upon the faith of the celestial light, to examine if the appearance of this new star might not be solved by natural causes; they do not assemble from every quarter scientific men, in order to reason on an event so uncommon; they sacrifice no time to vain difficulties, which generally arise, more from the repugnance we feel to truth, than from a sincere desire of enlightening ourselves, and of knowing it. Instructed by that tradition of their fathers which the captive Israelites had formerly carried into the east, and which Daniel and so many other prophets had announced there,

there, relative to the Star of Jacob which should one day appear, they, at once, comprehended, that the vain reflections of the human mind have no connection with the light of Heaven; that the portion of light which Heaven shews them is sufficient to determine and to conduct them; that grace always leaves obscurities in the ways to which it calls us, in order not to deprive faith of the merit of submission; and that, whenever we are so happy as to catch a single gleam of truth, the uprightness of the heart ought to supply whatever deficiency may yet remain in the evidence of the light.

Nevertheless, how many souls in the world, wavering upon faith, or rather enslaved by passions which render doubtful to them that truth which condemns them; how many souls, thus floating, clearly see, that, at bottom, the religion of our fathers hath marks of truth which the most high-flown and proudest reason would not dare to deny to it; that unbelief leads to too much; that, after all, we must hold to something; and, that total unbelief is a party still more incomprehensible to reason than the mysteries which shock it; who see it, and who struggle, by endless disputes, to lull that worm of the conscience which incessantly reproaches their error and their folly; who resist that truth, which proves itself in the bottom of their heart, under pretence of enlightening themselves; who apply for advice only that they may say

say to themselves, that their doubts are unanswerable; who have recourse to the most learned, only to have the power of alleging, as a fresh motive of unbelief, the having had recourse in vain? It would seem that religion is no longer but a matter of discourse; it is no longer considered as that important affair in which not a moment is to be lost; it is a simple matter of controversy, as formerly in the Arespagus; it fills up the idle time; it is one of those unimportant questions which fill up the vacancies of conversation, and amuse the languor and the vanity of general intercourse.

But, my brethren, " the kingdom of God cometh not with observation." Truth is not the fruit of controversy and dispute, but of tears and groanings; it is by purifying our heart in meditation and in prayer that we alone must expect, like the magi, the light of Heaven, and to become worthy of distinguishing and of knowing it. A corrupted heart, says St Augustin, may see the truth; but he is incapable of relishing or of loving it; in vain do you enlighten and instruct yourselves; your doubts are in your passions: religion will become evident and clear from the moment that you shall become chaste, temperate, and equitable; and you will have faith from the moment that you shall cease to have vice. Consequently, from the instant that you cease to have an interest in finding religion false, you will find it incontestable; no longer hate its maxims, and you will no longer contest its mysteries.

Augustin himself, already convinced of the truth of the gospel, still found, in the love of pleasure, a source of doubts and perplexities which checked him. It was no longer the dreams of the Manicheans which kept him removed from faith; he was fully sensible of their absurdity and fanaticism; it was no longer the pretended contradictions of our holy books; Ambrose had explained their purport and their adorable mysteries. Nevertheless, he still doubted; the sole thought of having to renounce his shameful passions in becoming a disciple of faith, rendered it still suspicious to him. He would have wished either that the doctrine of Jesus Christ had been an imposition, or that it had not condemned his voluptuous excesses, without which, indeed, he was then unable to comprehend how either an happy or a comfortable life could be led. Thus, always floating and unwilling to be settled; continually consulting, yet dreading to be instructed; by turns the disciple and admirer of Ambrose, and racked by the perplexities of a heart which shunned the truth, he dragged his chains, as he says himself, dreading to be delivered from it, he continued to start doubts merely to prolong his passions, he wished to be yet more enlightened, because he dreaded to be it too much; and, more the slave of his passion than of his errors, he rejected truth, which manifested itself to him,

him, merely becaufe he looked upon it as a victorious and irrefiftible hand which was at laft come to break afunder thofe fetters which he ftill loved. The light of Heaven finds, therefore, no doubts to diffipate in the minds of the magi, becaufe it finds no paffion in their hearts to overcome; and they well deferve to be the firft-fruits of the gentiles, and the firft difciples of that faith which was to fubjugate all nations to the gofpel.

Not but it is often neceffary to add, to our own light, the approbation of thofe who are eftablifhed to diftinguifh, whether it be the right fpirit which moves us; fallacy is fo fimilar to truth, that it is not eafy to avoid being fometimes deceived. Thus the magi, in order to be more furely confirmed in the truth of the prodigy which guides their fteps, come ftraight to Jerufalem : they confult the priefts and the fcribes, as the only perfons capable of difcovering to them that truth which they feek ; they boldly and openly demand, in the midft of that great city, " where is he that is born King of the " Jews ?" They propofe their queftion with no palliations, calculated to attract an equivocal anfwer : they are determined to be enlightened, and wifh not to be flattered ; from their heart they feek the truth, and, for that reafon, they find it.

New difpofition, fufficiently rare among believers. Alas! we find not truth, becaufe we never feek it with a fincere and upright heart : we diffufe a kind of mift over every attempt to find it,

which

which conceals it from our view: we confult, but we place our paffions in fo favourable a light, we hold them out in colours fo foftened, and fo fimilar to the truth, that we procure a reply of its being really fo: we wifh not to be inftructed; we wifh to be deceived, and to add, to the paffion which enflaves us, an authority which may calm us.

Such is the illufion of the majority of men, and frequently even of thofe who, become contrite, have quitted the errors of a worldly life. Yes, my brethren, let us fearch our own hearts, and we fhall find, that, however fincere our converfion may otherwife be, yet there is always within us fome particular point, fome fecret and privileged attachment, upon which we are not candid; upon which we never but very imperfectly inftruct the guide of our confcience; upon which we feek not with fincerity the truth; upon which, in a word, it would even grieve us to have found it: and from thence it is, that the weakneffes of the pious and good always furnifh fo many traits to the derifion of the worldy; from thence, we attract upon virtue continual reproaches and çenfures, which ought to light only upon ourfelves. Neverthelefs, to hear us fpeak, we love the truth; we are defirous of having it fhewn to us. But a convincing proof, of that being only a vain mode of fpeaking, is, that whatever concerns, or has any allufion to this cherifhed paffion, is carefully avoided by all around us; our friends are filent upon it; our fuperiors

periors are obliged to ufe an artful delicacy, not to injure our feelings; our inferiors are upon their guard, and employ continual precautions; we are never fpoken to, but with lenitives which draw a veil over our fore; we are almoft the only perfons ignorant of our defect: the whole world fees it, yet no one has the courage to make it known to ourfelves: it is clearly feen that we feek not with fincerity the truth; and that, far from curing us, the hand, which fhould dare to probe our fore, would only fucceed in making a frefh one.

David knew not, and refpected not the fanctity of Nathan, till after that prophet had fpoken to him, with fincerity, of the fcandal of his conduct; from that day, and ever afterwards, he confidered him as his father and deliverer; but, with us, a perfon lofes all his merit from the moment that he has forced us to know ourfelves. Before that, he was enlightened, prudent, full of charity; he poffeffed every talent calculated to attract efteem and confidence; the John the Baptifts were liftened to with pleafure, as formerly by an inceftuous king: but, from the moment that they have undifguifedly fpoken to us; from the moment that they have faid to us, " It is not lawful for thee," they are ftripped, in our opinion, of all their grand qualities: their zeal is no longer but whim; their charity but an oftentation, or a defire to cenfure and contradict: their piety but an imprudence or a cheat, with which they cover their pride; their

truth

truth but a mistaken phantom. Thus, frequently convinced in our own minds of the iniquity of our passions, we would wish others to give them their approbation; forced, by the inward testimony of the truth, to reproach them to ourselves, we cannot endure that they should be mentioned to us by others: we are hurt and irritated that others should join us against ourselves. Like Saul, we exact of the Samuels, that they approve, in public, what we inwardly condemn; and, through a corruption of the heart, perhaps more deplorable than our passions themselves, unable to silence truth in the bottom of our heart, we would wish to extinguish it in the hearts of all who approach us. I was right, therefore, in saying, that we all make a boast of loving the truth, but that few court it, like the magi, with an upright and a sincere heart.

Thus, the little attention which they pay to the difficulties, which seemed to dissuade them from that research, is a fresh proof of its sincerity and heartiness. For, my brethren, how singular must not this extraordinary step, which grace proposed to them, have at first appeared to their mind. They alone, of all their nation, among so many sages and learned men, without regard to friends and connections, in spite of public observations and derisions, while all others either contemn this miraculous star, or consider the attention paid to it, and the design of these three sages, as an absurd undertaking,

undertaking, and a popular weakness, unworthy of their mind and knowledge, they alone declare against the common opinion; they alone entrust themselves to the new guide which Heaven sends them; they alone abandon their country and their children, and reckon, as nothing, a singularity, the necessity and wisdom of which the celestial light discloses to them.

Last instruction. The cause, my brethren, of truth being always unavailingly shewn to us, is, that we judge not of it by the lights which it leaves in our soul, but by the impression which it makes on the rest of men with whom we live: we never consult the truth in our heart; we consult only the opinions which others have of it. Thus, in vain doth the light of Heaven a thousand times intrude upon us, and point out the ways in which we ought to go; the very first glance which we afterwards cast upon the example of others who live like us, revives us, and spreads a fresh mist over our heart. In those fortunate moments when we consult the sole truth of our own conscience, we condemn ourselves; we tremble over a futurity; we promise to ourselves a new life; yet, a moment after, when returned to the world, and no longer consulting but the general example, we justify ourselves, and regain that false security which we had lost. We have no confidence in the truth which the common example disproves; we sacrifice it to error and to the public opinion;

it becomes fufpicious to us, becaufe it has chofen out us alone to favour with its light, and the very fingularity of the bleffing is the caufe of our ingratitude and oppofition. We cannot comprehend, that, to work out our falvation, is to diftinguifh ourfelves from the reft of men; is to live fingle amidft the multitude; is to be an individual fupporter of our own caufe, in the midft of a world which either condemns or defpifes us; is, in a word, to count examples as nothing, and to be affected by our duty alone. We cannot comprehend, that, to devote ourfelves to deftruction, it requires only to live as others do; to conform to the multitude; to form with it only one body and one world; feeing the world is already judged; that it is that body of the antichrift which fhall perifh with its head and members; that criminal city, accurfed and condemned to an eternal anathema. Yes, my brethren, the greateft obftacle in our hearts, to grace and truth, is the public opinion. How many timid fouls, who have not the courage to adopt the righteous fide, merely becaufe the world, to whofe view they are expofed, would join againft them? Thus, the king of Affyria durft not declare himfelf for the God of Daniel, becaufe the grandees of his court would have reprobated fuch a ftep. How many weak fouls, who, difgufted with pleafures, only continue to purfue them through a falfe honour, and that they may not diftinguifh themfelves from thofe

who

who set an example of them? Thus, Aaron, in the midst of the Israelites, danced around the golden calf, and joined them in offering up incense to the idol which he detested, because he had not the courage, singly, to resist the public error and blindness. Fools that we are! it is the sole example of the public which confirms us against truth; as if men were our truth, or that it were upon the earth, and not in heaven, that we ought, like the magi, to search for that rule and that light which are to guide us.

It is true, that, frequently, it is not respect for the world's opinion, but the sufferings and self-denials it holds out to us, which extinguish truth in our heart: thus, it make us sorrowful like that young man of the gospel, and we do not receive it with that delight testified by the magi on seeing the miraculous star. They had beheld the magnificence of Jerusalem, the pomp of its buildings, the majesty of its temple, the splendor and grandeur of Herod's court; but the gospel makes no mention of their having been affected by that vain display of human pomp: they beheld all these grand objects of desire without attention, pleasure, or any exterior marks of admiration or surprise; they express no wish to view the treasures and the riches of the temple, as those ambassadors from Babylon formerly did to Hezekiah: solely taken up with the light of Heaven manifested to them, they have no eyes for any earthly object; feeling to the truth alone which has enlightened them, every thing elfe is an object of indifference, or a burden to them; and their heart, viewing all things in their proper light, no longer acknowledges either delight, intereft, or confolation to be found in any thing but the truth.

On our part, my brethren, the firft rays of truth which the goodnefs of God fhed on our heart, probably excited a fenfible delight. The project which we at firft formed of a new life; the novelty of the lights which fhone upon us, and upon which we had not as yet fully opened our eyes; the laffitude itfelf, and difguft of thofe paffions of which our heart now felt only the bitternefs, and the punifhment; the novelty of the occupations which we propofed to ourfelves in a change; all thefe offered fmiling images to our fancy; for novelty itfelf is pleafing: but this, as the gofpel fays, was only the joy of a feafon. In proportion as truth drew near, it affumed to us, as to Auguftin yet a finner, an appearance lefs captivating and fmiling. When, after our firft glance, as I may fay, of it, we had leifurely and minutely examined the various duties it prefcribed to us; the grievous feparations which were now to be a law to us; retirement, prayer, the felf-denials which it proved to be indifpenfible; that ferious, occupied, and private life in which we were to be engaged: ah! we immediately, like the young man of the gofpel, began to draw back forrowful and uneafy; all our paffions roufed up

frefh

fresh obstacles to it; every thing now presented itself in gloomy and totally different colours; and that, which we had at first thought to be so attractive, when brought near, was no longer in our eyes but a frightful object, a way rugged, terrifying, and impracticable to human weakness.

Where are the souls, who, like the magi, after having once known the truth, never afterwards wish to see but it alone; have no longer eyes for the world, for its empty pleasures, or for the vanity of its pompous shews; who feel no delight but in the contemplation of truth; in making it their resource in every affliction; the spur of their indolence; their succour against temptation; and the purest delight of their soul? And how vain, puerile, and disgusting doth the world, with all its pleasures, hopes, and grandeurs, indeed appear to a soul who hath known thee, O my God! and who hath felt the truth of thine eternal promises; to a soul who feels that whatever is not thee is unworthy of him; and who considers the earth only as the country of those who must perish for ever! Nothing is consolatory to him but what opens the prospect of real and lasting riches; nothing appears worthy of his regard but what is to endure for ever; nothing has the power of pleasing him but what shall eternally please him; nothing is longer capable of attaching him but that which he is no more to lose; and all the trifling objects of vanity are no longer, on his part, but the embarrassments

rassments of his piety, or gloomy monuments which recall the remembrance of his crimes.

Behold, in the instance of the magi, truth received with submission, with sincerity, and with delight; in the conduct of the priests let us see the truth dissembled; and, after being instructed in the use which we ought to make of truth with regard to ourselves, let us learn what is our duty, respecting it, to others.

Part II. The first duty required of us by the law of charity towards our brethren, is the duty of truth. We are not bound to bestow on all men our attentions, our cares, and our officious services; to all we owe the truth. The different situations in which rank and birth place us in the world, diversify our duties with regard to our fellow-creatures; in every situation of life that of truth is the same. We owe it to the great equally as to the humble; to our subjects as to our masters; to the lovers of it as to those who hate it; to those who mean to employ it against ourselves as to those who wish it only for their own benefit. There are conjunctures in which prudence permits to hide and to dissemble the love which we bear for our brethren; none can possibly exist in which we are permitted to dissemble the truth: in a word, truth is not our own property, we are only its witnesses, its defenders, and its depositaries. It is that spark, that light of God which should illuminate the whole world; and, when we dissemble

dissemble or obscure it, we are unjust towards our brethren, and ungrateful towards the Father of Light who hath spread it through our soul.

Nevertheless, the world is filled with dissemblers of the truth; we live, it would appear, only to deceive each other; and society, the first bond of which ought to be truth, is no longer but a commerce of dissimulation, duplicity, and cunning. Now, in the conduct of the priests of our gospel, let us view all the different kinds of dissimulation of which men render themselves every day culpable towards truth; we shall there find a dissimulation of silence, a dissimulation of compliance and palliation, a dissimulation of disguise and falsehood.

A dissimulation of silence. Consulted by Herod on the place in which the Christ was to be born, they made answer, it is true that Bethlehem was the place marked in the prophets for the fulfilment of that grand event; but they add not, that the star, foretold in the holy books, having at last appeared, and the kings of Saba and of Arabia coming with presents to worship the new chief who was to lead Israel, it was no longer to be doubted that the overshadowed had at last brought forth the righteous. They do not gather together the people in order to announce this blessed intelligence; they do not run the first to Bethlehem, in order, by their example, to animate Jerusalem. Wrapt up in their criminal timidity, they guard a profound silence;

silence; they iniquitously retain the truth; and, while strangers come from the extremities of the east loudly to proclaim in Jerusalem that the King of the Jews is born, the priests, the scribes are silent, and sacrifice, to the ambition of Herod, the interests of truth, the dearest hope of their nation, and the honour of their ministry.

What a shameful degradation of the ministers of truth! The good-will of the prince influences them more than the sacred deposit of the religion with which they are entrusted; the lustre of the throne stifles, in their heart, the light of Heaven; by a criminal silence they flatter a king who applies to them for the truth, and who can learn it from them alone; they confirm him in error by concealing that which might have undeceived him; and how, indeed, shall truth ever make its way to the ear of sovereigns, if even the Lord's anointed, who surround the throne, have not the courage to announce it, but join their efforts, with those who dwell in courts, to conceal and stifle it?

But this duty, my brethren, is, in certain respects, common to you as to us; yet, nevertheless, there are few persons in the world, even of those who set an example of piety, who do not, almost every day, render themselves culpable towards their brethren of the dissimulation of silence. They think that they render to truth all that they owe to it, when they do not declare against it; when they hear virtue continually decried by the world-

ly,

ly, the doctrine of the world maintained, its abuses and maxims justified, those of gospel opposed or weakened, the wicked often blaspheming what they know not, and setting themselves up as judges of that faith which shall judge them; that they listen to them, I say, without joining in their impiety, is true, but they do not boldly shew their disapprobation, and content themselves with merely not authorising their blasphemies or their prejudices by their suffrage.

Now, I say that, being all individually intrusted with the interests of truth, to be silent when it is openly attacked in our presence, is to become, in a measure, its persecutor and adversary. But, I add, that you, above all whom God hath enlightened, you then fail in that love which you owe to your brethren, seeing your obligations with regard to them augment in proportion to the grace with which God hath favoured you; you also render yourselves culpable towards God of ingratitude; you do not make a proper return for the blessing of grace and of truth with which he hath favoured you, in the midst of your extravagant passions. He hath illuminated your darkness; he hath recalled you to himself, while wandering in treacherous and iniquitous ways; he, no doubt, in thus shedding light through your heart, hath not had your benefit alone in view; he hath meant that it should operate as the instruction or as the reproach of your connections, your friends, your subjects, or your masters; he hath intended to favour your age, your nation, your country, in favouring you; for his chosen are formed only for the salvation or the condemnation of sinners. His design has been to place in you a light which might shine amid the surrounding darkness, and be a salutary guide to your fellow-creatures ; which might perpetuate truth among men, and render testimony to the righteousness and to the wisdom of his law, amidst all the prejudices, and all the vain conclusions of a profane world.

Now, by opposing only a cowardly and timid silence to the maxims which attack the truth, you do not enter into the views of God's mercy upon your brethren ; you render unavailing to his glory and to the aggrandisement of his kingdom, that talent of the truth which he had entrusted to you, and of which he will one day demand a particular and severe reckoning; I say, more particularly of you who had formerly, with so much eclat, supported the errors and profane maxims of the world, and who had once been its firmest and most avowed apologist. He surely had a right to exact of you, that you should declare yourselves with the same courage in favour of truth; nevertheless, from a zealous partisan of the world, his grace hath only succeeded in making a timid disciple of the gospel. That grand air of confidence and of intrepidity with which you formerly apologised for the passions, has forsaken you ever since you have
undertaken

undertaken the defence of the interests of virtue; that audacity which once imposed silence on truth, is now itself mute in the presence of error; and truth, which, as St Augustin says, gives confidence and intrepidity to all who have it on their side, has rendered you only weak and timid.

I admit, that there is a time to be silent as well as a time to speak; and that the zeal of truth hath its rules and measures; but I would not that the souls, who know God and serve him continually, hear the maxims of religion subverted, the reputation of their brethren attacked, the most criminal abuses of the world justified, without having the courage to adopt the cause of that truth which they dishonour. I would not that the world have its avowed partisans, and that Jesus Christ have no one to stand up for him. I would not that the pious and good, through a mistaken idea of good-breeding, dissemble upon those irregularities of sinners which they are daily witnessing; while sinners, on the contrary, consider it as giving themselves an important and fashionable air, to defend and to maintain them in their presence. I would that a faithful soul comprehend that he is responsible to the truth alone; that he is upon the earth solely to render glory to the truth: I would that he bear upon his countenance that noble and, I may say, lofty dignity, which grace inspires; that heroical candour which contempt of the world and all its glory produces; that generous and

Christian

Christian liberty, which expects only eternal riches, which has no hope but in God, which dreads nothing but the internal Judge, which pays court to, and spares nothing but the interests of righteousness and of charity, and which has no wish of making itself agreeable but by the truth. I would that the sole presence of a righteous soul impose silence on the enemies of virtue; that they respect that character of truth which he should bear engraven on his forehead; that they crouch under his holy greatness of soul, and that they render homage, at least by their silence and their confusion, to that virtue which they inwardly despise. Thus, the Israelites, taken up with their dances, their profane rejoicings, and their foolish and impious shouts around the golden calf, stop all in a moment, and keep a profound silence on the sole appearance of Moses, who comes down from the mountain, armed with the law of the Lord and with his eternal truth. First dissimulation of the truth: a dissimulation of silence.

The second manner in which it is dissembled, is that of softening it by modifications, and by condescensions which injure it. The magi, no doubt, could not be ignorant that the intelligence which they came to announce to Jerusalem would be highly displeasing to Herod. That foreigner, through his artifices, had seated himself on the throne of David; he did not so peaceably enjoy the fruit of his usurpation, but that he constantly

had

had a dread left some heir of the blood of the kings of Judah should expel him from the heritage of his fathers, and remount a throne promised to his posterity. With what eye must he then regard men who come to publish, in the midst of Jerusalem, that the King of the Jews is born, and to proclaim him to a people so attached to, and so zealous for the blood of David, and so impatient under every foreign rule? Nevertheless, the magi conceal nothing of what they had seen in the east; they do not soften that grand event by measured expressions less proper to arouse the jealousy of Herod. They might have called the Messiah whom they seek, the Messenger of Heaven, or the longed-for of nations; they might have designed him by titles less hateful to the ambition of Herod: but, full of the truth which hath appeared to them, they know none of these timid and servile time-servings; persuaded that those, who are determined to receive the truth only through the means of their errors, are unworthy of knowing it. They are unacquainted with the art of covering it with disguises and considerations for individuals, which dishonour it: they boldly come to the point, and demand, " where is he that is born King of the " Jews;" and, not satisfied with considering him as the Sovereign of Judea, they declare that heaven itself is his birth-right; that the stars are his, and make their appearance in the firmament only in obedience to his orders.

The

The priests and the scribes, on the contrary, forced, by the evidence of the scriptures, to render glory to the truth, soften it by guarded expressions. They endeavour to unite that respect which they owe to the truth, with that complaisance which they wish still to preserve for Herod: they suppress the title of king which the magi had given to him, and which had so often been bestowed by the prophets upon the Messiah; they design him by a title which might equally mark an authority of doctrine, or of superior power: they announce him rather as a legislator established to regulate the manners, than as a sovereign raised up for the deliverance of his people from bondage. And, notwithstanding that they themselves expect a Messiah, King, and Conqueror, they soften the truth which they wish to announce, and complete the blindness of Herod, with whom they temporise.

Deplorable destiny of the great! the lips of the priests quiver in speaking to them; from the moment that their passions are known they are temporised with; truth never offers itself to them but with a double face, of which one side is always favourable to them; the servants of God wish not avowedly to betray their ministry and the interests of truth; but they wish to conciliate them with their own interest: they endeavour to save, as it were, both the rule and their passions, as if the passions could subsist with that rule which condemns them. It seldom happens that the great

are

are inftructed, becaufe it feldom happens that the intention is not to pleafe in inftructing them. Neverthelefs, the greater part would love the truth were it once known to them: the paffions and the extravagancies of the age, nourifhed by all the pleafures which furround them, may lead them aftray; but a remaining principle of religion renders truth always refpectable to them. We may venture to fay, that ignorance condemns more princes and perfons of high rank than people of the loweft condition; and, that the mean complaifance which is paid to them, is more difhonourable to the miniftry, and is the caufe of more reproach to religion, than the moft notorious fcandals which afflict the church.

The conduct of thefe priefts appears bafe to you, my brethren: but, if you are difpofed to enter into judgment with yourfelves, and to follow yourfelves through the detail of your duties, of your friendfhips, of your converfations, you will fee that all your difcourfes, and all your proceedings, are merely mollifications of the truth, and temporifings in order to reconcile it with the prejudices, or the paffions of thofe with whom it is your lot to live. We never hold out the truth to them but in a point of view in which it may pleafe; in their moft defpicable vices we always find fome favourable fide; and, as all the paffions have always fome apparent refemblance to fome virtue, we never fail

to

to save ourselves through the assistance of that resemblance.

Thus, in the presence of an ambitious person, we never fail to hold forth the love of glory, and the desire of exalting one's self, only as tendencies which give birth to great men; we flatter his pride; we inflame his desires with hopes and with false and chimerical predictions; we nourish the error of his imagination by bringing phantoms within his reach, upon which he incessantly feasts himself. We perhaps venture, in general terms, to pity men who interest themselves so deeply for things which chance alone bestows, and of which death shall perhaps deprive us to-morrow; but we have not the courage to censure the madman who, to that vapour, sacrifices his quiet, his life, and his conscience. With a vindictive person we justify his resentment and anger; we justify his guilt in his mind, by countenancing the justice of his accusations; we spare his passion in exaggerating the injury and fault of his enemy. We perhaps venture to say, how noble it is to forgive; but we have not the courage to add, that the first step towards forgiveness is the ceasing to speak of the injury received.

With a courtier equally discontented with his own fortune, and jealous of that of others, we never fail to expose his rivals in the most unfavourable light: we artfully spread a cloud over their merit and their glory, least they should injure the jealous eyes of him who liſtens to us: we diminiſh, we caſt a ſhade over the fame of their talents and of their ſervices; and, by our iniquitous crouchings to his paſſion, we nouriſh it, we aſſiſt him in blinding himſelf, and induce him to conſider, as honours unjuſtly raviſhed from himſelf, all thoſe which are beſtowed upon his brethren. What ſhall I ſay? With a prodigal, his profuſions are no longer, in our mouths, but a diſplay of generoſity and magnificence. With a miſer, his ſordid calloufneſs of heart, in which every feeling is loſt, is no longer but a prudent moderation, and a laudable domeſtic economy. With a perſon of high rank, his prejudices and his errors always find in us ready apologies; we reſpect his paſſions equally as his authority, and his prejudices always become our own. Laſtly, We catch the infection, and imbibe the errors of all with whom we live; we transform ourſelves, as I may ſay, into otherſelves; our grand ſtudy is to find out their weakneſſes, that we may appropriate and apply them to our own purpoſes; we have, in fact, no language of our own; we always ſpeak the language of others; our diſcourſes are merely a repetition of their prejudices; and this infamous debaſement of truth we call knowledge of the world, a prudence which knows its own intereſt, the grand art of pleaſing and of ſucceeding in the world. "O ye "ſons of men! how long will ye love vanity, and "ſeek after leaſing?"

Yes, my brethren, by that we perpetuate error among men; we authorise every deceit; we justify every false maxim; we give an air of innocence to every vice; we maintain the reign of the world, and of its doctrine, against that of Jesus Christ; we corrupt society, of which truth ought to be the first tie; we pervert those duties and mutual offices of civil life, established to animate us to virtue, into snares, and inevitable occasions of a departure from righteousness; we change friendship, which ought to be a grand resource to us against our errors and irregularities, into a commerce of dissimulation and mutual deception: by that, in a word, we render truth hateful and ridiculous by rendering it rare among men; and, when I say we, I mean more especially the souls who belong to God, and who are intrusted with the interests of truth upon the earth. Yes, my brethren, I would that faithful souls had a language peculiar to them amid the world; that other maxims, other sentiments, were found in them than in the rest of men; and, while all others speak the language of the passions, that they alone speak the language of truth. I would that, while the world hath its Balaams, who, by their discourses and counsels, authorise irregularity and licentiousness, piety had its Phineases, who durst boldly adopt the interests of the law of God, and of the sanctity of its maxims: that, while the world hath its impious philosophers and false sages, who think that it does them

honour

honour openly to proclaim, that we ought to live only for the prefent, and that the end of man is, in no refpect, different from that of the beaft, piety had its Solomons, who, undeceived by their own experience, durft publicly avow, that, excepting the fear of the Lord and the obfervance of his commandments, all elfe is vanity and vexation of fpirit: that, while the world hath its charms and enchantments, which feduce kings and the people by their delufions and flatteries, piety had its Mofefes and Aarons, who had the courage to confound, by the fole force of truth, their impofition and artifice: in a word, that, while the world hath its priefts and its fcribes, who, like thofe of the gofpel, weaken the truth, piety had its magi, who dread not to announce it in the prefence even of thofe to whom it cannot but be difpleafing.

Not that I condemn the modifications of a fage prudence, which apparently gives up fomething to the prejudices of men, only that it may more furely recall them to rule and duty. I know that truth loves neither rafh nor indifcreet defenders; that the paffions of men require a certain deference and management; that they are in the fituation of fick perfons, to whom it is often neceffary to difguife and render palatable their medicines, and to cure them without their privity. I know that all deferences paid to the paffions, when their tendency is to eftablifh the truth, are not weakeners, but auxiliaries of it; and that the grand rule of the
zeal

zeal of truth, is prudence and charity. But such is not the intention when they weaken it by flattering and servile adulations; they seek to please, and not to edify; they substitute themselves in the place of truth; and their sole wish is to attract those suffrages which are due to it alone. And, let it not be said that it is more through sourness and ostentation, than through charity, that the just claim a merit in disdaining to betray truth. The world, which is always involved in deceit, of which the commerce and mutual ties revolve only upon dissimulation and artifice, which considers these even as an honourable science, and which is totally unacquainted with this noble rectitude of heart, cannot suppose it in others; it is its profound corruption which is the cause of its suspecting the sincerity and the courage of the upright; it is a mode of acting which appears ridiculous, because it is new to it; and, as it finds in it so marked a singularity, it loves better to suppose that it is rather the consequence of pride, or folly, than of virtue.

From thence it is that the truth is not only disguised, but it is likewise openly betrayed. Last dissimulation of the priests of our gospel: a dissimulation of falsehood. They are not satisfied with quoting the prophecies in obscure and mollified terms: but, seeing that the magi did not return to Jerusalem as they had intended, they add, no doubt in order to calm Herod, that, ashamed of not having been able to find that new King of

whom

whom they came in fearch, they have not had the courage to return: that they are ftrangers little verfed in the knowledge of the law and of the prophets; and that the light of Heaven, which they pretended to follow, was nothing but a vulgar illufion, and a fuperftitious prejudice of a rude and credulous nation. And fuch muft indeed have been their language to Herod, fince they themfelves act according to it, and do not run to Bethlehem to feek the new-born King, in order, it appears, to complete the perfuafion of Herod, that there was more credulity than truth in the fuperftitious refearch of thefe magi.

And behold to what we at laft come: in confequence of a fervile compliance with the paffions of men, and of continually wifhing to pleafe them at the expence of truth, we at laft openly abandon it; we cowardly and downrightly facrifice it to our intereft, our fortune, and our reputation; we betray our confcience, our duty, and our underftanding; and, confequently, from the moment that truth becomes irkfome to us, or renders us difpleafing, we difavow it, and deliver it up to oppreffion and iniquity; like Peter, we deny that we have ever been feen as its difciple. In this manner we change our heart into a cowardly and groveling one, to which any profitable falfehood cofts nothing; into an artificial and pliable heart, which affumes every form, and never poffeffes any determinate one; into a weak and flattering heart, which has not the courage to

refufe

refuse its suffrage to any thing but unprofitable and unfortunate virtue; into a corrupted and interested heart, which makes subservient to its purposes, religion, truth, justice, and all that is most sacred among men; in a word, a heart capable of every thing except that of being true, noble, and sincere. And think not that sinners of this description are so very rare in the world. We shun only the notoriety and shame of these faults; secret and secure basenesses find few scrupulous hearts; we often love only the reputation and glory of truth.

It is only proper to take care that, in pretending to defend the truth, we are not defending the mere illusions of our own mind. Pride, ignorance, and self-conceit, every day furnish defenders to error, equally intrepid and obstinate as any of whom faith can boast. The only truth worthy of our love, of our zeal, and of our courage, is that held out to us by the church: for it alone we ought to endure every thing; beyond that, we are no longer but the martyrs of our own obstinacy and vanity.

O my God! pour then through my soul that humble and generous love of the truth, with which thy chosen are filled in heaven, and which is the only characteristic mark of the just upon the earth. Let my life be only such as to render glory to thine eternal truths; let me honour them through the sanctity of my manners; let me defend them through zeal for thy interests alone, and enable me continually to oppose them to error and vanity:

annihilate

annihilate in my heart thofe human fears, that prudence of the flefh which dreads to lay open to perfons their errors and their vices. Suffer not that I be a feeble reed which bends to every blaft, nor that I ever blufh to bear the truth imprinted on my forehead, as the moft illuftrious title with which thy creature can glorify himfelf, and as the moft glorious mark of thy mercies upon my foul. In effect, it is not fufficient to be the witnefs and depofitary of it, it is alfo neceffary to be its defender: character contrafted with that of Herod, who is, in our gofpel at prefent, its enemy and perfecutor. Laft inftruction with which our gofpel furnifhes us: the truth perfecuted.

PART III. If it is a crime to withftand the truth when it fhines upon us; iniquitoufly to withhold it when we owe it to others; it is the fulnefs of iniquity, and the moft diftinguifhed character of reprobation, to perfecute and combat it. Neverthelefs, nothing more common in the world than this perfecution of truth; and the impious Herod, who, on the prefent occafion, fets himfelf up againft it, has more imitators than is fuppofed.

For, in the firft place, he perfecutes it through that repugnancy which he vifibly fhews to the truth, and which induces all Jerufalem to follow his example; and this is what I call a perfecution of fcandal. Secondly, He perfecutes it by endeavouring to corrupt the priefts, and even by laying fnares for the piety of the magi; and this is what

I call

I call a persecution of seduction. Lastly, He persecutes it by shedding innocent blood; and this is a persecution of power and violence. Now, my brethren, if the brevity of a discourse permitted me to examine these three descriptions of persecution of the truth, there is not perhaps one of them of which you would not find yourselves culpable.

For, 1*stly*, Who can flatter himself with not being among the number of the persecutors of truth, under the description of scandals? I even speak not of those disorderly souls who have erected the standard of guilt and licentiousness, and who pay little, if indeed any, attention to the public opinion: the most notorious scandals are not always those which are most to be dreaded; and avowed debauchery, when carried to a certain degree, occasions, in general, more censures upon our conduct than imitations of our excesses. I speak of those souls delivered up to the pleasures, to the vanities, and to all the abuses of the age, and whose conduct, in other respects regular, is not only irreproachable in the sight of the world, but attracts even the praises and the esteem of men; and I say that they persecute the truth through their sole examples, that they undo, as much as in them lies, the maxims of the gospel in every heart; that they cry out to all men, that shunning of pleasures is a needless precaution; that love of the world and the love of virtue are not at all incompatible; that a taste for theatres, for dress, and for all public amusements,

ments, is entirely innocent; and that it is eafy to
to lead a good life even while living like the reft
of the world. This worldly regularity is therefore
a continual perfecution of the truth; and fo much
the more dangerous, as it is an authorifed perfecution which has nothing odious in it, and againft
which no precaution is taken; which attacks the
truth without violence, without effufion of blood,
under the fmiling image of peace and fociety; and
which, through thefe means, occafions more deferters from the truth than ever all tyrants and tortures formerly did.

I fpeak even of thofe good characters who only
imperfectly fulfil the duties of piety, who ftill retain,
too, public remains of the paffions of the world
and of its maxims: and, I fay, that they perfecute
the truth through thefe unfortunate remains of infidelity and weaknefs; that they are the occafion
of its being blafphemed by the impious and other
finners; that they authorife the fenfelefs difcourfes
of the world againft the piety of the fervants of
God; that they are the caufe of fouls being difgufted with virtue, who might otherwife feel themfelves difpofed to it; that they confirm, in the
path of error, thofe who feek pretexts to remain
in it: in a word, that they render virtue either
fufpicious or ridiculous. Thus, ftill every day, as
the Lord formerly complained through his prophet Jeremiah, the backfliding Ifrael, that is to
fay, the world, juftifies herfelf more than trea-

Vol. III.   F f   cherous

cherous Judah, that is to say, the weaknesses of the good : I mean to say, that the world thinks itself secure when it sees that those souls, who profess piety, join in its pleasures and frivolities ; are warm, like the rest of men, upon fortune, upon favour, upon preferences, and upon injuries ; pursue their own ends, have still a desire of pleasing, eagerly seek after distinctions and favours, and sometimes make even piety subservient towards more surely attaining them. Ah ! it is then that the world triumphs, and that it feels itself comforted in the comparison ; it is then that, finding such a resemblance between the virtue of the good and its own vices, it feels tranquil upon its situation, and thinks that it is needless to change, since, in changing the name, the same things are still retained.

And it is here that I cannot prevent myself from saying, with the apostle Peter, to you, whom God hath recalled from the ways of the world and of the passions, to those of truth and righteousness ; let us act in such a manner among the worldly, that, in place of decrying virtue as they have hitherto done, and of despising or censuring those who practice it ; the good works which they shall behold in us, our pure and holy manners, our patience under scorn, our wisdom and our circumspection in discourse, our modesty and humility in exaltation, our equality of mind and submission under disgrace, our gentleness towards our inferiors,

riors, our regard for our equals, our fidelity towards our masters, our universal charity towards our brethren, force them to render glory to God, make them to respect and even to envy the destiny of virtue, and dispose their hearts to receive the grace of light and of truth when it shall deign to visit them, and to enlighten them upon their erroneous ways. Let us shut up the mouth of all the enemies of virtue by the sight of an irreprehensible life: let us honour piety, that it may honour us: let us render it respectable if we wish to gain partisans to it: let us furnish to the world examples which condemn it, and not censures which justify it: let us accustom it to think, that godliness is profitable unto all things, having promise not only of the life to come, but also peace, satisfaction, and content, which are the only good, and the only real pleasures of the present life.

To this persecution of scandal Herod adds a persecution of seduction: he tempts the sanctity and the fidelity of the ministers of the law: he wishes to make the zeal and the holy boldness of the magi instrumental to his impious designs: in a word, he neglects nothing to undo the truth before he openly attacks it.

And behold a fresh manner in which we continually persecute the truth. In the *first* place, We weaken the piety of the just by accusing their fervor of excess, and by struggling to persuade them that they do too much; we exhort them, like the grand

grand tempter, to change their stones into bread; that is to say, to abate from their austerity, and to change that retired, gloomy, and laborious life, into a more ordinary and comfortable one: we give them room to dread, that the sequel will not correspond with these beginnings: in a word, we endeavour to draw them nearer to us, being unwilling to raise ourselves to a level with them. 2*dly*, We perhaps tempt even their fidelity and their innocence, by giving the most animated descriptions of those pleasures from which they fly: like the wife of Job, we blame their simplicity and weakness: we exaggerate to them the inconveniences of virtue and the difficulties of perseverance: we shake them by the example of unfaithful souls, who, after putting their hand to the plough, have cast a look behind, and abandoned their labour: what shall I say? We perhaps attack even the immovable ground-work of faith, and we insinuate the inutility of the self-denials it proposes, from the uncertainty of its promises. 3*dly*, We harass, by our authority, the zeal and the piety of those persons who are dependent upon us: we exact duties of them, either incompatible with their innocence, or dangerous to their virtue: we place them in situations either painful or trying to their faith: we interdict them from practices and observances, either necessary for their support in piety, or profitable towards their progress in it: in a word, we become domestic tempters

with

with respect to them, being neither capable of tasting good ourselves nor of suffering it in others, and performing, towards these souls, the office of the demon, who only watches in order to destroy. *Lastly,* We render ourselves culpable of this persecution of seduction, by making our talents instrumental to the destruction of the reign of Jesus Christ: the talents of the body in inspiring iniquitous passions; in placing ourselves in hearts where God alone ought to be; in corrupting the souls for whom Jesus Christ gave his blood: the talents of the mind in inducing to vice; in embellishing it with all the charms most calculated to hide its infamy and horror; in presenting the poison under the most alluring and seductive form; and in rendering it immortal by lascivious works, through the means of which a miserable author shall, to the end of ages, preach up vice, corrupt hearts, and inspire his brethren with every deplorable passion which had enslaved himself during life; shall see his punishment and his torments increased in proportion as the impious fire he has lighted up shall spread upon the earth; shall have the shocking consolation of declaring himself, even after death, against his God, of gaining souls from him whom he had redeemed, of still insulting his holiness and majesty, of perpetuating his own rebellion and disorders even beyond the tomb, and of making, even to the fulfilment of time, the crimes of all men his own crimes. Wo, saith the Lord, to

all

all those who rise up against my name and glory, and who lay snares for my people. I will take vengeance of them on the day of my judgment: I will demand of them the blood of their brethren whom they have seduced, and whom they have caused to perish: and I will multiply upon them, and make them for ever to feel the most dreadful evils, in return for that glory which they have ravished from me.

But, a last description of persecution, still more fatal to truth, is that which I call a persecution of power and violence. Herod, having gained nothing by his artifices, at last throws off the mask, openly declares himself the persecutor of Jesus Christ, and wishes to extinguish in its birth that light which comes to illuminate the whole world.

The sole mention of the cruelty of that impious prince strikes us with horror; and it does not appear that so barbarous an example can ever find imitators among us: nevertheless, the world is full of these kinds of public and avowed persecutors of the truth; and, if the church be no longer afflicted with the barbarity of tyrants, and with the effusion of her children's blood, she is still every day persecuted by the public derisions which the worldly make of virtue, and by the ruin of those faithful souls whom she, with grief, so often beholds sinking under the dread of their derisions and censures.

Yes, my brethren, those discourses which you so readily allow yourselves against the piety of the
servants

servants of God, of those souls who, by their fervent homages, recompense his glory for your crimes and insults; those derisions of their zeal and of their holy intoxication for their God; those biting sarcasms which rebound from their person upon virtue itself, and are the most dangerous temptation of their penitence: that severity on their account, which forgives them nothing, and changes even their virtues into vices; that language of blasphemy and of mockery, which throws an air of ridicule over the seriousness of their compunction; which gives appellations of irony and contempt to the most respectable practices of their piety; which shakes their faith, checks their holy resolutions, disheartens their weakness, makes them, as it were, ashamed of virtue, and often is the cause of their returning to vice: behold what, with the saints, I call an open and declared persecution of the truth. You persecute in your brother, says St Augustin, that which the tyrants themselves have never persecuted; they have deprived him only of life; your scheme is to deprive him of innocence and virtue: their persecution extended only to the body; you carry yours even to the destruction of his soul.

What, my brethren! is it not enough that you do not yourselves serve the God for whom you are created? (This is what the first defenders of faith, the Tertullians and the Cyprians, formerly said to the Pagan persecutors of the faithful; and must it be that we, alas! have the same complaints to make
against

against Christians?) Is it not enough? Must you also persecute those who serve him? You are then determined neither to adore him yourselves nor to suffer that others do it? You every day forgive so many extravagancies to the followers of the world, so many unreasonable passions; you excuse them; what do I say? You applaud them in the inordinate desires of their heart: in their most shameful passions you find constancy, fidelity, and dignity: You give honourable names to their most infamous vices; and it is a just and faithful soul alone, a servant of the true God, who has no indulgence to expect from you, and is certain of attracting upon himself your contempt and censures? But, my brethren, theatrical and other amusements are publicly licensed, and nothing is said against them: the madness of gambling has its declared partisans, and they are quietly put up with: ambition has its worshippers and slaves, and they are even commended: voluptuousness has its altars and victims, and no one contests them: avarice has its idolaters, and not a word is said against them: all the passions, like so many sacrilegious divinities, have their established worship, without the smallest exception being taken; and the sole Lord of the universe, and the Sovereign of all men, and the only God upon the earth, either shall not be served at all, or shall not be it with impunity, and without every obstacle being placed in the way of his service?

Great

Great God! avenge then thine own glory: render again to thy servants that honour and that lustre which the impious unceasingly ravish from them: do not, as formerly, send ferocious beasts from the depths of their forests to devour the contemners of virtue, and of the holy simplicity of thy prophets; but deliver them up to their inordinate desires, still more cruel and insatiable than the lion or the bear, in order that, worn out, racked by the internal convulsions and the frenzies of their own passions, they may know all the value and all the excellence of that virtue which they contemn, and aspire to the felicity and to the destiny of those souls who serve thee.

For, my brethren, you whom this discourse regards, allow me, and with grief, to say it here: must you be the instruments which the demon employs to tempt the chosen of God, and, if it were possible, to lead them astray? Must it be that you appear upon the earth merely in order to justify the prophecies of the holy books with regard to the persecutions, which, even to the end, are inevitable to all those who shall wish to live in godliness which is in Jesus Christ? Must you alone be the means of sustaining the perpetuity of that frightful succession of persecutors of faith and of virtue, which is to endure as long as the church? Must you, in default now of tyrants and of tortures, continue to be the rock and the scandal of the gospel? Renounce then yourselves the hope which

which is in Jesus Christ; join yourselves with those barbarous nations, or with those impious characters who blaspheme his glory and his divinity, if to you it appears so worthy of derision and laughter to live under his laws, and according to his maxims. An infidel or a savage might suppose that we, who serve and who worship him, are under delusion; he might pity our credulity and weakness, when he sees us sacrificing the present to a futurity, and an hope which, in his eyes, might appear fabulous and chimerical; but he would be forced, at least, to confess that, if we do not deceive ourselves, and if our faith be justly grounded, we are the wisest and the most estimable of all men. But for you, who would not dare to start a doubt of the certitude of faith, and of the hope which is in Jesus Christ, with what eyes, with what astonishment would that infidel regard the censures which you so plentifully bestow upon his servants? You prostrate yourselves before his cross, he would say to you, as before the pledge of your salvation; and you laugh at those who bear it in their heart, and who ground their whole hope and expectation in it! You worship him as your Judge; and you contemn and load with ridicule those who dread him, and who anxiously labour to render him favourable to their interests! You believe him to be sincere and faithful in his word; and you look upon, as weak minds, those who place their trust in him, and who sacrifice every thing to the grandeur and

to

to the certainty of his promises! O man, so astonishing, so full of contradictions, so little in unison with thyself, would the infidel exclaim, how great and how holy must the God of the Christians therefore be, seeing that, among all those who know him, he hath no enemies but such as are of thy description!

Let us, therefore, respect virtue, my brethren; let us honour, in his servants, the gifts of God, and the wonders of his grace. Let us merit, by our deference and our esteem for piety, the blessing of piety itself. Let us regard the worthy and pious as the souls who alone continue to draw down the favours of Heaven upon the earth, as resources established to reconcile us one day with God, as blessed signs, which prove to us that the Lord still looketh upon men with pity, and continueth his mercies upon his church. Let us encourage by our praises, if we cannot strengthen by our example, the souls who return to him: let us applaud their change, if we think it impossible, as yet, to change ourselves: let us glory in defending them, if our passions will not, as yet, permit us to imitate them. Let us reverence and esteem virtue. Let us have no friends but the friends of God: let us count upon the fidelity of men only in proportion as they are faithful to their Master and Creator: let us confide our sorrows and our sufferings only to those who can present them to him, who alone can console them: let us believe to be in our real

interests

interests only those who are in the interests of our salvation. Let us smooth the way to our conversion: let us, by our respect for the just, prepare the world to behold us one day, without surprise, just ourselves. Let us not, by our derisions and censures, raise up an invincible stumbling-block of human respect, which shall for ever prevent us from declaring ourselves disciples of that piety which we have so loudly and so publicly decried. Let us render glory to the truth; and, in order that it may deliver us, let us religiously receive it, like the magi, from the moment that it is manifested to us: let us not dissemble it, like the priests, when we owe it to our brethren: let us not declare against it, like Herod, when we can no longer dissemble it to ourselves, in order that, after having walked in the ways of truth upon the earth, we may all together one day be sanctified in truth, and perfected in charity.

SERMON VII.

THE DIVINITY OF JESUS CHRIST.

Luke ii. 21.

His name was called Jesus, which was so named of the angel.

A God lowering himself so far as even to become man, astonishes and confounds reason; and into what an abyss of errors is it not plunged, if the light of faith come not speedily to its aid, to discover the depth of the divine wisdom concealed under the apparent absurdity of the mystery of a Man-God? Thus, in all times, this fundamental point of our holy religion, I mean the divinity of Jesus Christ, hath been the object most exposed to the foolish oppositions of the human mind. Men, full of pride, whose mouths ought to be filled with

only

only thankſgivings for the ineffable gift, made to them by the Father of mercies, of his only Son, have continually infulted him, by vomiting forth the moſt impious blaſphemies againſt that adorable Son. Full of blindneſs, who have not ſeen that the ſole name of Jeſus, which is given to him on this day, that name which he at firſt receives in heaven, and which an angel conveys to the earth, to Mary and Joſeph, is the inconteſtable proof of his divinity. That ſacred name eſtabliſhes him the Saviour of mankind; Saviour, in that, through the effuſion of blood, which becomes our ranſom, he delivers us from ſin, and from the conſequences inſeparable from it, viz. the tyranny of the demon and of hell: Saviour, in that, attracting upon his own head the chaſtiſement due to our prevarications, he reconciles us with God, and opens to us afreſh the entry of the eternal ſanctuary, which ſin had ſhut againſt us. But, my brethren, if the Son of Mary be but a mere man, of what value, in the eyes of God, will be the oblation of his blood? If Jeſus Chriſt be not God, how will his mediation be accepted, while he would himſelf have occaſion for a mediator to reconcile him with God?

This proof, which I only touch upon here, and ſo many others with which religion furniſhes me, would quickly ſtop the mouth of the ungodly, and confound his impiety, if I undertook to ſhew them in all their light, and to give an extenſion in proportion to their importance. But, God-forbid that

that I should come here, into the holy temple where the altars of our divine Saviour are raised up, where his worshippers assemble, to enter into contestation, as if I spake in the presence of his enemies, or, to make the apology of the mystery of the Man-God, before a believing people, and a sovereign whose most illustrious and most cherished title is that of Christian. It is not, therefore, to combat these ungodly, that, on this day, I consecrate my discourse to the divinity and to the eternal glory of Jesus, Son of the living God; I come for the sole purpose of consoling our faith, while recounting the wonders of him who is its Author and Perfecter; and to reanimate our piety in exposing to you the glory and the divinity of our Mediator who is its object and its sweetest hope.

It is even proper to renew, from time to time, these grand truths in the minds of the great and of the princes of the people, in order to strengthen them against those discourses of infidelity which they, in general, are only too much in the way of hearing; and it is expedient sometimes to raise up the veil which covers the sanctuary, that they may have a view of those hidden beauties which religion only holds out to their respect and their homages.

Now, the divinity of the Mediator can only be proven by his ministry; his titles can appear only in his functions: and, in order to know whether

he

he be defcended from heaven, and equal with the moſt High, it requires only to relate the purpoſes for which he came upon the earth. He came, my brethren, to form an holy and a believing people; a believing people, who ſubject their reaſon to the ſacred yoke of faith; an holy people, whoſe converſation is in heaven, and who are no longer reſponſible to the fleſh, to live according to the fleſh: ſuch is the grand deſign of his temporal miſſion.

The luſtre of his miniſtry is the firmeſt foundation of our faith: the ſpirit of his miniſtry, the ſole rule of our morals. Now, if he was only a man commiſſioned of God, the luſtre of his miniſtry would be the inevitable occaſion of our ſuperſtition and idolatry; the ſpirit of his miniſtry would be the fatal ſnare to entrap our innocence. Thus, whether we conſider the luſtre or the ſpirit of his miniſtry, the glory of his divinity remains equally and invincibly eſtabliſhed.

O Jeſus, ſole Lord of all, accept this public homage of our confeſſion and of our faith! While impiety blaſphemes in ſecret, and under the ſhades of darkneſs againſt thy glory, allow us the conſolation of publiſhing it with the voice of all ages in the face of theſe altars; and form, in our heart, not only that faith which confeſſes and worſhips thee, but alſo that which follows and which imitates thee.

Part I. God can manifeſt himſelf to men, only in order to teach them what he is, and what men

owe

owe to him; and religion is, properly speaking, but a divine light, which difcovers God to man, and which regulates the duties of man towards God. Whether the moft High fhew himfelf to the earth, or whether he fill extraordinary men with his fpirit, the end of all his proceedings can be only the knowledge and the fanctification of his name in the univerfe, and the eftablifhment of a worfhip in which they render to him what is due to him alone.

Now, if the Lord Jefus, come in the fulnefs of time, was nothing more than an upright and innocent man, only chofen to be the meffenger of God upon the earth; the principal end of his miniftry would have been that of rendering the world idolatrous, and of ravifhing from the divinity that glory which is his due, in order to appropriate it to himfelf.

In effect, my brethren, whether we confider the luftre of his miniftry in that pompous train of oracles and of figurative allufions which have preceded him in the wonderful circumftances which have accompanied him, and, laftly, in the works which he hath operated; the luftre of it is fuch, that, if Jefus Chrift was only a man fimilar to us, God, who hath fent him upon the earth arrayed in fuch glory and power, would himfelf have deceived us, and would be culpable of the idolatry of thofe who worfhip him.

The first signal character of the ministry of Jesus Christ, is that, from the beginning of the world, it was foretold and promised to men. Scarcely had the fall of Adam taken place, when the Restorer, whom his guilt had rendered necessary to the earth, is shewn to him from afar. In the following ages, God, it would appear, is only occupied in preparing mankind for his coming: if he manifest himself to the patriarchs, it is in order to confirm their faith in that expectation; if he inspire prophets, it is in order to announce him; if he choose to himself a people, it is for the purpose of making it the depositary of that grand promise; if he prescribe sacrifices and religious ceremonies to men, it is in order to trace out in them, as from afar, the history of him who was to come. Whatever took place upon the earth seems to lead to that grand event: empires and kingdoms fall or rise only in order to prepare the way for it: the heavens are only opened to promise it: and, as St Paul says, the whole creation groaneth and travaileth in pain to bring forth the righteous, who is to come for the redemption of our body from the bondage of corruption and sin.

Now, my brethren, to inspire, from the beginning of all ages, the earth with the expectation of a man, and to announce him to it from heaven, is already, in fact, to prepare men to receive him with a kind of religion and worship; and, even granting that Jesus Christ were to have only the eclat

eclat of that particular circumſtance which diſtinguiſhes him from all other men, the ſuperſtition of the people, with regard to him, were he only a ſimple creature, had been to dread. But, even the circumſtance of Jeſus Chriſt being foretold is not ſo wonderful as thoſe in which he hath been it, which are more ſurpriſing than even the prophecies themſelves. In effect, if Cyrus and John the Baptiſt have been foretold, long before their birth, in the prophecies of Iſaiah and of Malachi, theſe are only individual prophecies, without conſequence or train, and which are found in a ſingle prophet; predictions which announce only particular events, and by which the religion of the people could never be caught or ſurpriſed; Cyrus to be the re-eſtabliſher of the walls of Jeruſalem; John the Baptiſt to prepare the way for him who was to come; both in order to confirm, by the accompliſhment of their particular prophecies, the truth and the divinity of all the prophecies which announce Jeſus Chriſt.

But here, my brethren, it is a Meſſenger of Heaven, foretold by a whole people, announced, during four thouſand years, by a long train of prophecies, deſired of all nations, figured by all the ceremonies, expected by all the juſt, and ſhewn from afar in all ages. The patriarchs expire in wiſhing to ſee him: the juſt live in that expectation: fathers inſtruct their children to wiſh for him; and this deſire is like a domeſtic religion which is

perpetuated

perpetuated from age to age. The prophets themselves of the gentiles fee the Star of Jacob shining from afar; and this great event is announced even in the oracles of idols. Here, it is not for a particular event; it is to be the resource of the condemned world, the legislator of all people, the light of nations, the salvation of Israel; it is in order to blot out iniquity from the earth, to bring an eternal righteousness, to fill the universe with the spirit of God, and to be the blessed bearer of an immortal peace to all men. What a pompous train! What a snare for the religion of all ages, if such magnificent preparations announce only a simple creature; and, more especially, in times when the credulity of the people so easily placed extraordinary men in the rank of gods!

Besides, when John the Baptist appears on the borders of the Jordan affraid, it would seem, that the single oracle which had foretold him might become an occasion of idolatry to the people whom the fame of his sanctity attracted round him, he performs no miracles; he never ceases to say: " I " am not he whom you expect; but one mightier " than me cometh, the latchet of whose shoes I am " not worthy to unloose;" he is only watchful, it would appear, to prevent superstitious honours. Jesus Christ, on the contrary, whom four thousand years of expectation, of allusions, of prophecies, of promises, had, with so much magnificence, announced to the earth; Jesus Christ, far from preventing

venting the superstition of the people with regard to himself, comes in full authority and might; he does miracles and deeds which no one had ever done before him; and, not only he raises himself above John the Baptist, but he gives out that he is equal with God himself. Had the error been to dread, and, if to render to him divine honours had been an idolatry, where would be his zeal for the glory of him who sends him, or where would be his love for men?

And yet more, my brethren, all the extraordinary men of which the preceding ages could boast, all the just of the law and of the age of the patriarchs, had been only the imperfect types of the Christ; and again, each of them represented only some individual trait of his life and ministry; Melchisedec, his priesthood; Abraham, his quality of Head and Father of believers; Isaac, his sacrifice; Job, his persecutions and sufferings; Moses, his office of Mediator; Joshua, his triumphant entry into the land of the living with a chosen people. All these men, however, so venerable and so miraculous, were only rude sketches of the Messiah to come; and how great must that Messiah himself have been to be, seeing his figures were so illustrious and so shining! But, deprive Jesus Christ of his divinity and of his eternal origin, and the reality has nothing superior to the figure. I know, as we shall afterwards say, that, when we narrowly examine the lustre of his wonders, we shall

see

see them marked with divine characters which are only to be found in the life of those great men. But, to judge of them by the eyes of the senses alone, the parallel would not be favourable to Jesus Christ. Is he greater than Abraham? That man so great, that the Lord himself, among his most pompous names, had taken that of the God of Abraham, as if in order to proclaim to the world that the homages of a man, so righteous and so extraordinary, were more glorious to his sovereignty than the title of God of empires and of nations: so great, that the Jews believed themselves superior to all other nations of the earth, only because they were the posterity of that famous chief so cherished of Heaven; and that fathers, in recounting to their children the wonders of their nation and the history of their ancestors, animated them to virtue, only by putting them in remembrance that they were the children of Abraham and the members of a holy race? Is he more wonderful than Moses? That man, mighty in words and in deeds, mediator of an holy covenant, who broke the yoke of Egypt and delivered his people from bondage: that man, who was established the god of Pharaoh, who seemed the master of nature, who covered the earth with plagues, who divided seas, who made a new nourishment to be showered from heaven; that man, who saw the Lord face to face upon the holy mountain, and who appeared before Israel all resplendent in light? What is

there

there more aftonifhing or more magnificent in the life of Jefus Chrift ? Neverthelefs, thefe were only rude fketches of his glory and might : he was to be the laft finifhing and perfection of them. Now, if Jefus Chrift were not the image of the fubftance of his Father, and the eternal fplendour of his glory, he, at the utmoft, could only be equalled with thefe firft men ; and the incredulity of the Jews might, without blafphemy, demand of him : " Art " thou greater than our father Abraham, or, than " the prophets which are dead: whom makeft " thou thyfelf?" I have then juftly faid, that if, in the firft place, you will eftimate his miniftry from that pompous train of oracles and of figures which have announced him, the fplendour is fuch, that, if Jefus Chrift be but a man fimilar to us, the wifdom itfelf of God would be culpable of the miftake of thofe who worfhip him.

But, my brethren, the Chrift hath been foretold with his members : we are comprifed in the prophecies which have announced him to the earth : we have been promifed as an holy race, a fpiritual people, who were to bear the law engraven on their heart, who were to figh after only eternal riches, and who were to adore in fpirit and in truth : like Jefus Chrift, we have compofed the expectation of the juft of ancient times, and the defire of nations: we are that new Jerufalem, pure and undefiled, fo often announced in the prophets, where God alone was to be known and worfhipped ; where

faith

faith was to be the sole light to illuminate us; charity the only bond of union; and the land of promise the only hope to animates us. Now, do we answer an expectation so illustrious and so holy? Are we worthy of having been the earnest desire of all those distant ages which have preceded us? Do we merit to have been looked forward to like celestial men, who were to fill the earth with sanctity and righteousness? Have not those ages been deceived in their expectation of the Christian people? Were the just of those distant times to return upon the earth, could we present ourselves to them, and say: Behold those celestial, spiritual, temperate, believing, and charitable men, whom you expected? Alas! my brethren, the just of former times were Christians before the birth of faith; and we are still Jews, under all the advantages of the gospel: we live solely for the earth: we know no true riches but the present good: our whole religion is grounded in the senses: we have received more assistances, but we are not more believing.

To the lustre of the prophecies which have announced Jesus Christ, we must add that of his works and of his miracles: second resplendent character of his ministry. Yes, my brethren, even admitting that Heaven had not promised him to the earth with such magnificence; that the manner in which he was to appear to the earth had not constituted, during all these first ages, the sole occupation

cupation and expectation of the univerfe; did ever man appear more wonderful, more divine in his actions, and in all the circumftances of his life?

I fay, 1/tly, in his actions and in his miracles. I know, and we come from faying it, that, in the ages which preceded him, extraordinary men had appeared upon the earth, to whom the Lord feemed to have delegated his omnipotence and virtue: in Egypt and in the defert Mofes appeared the mafter of heaven and earth; in the following ages Elijah came to prefent the fame fight to men. But, when we narrowly examine their power itfelf, we find that all thefe miraculous men always bore with them the marks of weaknefs and dependance.

Mofes only operated his miracles with his myfterious rod; without it he was no longer but a weak and powerlefs man; and it would feem that the Lord had attached the virtue of miracles to that morfel of parched wood for the purpofe of making the Ifraelites fenfible that, in his hands, Mofes himfelf was but a weak and fragile inftrument, whom he was pleafed to employ in the operation of grand effects. Jefus Chrift operates the grandeft miracles, even without fpeaking; and the fole touch of his garment cures inveterate infirmities. Mofes communicates not to his difciples the power of operating miracles; for it was an extraneous gift which he had received from Heaven, and which he had not the power of delegating: Jefus Chrift leaves to his a ftill greater efficacy than had appeared ed even in himself. Moses always acts in the name of the Lord: Jesus Christ operates all in his own name; and the works of his Father are his. Nevertheless, this Moses, who had not been prophecied like Jesus Christ, who remitted not sins as he did, who never gave himself out as equal to God, but only as his faithful servant; this Moses, dreading that, after his death, his miracles should make him pass for a god, takes precautions lest, in the revolution of ages, the credulity of his people render to him divine honours: he goes up alone to the mountain, to expire far from the sight of his brethren, in the fear of their coming to offer up victims upon his tomb; and for ever removes his body from the superstition of the tribes: he does not shew himself to his disciples after his death; he contents himself with leaving to them the law of God, and employs every mean to obliterate himself from their remembrance. And Jesus Christ, after all the miracles which he operates in Judea, after all the prophecies which had announced him, after having appeared as a God upon the earth, his tomb is known to all the universe, exposed to the veneration of all people and ages; even after his death he shews himself to his disciples. Was superstition, then, less to be dreaded here? Or is Jesus Christ less zealous than Moses for the glory of the supreme Being, and for the salvation of men?

Elijah,

Elijah, it is true, raifes up the dead; but he is obliged to ftretch himfelf out upon the body of the child whom he recalls to life; and it is eafily feen that he invokes a foreign power; that he withdraws from the empire of death a foul which is not fubjugated to him; and that he is not himfelf the mafter of life and death. Jefus Chrift raifes up the dead as eafily as he performs the moft common actions; he fpeaks as mafter of thofe who repofe in an eternal fleep; and it is thoroughly felt that he is the God of the dead as of the living, never more tranquil and calm than when he is operating the grandeft things.

Laftly, The poets reprefented to us their fybils and their prieftefles as mad women while foretelling the future: it would feem that they were unable to fuftain the prefence of the falfe fpirit which dwelt within them. Even our own prophets, when announcing future things, without lofing the ufe of their reafon, or departing from the folemnity and the decency of their miniftry, partook of a divine enthufiafm: the foft founds of the lyre were often neceflary to aroufe in them the prophetic fpirit: it was eafily to be feen that they were animated by a foreign impulfe; and that it was not from their own funds they drew the knowledge of the future, and thofe hidden myfteries which they announced to men. Jefus Chrift prophecies as he fpeaks; the knowledge of the future has nothing either to move, difquiet, or furprife surprise him, because all times are contained in his mind; the future mysteries which he announces are not sudden and infused lights to his soul; they are familiar objects to him, always present to his view, and the images of which he finds within himself; and all ages to come, under the immensity of his regards, are as the present day which illuminates us. Thus, neither the resurrection of the dead, nor the foretelling of the future, ever injures his natural tranquility; he sports himself, if I may venture to say so, in operating miracles in the universe; and if he, at times, appear to tremble and to be troubled, it is solely when viewing the sin and the perversity of his people; because the more exalted one is in sanctity, the more does sin offer new horrors; and that the only thing which a Man-God can view with trembling, is the spectacle of a conscience stained with crimes.

Such is the omnipotency of Jesus Christ: his miracles bear no mark of dependance: and, not satisfied with thereby shewing to us that he is equal to God, he also advertises us, that, whatever wonder is operated by his Father upon the earth, he likewise operates; and that his Father's works are his. Hath any prophet, down to the period of Jesus Christ, spoken in this manner; and who, far from rendering glory to God as the author of every excellent gift, hath attributed to himself all the grand things which it had pleased the Lord to operate through his ministry?

But,

But, my brethren, if we have also been prophecied with Jesus Christ, we are moreover participators of his sovereignty over all creatures. Through faith the Christian is master of nature; all is subjected to him, because he himself is inferior only to God; all his actions ought to be miraculous, because they ought all to proceed from a sublime and a divine principle, and far above the powers of human weakness: we ought to be, as I may say, miraculous men, masters of the world in contemning it; exalted above the laws of nature by overcoming them; sovereign disposers of events by a thorough and tranquil submission to them; more powerful than death itself by wishing for it. Such is the sublimity of the Christian: and, how great must Jesus Christ have been, to have exalted human weakness to such a pinnacle of grandeur and might!

Finally, The last splendid character of his ministry is the marvellous and, till then, unheard-of circumstances which compose the whole course of his mortal life. I know that he came in nakedness and humiliation; but, through these obscure and contemptible externals, what lustre are not even the enemies of his divinity forced to acknowledge there?

In the *first* place, although they consider him as a man similar to us, they, nevertheless, believe him to have been formed, through the invisible operation of the most High, in the womb of a virgin

gin of Judah, in opposition to the common law of the children of Adam. What glory already for a simple creature!

Secondly, Scarcely is he born, when celestial legions sing the praises of the Lord, and give us to understand, that this birth renders his glory to the most High, and brings an eternal peace upon the earth. What then is this creature who can render glory to the most High, whose glory is in himself alone? Immediately after this a new star calls the wise men from the heart of the East; and, guided by that miraculous light, those righteous men come from the extremities of the earth to worship the new King of the Jews.

Trace all the circumstances of his life. If Mary bring him to the temple, a righteous man and an holy woman proclaim his future greatness; and, transported with an holy joy, they die with pleasure, after having seen him whom they call the salvation of the world, the light of nations, and the glory of Israel. The doctors, assembled in the temple, behold, with terror, his infancy to be wiser and more enlightened than all the wisdom of old men. In proportion as he grows up, his glory unfolds itself: John the Baptist, that man, the greatest of the children of men, humbles himself before him, and says that he is not worthy of performing the meanest offices to him. A voice from Heaven declares that he is the well-beloved Son. The affrighted demons fly from before him, are unable to support the sole presence of his sanctity, and confess that he is the holy of God. Collect together testimonies so different and so new, circumstances so unheard-of, and so extraordinary : what is this man who appears upon the earth with so much eclat ? And are not the people who have worshipped him at least excusable ?

But these are only weak preludes of his glory. If he privately withdraw himself upon the Tabor, accompanied with three disciples, his glory, impatient, if I dare to say it, at having hitherto been held captive under the veil of humanity, openly bursts forth : he appears all resplendent in light: the heavenly Father, who then, it would appear, lest the glory of Jesus Christ should become an occasion of error and idolatry to the astonished disciples, spectators of this sight, ought to have warned them that this Jesus, whom they beheld so glorious, was nevertheless only his servant and messenger, declares to them, on the contrary, that this is his well-beloved Son, in whom he is well pleased, and affixes no bounds to the homages which, according to his pleasure, they are to render to him. When Moses appeared surrounded with glory, and, as it were, transfigured on mount Sinai, afraid lest the Israelites, always superstitious, should consider him as a god descended upon the earth, the Lord, amid a flame of fire, declared at the same time from on high, " I am that I am, and thou shalt worship " only me." Moses himself appears before the

people

people with only the tables of the law in his hands, as if to let them know that, notwithstanding the glory with which they had seen him arrayed, he nevertheless was only the minister, and not the author of the holy law; that he could offer it to them only engraven on stone, and that it belonged solely to God to engrave it on hearts. But, on the Tabor, Jesus Christ appears as the legislator himself: the new law is not given to him by his Father to bear it to men; he only commandeth them to listen to him, and from his own mouth he proposeth him as their legislator, or rather as their living and eternal law.

What more shall I say, my brethren? If from the Tabor we pass to mount Calvary; that place, in which all the ignominy of the Son of Man was to be consummated, is not less, however, the theatre of his glory and divinity. All nature disorganised, confesses its Author in him; the stars which are hidden; the dead who arise; the stones of the tombs, which open of their own accord, and break in pieces; the veil of the temple, which is rent from top to bottom; even incredulity itself, which confesses him through the mouth of the centurion: all feel that it is not an ordinary man who dies, and that things take place upon that mount totally new and extraordinary.

Many righteous before him had died for the truth, by the hands of the impious: the head of the forerunner had lately been seen in the palace

of

of Herod, as the price of voluptuousness: Isaiah, by a grievous death, had rendered glory to God; and, notwithstanding his royal blood, his august birth was ineffectual in sheltering him from those persecutions which are always the recompense of truth and zeal: many others had died for the sake of righteousness; but nature seemed not wholly interested in their sufferings; the dead forsook not their tombs to come and, as it were, reproach to the living their sacrilege: nothing, in any degree similar, had, as yet, appeared upon the earth.

Survey the rest of his mysteries; every where you will find traits which distinguish him from all other men. If he rise up from among the dead, besides that it is through his own efficiency, (which no eye had ever yet beheld), it is not, like so many others, who had been raised up through the ministry of the prophets, to return once more into the empire of death: he arises, never more to die; and, even here below, he receives an immortal life, which is what had never yet been accorded to any creature.

If he is carried up into heaven, it is not in a flaming chariot that he vanishes in the twinkling of an eye; he ascends with majesty, and allows all leisure to his affectionate disciples to worship him, and to accompany their divine Master with their eyes and their homages. The angels, as if to receive him into his empire, come to greet this King of glory, and comfort the affliction of the disciples, by promising him once more to the earth, surrounded with glory and immortality. All here announces the God of heaven, who returns to the place from whence he came, and who goes to resume the possession of his own glory; at least, every thing inclines men to believe so.

And, in truth, my brethren, when Elijah is taken up to heaven in a fiery chariot, a single disciple is the only spectator of that miraculous ascension; it takes place in a retired spot, removed from the view of the other children of the prophets, who, perhaps more credulous and less enlightened than Eliseus, might have been inclined to render divine honours to that miraculous man. But Jesus Christ, surrounded with glory, mounts up to heaven before the eyes of five hundred disciples: the weakest, and those who were least confirmed in the faith of his resurrection, are the first who are invited to the holy mountain: nothing is dreaded from their credulity: on the contrary, their adorations are equally permitted as their regrets and tears; and a life full of prodigies, till then so unheard-of on the earth, is at last terminated by a circumstance still more wonderful, and sufficient of itself to make him to be regarded as a God, and to immortalise error and idolatry among men.

In effect, if the pagan ages, in order to justify the ridiculous and impious homages which they paid to their legislators, to the founders of empires,

and

and to other celebrated men, gave it out, in their historians and poets, that these heroes were not dead, but had only difappeared from the earth; and that, being of the fame nature with the gods, they had afcended to heaven, in order to affume their ftation among the other ftars, which, according to them, were fo many divinities who enlighten us, and for the purpofe of there enjoying that immortality to which their divine birth entitled them : if fo very vulgar a fiction had of itfelf been able to render men fo long idolatrous, what impreffion muft the reality of that fable not have made upon the people? And if the univerfe had worshipped impoftors, who were falfely faid to have mounted up to heaven, would it not have been excufable to worfhip a miraculous man, whom men, with their own eyes, had feen exalted above the ftars?

But obferve, my brethren, that the occafion of error finifhes not with Jefus Chrift ; it is announced to us, that, at the end of ages, he will again appear in the heavens furrounded with power and majefty, and accompanied with all the heavenly hoft : all affembled nations fhall, with trembling, await at his feet the decifion of their eternal deftiny : he will fovereignly pronounce their decifive fentence. The Abrahams, the Mofefes, the Davids, the Elijahs, the John the Baptifts, and all that ages have produced of great and moft wonderful, fhall be fubmitted to his judgment and to his empire ;

he

he will himself be exalted above all power, all dominion, and all which is termed great in heaven and in the earth : he will erect his throne above the clouds, and fit on the right hand of the moſt High: he will appear Maſter, not only of life and death, but the immortal King of ages, the Prince of eternity, the Chief of an holy people, the ſupreme Arbiter of all the created. What then is this man to whom the Lord hath delegated ſuch power? And the dead themſelves, who ſhall appear in judgment before him, ſhall they be condemned for having worſhipped him, when they ſhall ſee him clothed with ſuch glory, majeſty, and power?

And one reflection, which I beg you to make in finiſhing this part of my diſcourſe, is that, if only one extraordinary and divine trait were to be found here in the courſe of a long life, we might be inclined to believe, that it ſometimes pleaſeth the Lord to allow his glory and his power to ſhine forth in his ſervants. Thus, Enoch was carried up, Moſes appeared transfigured on the holy mountain, Elijah was raiſed up to heaven in a fiery chariot, John the Baptiſt was foretold. But, beſides that theſe were individual circumſtances, and that the language of thoſe miraculous men and of their diſciples, with reſpect to the divinity and to themſelves, left no room for ſuperſtition and miſtake; here, it is an aſſemblage of wonders, which all, or even taken ſeparately, would have been ſufficient to deceive the credulity of men : here, all the different

ferent traits, difperfed among all thefe extraordinary men who had been confidered almoft as gods upon the earth, are collected together in Jefus Chrift, but in a manner a thoufand times more glorious and more divine. He prophecies, but more loftily, and with more ftriking characters, then John the Baptift: he appears transfigured in the holy mount, but furrounded with more glory than Mofes: he afcends to heaven, but with more marks of power and majefty than Elijah: he penetrates into the future, but with more accuracy and clearnefs than all the prophets: he is produced, not only from a barren womb like Samuel, but likewife by a pure and innocent virgin: what fhall I fay? And not only he does not undeceive men by certain and precife expreffions upon his origin as purely human; but his fole language, with refpect to his equality to the moft High; but the fole doctrine of his difciples, who tell us that he was in the bofom of God from all eternity, and that all hath been made through him, who call him their Lord and their God, who inform us that he is all in all things, would juftify the error of thofe who worfhip him, had even his life been, in other refpects, an ordinary one, and fimilar to that of other men.

O you! who refufe to him his glory and his divinity, yet, neverthelefs, confider him as a meffenger fent by God to inftruct men, complete the blafphemy; and confound him with thofe impoftors

tors who have come to seduce the world, since, far from tending to establish the glory of God and the knowledge of his name, the splendour of his ministry has answered the sole purpose of erecting himself into a divinity, of placing him at the side of the most High, and of plunging the whole universe into the most dangerous, the most durable, the most inevitable, and the most universal of all idolatries.

For our part, my brethren, we who believe in him, and to whom the mystery of the Christ hath been revealed, let us never lose sight of that divine model which the Father shews to us from on high on the holy mount. Let us enter into the spirit of the mysteries of which his whole mortal life is composed; they are merely the different states of the life of the Christian on this earth: let us confess the new empire which Jesus Christ came to form in our hearts. The world, which we have hitherto served, hath never been able to deliver us from our grievances and wretchedness. We vainly sought in it, freedom, peace, and comfort of life; and we have found only slavery, disquiet, bitterness, and the curse of life. Behold a new Redeemer, who comes to bring peace to the earth; but it is not as the world promises it that he gives it to us. The world had wished to conduct us to peace and happiness through the pleasures of the senses, indolence, and a vain philosophy; it hath not been successful; by favouring our passions it hath

hath only augmented our punishments: Jesus Christ comes to propose a new way for the attainment of that peace and happiness which we search after; detachment from and contempt of the world, mortification of the senses, self-denial, behold the new riches which he comes to display to men. Let us be undeceived: we have no happiness to expect, even in this life, but by repressing our passions, and by refusing ourselves the gratification of every pleasure which disquiets and corrupts the heart: there is no philosophy, but that of the gospel, which can bestow happiness, or make real sages, because it alone regulates the mind, fixes the heart, and, by restoring man to God, restores him to himself. All those who have pursued other ways, have found only vanity and vexation of spirit; and Jesus Christ alone, in bringing the sword and separation, is come to bring peace among men.

O my God! I know only too well that the world and its pleasures make none happy! Come then and resume thy influence over a heart which in vain endeavours to fly from thee; and which its own disgusts recall to thee in spite of itself: come to be its Redeemer, its peace, and its light, and pay more regard to its wretchedness than to its crimes.

Behold how the lustre of the ministry of Jesus Christ would operate as an inevitable occasion of idolatry in men, were he only a simple creature.

Let

Let us now see how the spirit of his ministry would become the snare of our innocence.

PART II. The lustre of the ministry of Jesus Christ is not the most august and most magnificent side of it. However dignified he hath appeared, in consequence of all the oracles which have announced him, the works which he hath operated, and the shining circumstances of his mysteries, these are merely the outward appearances, as I may say, of his glory and of his grandeur; and, in order to know all that he is, we must enter into the principle and spirit of his ministry. Now, in the spirit of his ministry are comprised his doctrine, his favours, and his promises. Let us display these in their proper extent, and prove, either that we must deny to Jesus Christ his quality of a righteous man, and of a messenger of the almighty God, which the enemies of his divinity grant him to have been, or we must admit that he is himself a God manifested in the flesh, and come down upon the earth in order to save mankind.

Yes, my brethren, this is an inevitable alternative: if Jesus Christ be holy, he is God; and, if his ministry be not a ministry of deceit and imposition, it is the ministry of eternal Truth itself which hath been manifested for our instruction. Now, the enemies of his divine birth are forced to admit, that he hath been a man righteous, innocent, and friend of God: and if the world hath beheld dark and impious minds, who have likewise wife dared to blafpheme againft his innocence and to confound him with feducers, thefe have been only fome individual monfters who were held in abhorrence by the human race, and whofe names, too odious to all nature, are for ever buried in the fame darknefs from which the horror of their impiety originally came.

In effect, what man, till then, had appeared upon the earth with more inconteftable marks of innocence and fanctity than Jefus, Son of the living God? In what philofopher had ever been obferved fuch a love of virtue, fo fincere a contempt of the world, fo much charity towards men, fuch indifference for human glory, fuch zeal for the glory of the fupreme Being, fuch elevation above whatever is admired or fought after by men? How great is his zeal for the falvation of men! It is to that object that he directs all his difcourfes, all his cares, all his defires, and all his anxieties. The philofophers criticifed only the men, and folely endeavoured to expofe their weaknefs or their abfurdities: Jefus Chrift never fpeaks of their vices but in order to point out their remedies. The former were the cenfurers of human weakneffes; Jefus Chrift is their phyfician: the former gloried in being able to point out vices in others, from which they themfelves were not exempted; he never fpeaks, but with the bittereft forrow, of faults, from which his own innocence protects him, and even fheds tears over the diforders of an unbelieving city: it is easily seen that the former had no intention to reclaim men, but merely to attract esteem to themselves, by pretending to contemn them; and that the only wish of the latter is to save them, and that he is little affected with their applauses or esteem.

Pursue the whole detail of his manners and of his conduct, and see if any righteous character hath ever appeared on the earth more generally exempted from all the most inseparable weaknesses of humanity. The more narrowly he is examined, the more is his sanctity displayed. His disciples, who have it best in their power to know him, are the most affected with the innocence of his life; and familiarity, so dangerous to the most heroical virtue, serves only in his to discover fresh matter of wonder. He speaks only the language of Heaven: he never replies but when his answers may be useful towards the salvation of those who interrogate him. We see not in him those intervals, as I may say, in which the man re-appears; on every occasion he is the messenger of the Most High. The commonest actions are extraordinary in him, through the novelty and the sublimity of the dispositions with which he accompanies them; and, when he eats with the pharisee, he does not appear a man less divine than when he raises up Lazarus. Surely, my brethren, nature alone could never lead human weakness so far; this is not a philosopher who enjoins to others what he doth

not

not himself, it is a righteous character who, in his own examples, adopts the rules and precepts of his doctrine; and holy must he indeed be, seeing the very disciple who betrayed him, so interested to justify his own perfidy by an exposure of his faults, renders public testimony, however, to his innocence and sanctity; and that the whole challenged malice of his enemies hath never been able to convict him of sin.

Now, I say that, if Jesus Christ be holy, he is God; and that, whether you should consider the doctrine which he hath taught us with respect to his Father or with respect to men, it is no longer but a mass of equivocations or qualified blasphemies, if he be only an ordinary man, merely deputed by God for the instruction of men.

I say, whether you should consider it with respect to his Father. In effect, if Jesus Christ be but a simple messenger of the Most High, he comes, then, for the sole purpose of manifesting to idolatrous nations the unity of the divine essence. But, besides that his mission principally regards the Jews, who, for a long time past, had not returned to idolatry, and, consequently, needed not that God should raise up a prophet to reclaim them from an error of which they were not guilty, and a prophet whom they were taught from the beginning of the world to expect as the light of Israel, and the Redeemer of his people; and, besides, in what manner doth Jesus Christ fulfil his ministry, and what is his language

guage with regard to the supreme Being? Moses and the prophets, charged with the same mission, never cease to proclaim that the Lord was one and the same; that it was impious to compare him to the similitude of the creature; and that they themselves were only his servants and messengers, vile instruments in the hands of a God, who, through them, operated great things. No dubious expression escapes from their mouth on so essential a point of their mission; no comparison of themselves to the supreme Being, always dangerous, in consequence of the natural tendency of man to prostitute his homages to men, and to raise up for himself palpable and visible gods; no equivocal term which might have blended themselves with the Lord, in whose name they spake, and have given birth to a superstition and an idolatry, to combat which they only came.

But, if Jesus Christ be only a messenger such as they were, with how much less fidelity doth he fulfil his ministry! He continually says that he is equal to his Father; he acquaints us, that he hath come down from heaven, and that he hath quitted the bosom of God; that he was before Abraham; that he was before all things; that the Father and he are one; that eternal life consists in the knowledge of the Son, as well as in the knowledge of the Father; that whatever is done by the Father, the Son also doth. Had any prophet, down to Jesus Christ, spoken in a language so new, so

strange,

strange, so disrespectful towards the supreme God; and who, far from rendering glory to God as the author of every good gift, hath attributed to his own efficiency the great things which the Lord had deigned to operate through his ministry. Every where he compares himself to the sovereign God; on one occasion, indeed, he says that the Father is greater than he; but what language is that, if he be not himself a God manifested in flesh? And would we not consider as a fool any man who should seriously tell us that the supreme Being is greater than he? Even to dare to compare himself with the divinity, is it not equalling himself to him? Is there any proportion either of greater or less betwixt God and man, betwixt the whole and nothing? But what do I say? Jesus Christ is not content with saying that he is equal to God; he even justifies the novelty of these expressions against the murmurings of the Jews who are offended at them; far from clearly undeceiving them, he confirms them in the offence: on every occasion he affects a language, which, unless cleared up and justified by his equality to his Father, becomes either foolish or impious. If he be not God, what came he to do upon the earth? He comes to scandalise the Jews, by giving them room to believe that he compares himself to the most High: he comes to seduce nations, by procuring to himself the adoration of the whole earth after his death: he comes to spread fresh obscurity over the universe,

verse, and not, as he hath vaunted, to spread understanding, light, and the knowledge of God. What! my brethren, Paul and Barnabas rend their garments when they are taken for gods; they loudly proclaim to the people who wished to offer up victims to them: Worship the Lord alone, whose servants and ministers we are. The angel in the Revelation, when St John prostrates himself to worship him, rejects the homage with horror, and says to him: " Worship God alone; I am " only thy fellow-servant, and of thy brethren " that have the testimony of Jesus." And Jesus Christ tranquilly suffers, that they render divine honours to him! And Jesus Christ praises the faith of the disciples who worship him, and who, with Thomas, call him their Lord and their God! And Jesus Christ even confutes his enemies who contest his divinity and divine origin! Is he then less zealous than his disciples for the glory of him who sends him? Or is it a matter of less importance to him, pointedly to undeceive the people on a mistake so injurious to the supreme Being, and which, in fact, destroys the whole fruit of his ministry?

Yes, my brethren, what blessing hath the coming of Jesus Christ brought to the world, if those who worship him be idolatrous and profane? All who have believed in him have worshipped him as the eternal Son of the Father, the image of his substance, and the splendour of his glory. There

is

is but a small number of men in Christianity, who, though they acknowledge him as a messenger of God, yet refuse to him divine honours: even this sect, universally banished, and execrable even in those places where every error finds an asylum, is reduced to a few obscure and concealed followers; every where punished as an impiety from the instant that it dares to avow itself; and forced to hide itself in obscurity, and in the extremities of the most distant provinces and kingdoms. Is it, then, that numerous people of every tongue, of every tribe, and of every nation, which Jesus Christ came to form upon the earth? Is it a Jerusalem, formerly barren, and become fruitful, which was to contain tribes and nations in its bosom, and where the most distant isles, princes, and kings, were to come to worship? Are these the grand advantages which the world was to reap from the ministry of Jesus Christ? Is this, then, that abundance of grace, that plenitude of the spirit of God shed over all men, that universal regeneration, that spiritual and lasting reign which the prophets had foretold with such majesty, and which was to attend the coming of the Redeemer? What! my brethren, an expectation so magnificent is then reduced to the miserable sight of the world plunged into a new idolatry? That event, so blessed for the earth, promised for so many ages, announced with so much pomp, so earnestly longed for by all the righteous, and held out from afar to the whole

universe

universe as its only resource, was then to corrupt and to pervert it for ever? That church, so fruitful, of which kings and Cesars, at the head of their people, were to be the children, was then to contain, in its bosom, only a small number of men, equally odious to heaven and to the earth, the disgrace of nature and of religion, and obliged to seek, in obscurity, a shelter for the horror of their blasphemy? And all the future magnificence of the gospel was then to be limited to the formation of the detestable sect of an impious Socinus?

O God! how wise and reasonable doth the faith of thy church appear, when opposed to the absurd contradictions of unbelief! And how consoling for those who believe in Jesus Christ, and who place their hope in him, to behold the abysses which pride digs for itself when it pretends to open new ways, and to sap the only foundation of the faith and of the hope of Christians.

Behold, my brethren, how the doctrine of Jesus Christ, with relation to his Father, establishes the glory of his eternal origin. Thus, when the prophets speak of the God of heaven and of the earth, their expressions are too weak for the magnificence and the grandeur of their ideas. Full of the immensity, the omnipotence, and the majesty of the supreme Being, they exhaust the weakness of the human language in order, if possible, to correspond with the sublimity of these images. That God, is he who measures the waters of the ocean

in

in the hollow of his hand, who weighs the mountains in his balance, in whofe hands are the thunders and the tempefts, who fpeaks, and all is done; who amufes himfelf in upholding the univerfe. It was natural for fimple men to fpeak in this manner of the glory of the moft High; the infinite difproportion betwixt the immenfity of the fupreme Being and the weaknefs of the human mind muft ftrike, dazzle, and confound it; and the moft pompous expreffions are too feeble to convey its aftonifhment and admiration.

But, when Jefus Chrift fpeaks of the glory of the Lord, it is no longer in the pompous ftile of the prophets: he calls him an holy Father, a righteous Father, a merciful Father, a Shepherd who purfues a ftrayed fheep, and kindly bears it home himfelf; a Friend who yields to the importunities of his friend; a Father feelingly affected with the return and the amendment of his fon: it is clearly feen that this is a Child who fpeaks a domeftic language; that the familiarity and the fimplicity of his expreffions fuppofe in him a fublimity of knowledge which renders the idea of the fupreme Being familiar to him, and prevents him from being ftruck and dazzled, as we are, with his majefty and glory; and, laftly, that he only fpeaks of what is laid open to his view, and which he poffeffes himfelf. A perfon is much lefs ftruck with the eclat of titles which he has borne, as I may fay, from his birth: the children of kings fpeak, without emotion, of sceptres and crowns; and it is likewise the eternal Son alone of the living God who can speak so familiarly of the glory of God himself.

Behold, my brethren, seeing we participate with Jesus Christ in all his blessings, the right which he hath acquired for us, of considering God as our Father, of daring to call ourselves his children, and of loving rather than of fearing him. Nevertheless, we serve him like slaves and hirelings: we dread his chastisements; but we are little affected by his love and his promises: his law, so righteous, so holy, has nothing pleasing for us; it is a yoke which oppresses us, which excites our murmurs, and which we would soon free ourselves from were our transgressions against it to go unpunished: nothing is heard but complaints against the severity of its precepts, but contentions in order to support the propriety of those softenings which the world always mingles with their practice: in a word, were he not an avenging God we would never confess him; and it is to his justice and to his chastisements alone that he is indebted for our respect and homages.

But the doctrine of Jesus Christ, with relation to men, whom he came to instruct, doth not less establish the truth of his divine birth. For I speak not here of the wisdom, the sanctity, and the sublimity of that doctrine: in it, every thing is worthy of reason, and of the soundest philosophy:

every

every thing is proportioned to the wretchednefs and to the excellency of man, to his wants and to his exalted lot; every thing there infpires contempt for perifhable things, and the love of eternal riches: every thing there maintains good order, and the peace and tranquility of ftates: every thing there is grand, becaufe every thing is true: the glory of the deeds is more real and more fhining in the heart than the deeds themfelves. The wife man of the gofpel feeks, from his virtue here below, only the fatisfaction of obeying God, who will one day amply recompenfe him for it, and he prefers the teftimony of his own confcience to all the applaufes of men: he is greater than the entire world, through his exalted faith; and he is below the leaft of men, through the modefty of his fentiments. His virtue feeks not, in pride, the indemnity of its fufferings; that is the firft enemy which it attacks; and, in that divine philofophy, the moft heroical actions are nothing, from the moment that we count them as any thing ourfelves: it confiders glory as an error, profperity as a misfortune, elevation as a precipice, afflictions as favours, the earth as a place of exilement, all that happens as a dream. What is this new language? What man prior to Jefus Chrift had ever fpoken in this manner? And if his difciples, merely in confequence of having announced this divine doctrine, were taken by a whole people for gods defcended upon the earth, what worfhip fhall they

have

have it in their power to refuse to him who is the Author of it, and in whose name they announce it?

But, let us leave these general reflections, and come to the more precise duties of that love and dependance which his doctrine exacts of men with regard to himself. He commands us to love him, as he commands us to love his Father: he insists that we dwell in him, that is to say, that we establish ourselves in him, that we seek our happiness in him, as in his Father; that we direct all our actions, all our thoughts, all our desires, that we direct ourselves to his glory, as to the glory of his Father; sins themselves are not remitted but to those who sincerely love him; and all the righteousness of the just, and the reconciliation of the sinner, are the effects of the love which we have for him. What is this man who comes to usurp the place of God in our hearts? Is a creature worthy of being loved for itself, and every noble and estimable quality which it may possess, is it not the sole gift of him who alone is worthy of all love?

What prophet prior to Jesus Christ had ever spoken thus to men: You shall love me; whatever you do, you shall do it for my glory. You shall love the Lord your God, said Moses to the children of Israel. Nothing is amiable in itself but what can bestow happiness upon us: now, no creature can be our happiness or our perfection: no creature, consequently, is worthy of being loved for itself; it would be an idolatry. Any man, who comes

comes to propose himself to men as the object of their love, is impious, and an impostor who seeks to usurp the most essential right of the supreme Being: he is a monster of pride and folly, who wants to erect altars to himself, even in hearts, the only sanctuary which the divinity had never yielded up to profane idols. The doctrine of Jesus Christ, that doctrine so divine, and so much admired even by the pagans, would no longer, in that case, be but a monstrous mixture of impiety, of presumption, and of folly, if, not being himself the God blessed in all ages, he had made that love which he exacted of his disciples, the most essential precept of his morality; and it would be a ridiculous mark of ostentation in him, to have held himself out to men as a model of humility and modesty, while, in fact, he was carrying presumption and unlimited compliance to a degree far beyond all the proudest philosophers, who had never aspired to more than the esteem and the applauses of men.

Nor is this all: not only Jesus Christ insists that we love him, but he also exacts of men marks of the most disinterested and most heroical love. He insists that we love him more than our relations, than our friends, than our fortune, than our life, than the whole world, than ourselves; that we suffer all for his sake, that we renounce all for him, that we shed, even to the last drop of our blood for him: whoever renders not to him these
grand

grand homages, is unworthy of him; whoever puts him in competition with any creature, or with himself, insults and dishonours him, and forfeits every pretension to his promises.

What! my brethren, he is not satisfied, as the idols, and even the true God himself had appeared to be, with the sacrifices of goats and bulls? He carries his pretensions still further, and requires of man the sacrifice of himself; that he fly to gibbets; that he offer himself to death and to martyrdom for the glory of his name! But, if he be not the Master of our life, by what right doth he exact it of us? If our soul be not originally come from him, is it to him that we ought to return it? Is that regaining it, to have lost it for his sake? If he be not the Author of our being, do we not become sacrilegious and murderers when we sacrifice ourselves for his glory, and when we transfer to a creature, and to a simple messenger of God, the grand sacrifice of our being, solely destined to confess the sovereignty and the power of the eternal Maker, who hath drawn us from nothing? That Jesus Christ die himself, well and good, for the glory of God, and even that he exhort us to follow his example; many prophets before him had died for the Lord's sake, and had exhorted their disciples to walk in their steps. But that Jesus Christ, if he be not God himself, should order us to die for himself, should exact of men that last proof of love; that he should command us to offer

up

up a life for him which we hold not of him; is it possible that men should have ever existed upon the earth so vulgar and so stupid as to allow themselves to be led away by the extravagance of such a doctrine? Is it possible that maxims so ridiculous and so impious should have been able to triumph over the whole universe, to overthrow all sects, to recall all minds, and to prevail over every thing which had hitherto appeared exalted, either in learning, in doctrine, or in the wisdom of the earth? And, if we consider as barbarians those savage nations who make a sacrifice of themselves upon the tombs and ashes of their relations and friends, why should we view, in a more respectable light, those disciples of Jesus Christ who have sacrificed themselves for his sake? And shall not his religion be equally a religion of barbarity and of blood?

Yes, my brethren, the Agnes', the Lucias, the Agathas, those first martyrs of faith and of modesty, would then have sacrificed themselves to a mortal man? And, in preferring to shed their blood rather than to bend the knee before vain idols, they would have shunned one idolatry only in order to fall into another more condemnable, in dying for Jesus Christ? The generous avowers of faith would then have been only a set of desperate and fanatical men, who, like madmen, had run to death? The tradition of the martyrs would then be no longer but the list of an impious and bloody scene?

scene? The tyrants and persecutors would then have been the defenders of righteousness, and of the glory of the divinity? Christianity itself a sacrilegious and profane sect? The human race would then have totally erred? And the blood of the martyrs, far from having been the seed of believers, would have answered the sole purpose of inundating the whole universe with superstition and idolatry? O God! can the ear of man listen to such blasphemies without horror? And what more is necessary to overthrow unbelief than to shew it to itself?

Such are our first duties towards Jesus Christ; to sacrifice to him our inclinations, our friends, our relations, our fortune, our life itself, and, in a word, whatever may stand in the way of our salvation; it is to confess his divinity; it is to acknowledge that he alone can supply the place of all that we forsake for him, and render to us even more than we quit, by giving to us himself. It is he alone, says the apostle John, who contemns the world and all its pleasures, who confesses that Jesus Christ is the Son of God, because he thereby pronounces that Jesus Christ is greater than the world, more capable of rendering us happy, and consequently more worthy of our love.

But it is not sufficient to have considered the spirit of the ministry of Jesus Christ in his doctrine; it is necessary to consider it, secondly, in the special favours and blessings which the universe has received

received from him. He came to deliver all men from eternal death; from enemies of God, as they were, he hath rendered them his children: he hath secured to them the possession of the kingdom of God, and of immutable riches: he hath brought to them the knowledge of salvation and the doctrine of truth. These gifts, so magnificent, have not ended even with him; seated on the right hand of his Father, he still sheds them over our hearts; all our miseries still find their remedy in him: he nourishes us with his body; he washes us from our stains by continually applying to us the price of his blood; he forms pastors to conduct us; he inspires prophets to instruct us; he sanctifies righteous characters to animate us by their example; he is continually present in our hearts to comfort all their wants: man hath no passion which his grace doth not cure, no affliction which it doth not render pleasing, no power but what springs from him: in a word, he assures us himself that he is our way, our truth, our life, our righteousness, our redemption, our light. What new doctrine is this? Can a single man be the source of so many benefits to other men? Can the sovereign God, so jealous of his glory, attach us to a creature, by duties and ties so intimate and sacred, that we depend almost more upon that creature than upon himself? Would there be no danger that a man, become so beneficial and so necessary to other men, should at last become their idol?

That a man, author and difpenfer of fo many bleſſings, and who difcharges, with regard to us, the office and all the functions of a god, fhould likewife, in a little time, occupy his place in our hearts?

For obferve, my brethren, that it is gratitude alone which hath formerly made fo many gods. Men, neglecting the Author of their being and of the univerfe, worfhipped, at firſt, the air which enabled them to live, the earth which nourifhed them, the ſun which gave them light, and the moon which prefided over the night: fuch were their Cybeles, their Apollos, their Dianas. They worſhipped thofe conquerors who had delivered them from their enemies; thofe benevolent and upright princes who had rendered their fubjects happy, and the memory of their immortal reign; and Jupiter and Hercules were placed in the rank of gods, the one for the number of his victories, and the other in confequence of the happinefs and tranquility of his reign: in the ages of fuperftition and credulity, men knew no other gods than thofe who were ferviceable to them. And fuch is the character of man; his worfhip is but his love and his gratitude.

Now, what man hath ever benefited mankind fo much as Jefus Chriſt? Recollect all that the pagan ages have told us of the hiftory of their gods, and fee if they believed themfelves indebted to them what unbelief itfelf acknowledges, with the holy books, the world to be indebted to Jefus Chriſt.

To

To fome they thought themfelves indebted for favourable winds and a fortunate navigation; to o-
thers for the fertility of feafons; to their Mars for
fuccefs in battle; to their Janus for the peace and
the tranquility of the people; to Efculapius for
their health. But what are thefe weak benefits,
if you compare them to thofe which Jefus Chrift
hath fhowered upon the earth? He hath brought
to it an eternal peace, a lafting happinefs, righteoufnefs and truth; he hath made of it a new
world and a new earth; he hath not loaded a fingle people with his benefits, he hath loaded all nations, the whole univerfe; and what is more, he
hath become our benefactor only by fuffering as
our victim. What could he do more exalted or
more noble for the earth? If gratitude hath made
gods, could Jefus Chrift fail to find worfhippers a-
mong men? And, were it poffible that any excefs
could take place in our love and in our gratitude
to him, was it at all proper that we fhould be fo
deeply indebted to him?

Again, if Jefus Chrift, in dying, had informed
his difciples that to the Lord alone they were indebted for fo many benefits, that he himfelf had
been merely the inftrument, and not the author
and fource of all thefe fpecial favours, and that
they ought, confequently, to forget him, and to render to God that glory which was due to him alone:
but very differently than with fuch inftructions
doth Jefus Chrift terminate his wonders and his
miniftry.

ministry. He not only requires that his disciples forget him not, and that they do not cease, even after his death, to hope in him; but, on the point of quitting them, he assures them that, even to the consummation of time, he will be present with them; he promises still more than he hath already bestowed upon them, and attaches them for ever to himself by indissoluble and immortal ties.

In effect, the promises which, in that last moment, he makes to them, are still more astonishing than all the favours he had granted to them during his life. In the *first* place, he promises to them the consoling Spirit, which he calls the Spirit of his Father: that Spirit of the truth which the world cannot receive; that Spirit of energy which was to form the martyrs; that Spirit of intelligence which was to enlighten the prophets; that Spirit of wisdom which was to conduct the pastors; that Spirit of peace and of charity which, of all believers, was to make only one heart and one soul. What right hath Jesus Christ over the Spirit of God, to dispose of it at his pleasure, and to promise it to men, if it be not his own Spirit? Elijah, ascending to heaven, looks upon it as a thing hardly possible to promise to Eliseus, individually, his twofold spirit of zeal and prophecy: how far was he from promising to him the eternal Spirit of the heavenly Father, that Spirit of liberty which agitates where he thinks fit! Nevertheless, the promises of Jesus Christ are accomplished;

scarcely

scarcely hath he afcended to heaven when the Spirit of God defcends upon the difciples; the illiterate become at once more learned than all the fages and philofophers; the weak more powerful than the tyrants; the foolifh, according to the world, more prudent than all the wifdom of the age. New men, animated with a new Spirit, appear upon the earth; they attract all to walk in their fteps; they change the face of the univerfe; and, even to the end of ages, fhall that Spirit animate his church, form righteous fouls, overthrow the unbelieving, confole his difciples, fuftain them amid perfecutions and difgraces, and fhall bear witnefs in the bottom of their heart that they are children of God, and that they are entitled, through that auguft title, to more real and more folid riches than all thofe of which the world can ever defpoil them.

Secondly, Jefus Chrift promifes to his difciples the keys of heaven and of hell, and the power of remitting fins. What! my brethren, the Jews are deeply offended when he pretends to remit them himfelf, and when he feems to attribute to himfelf a power referved to God alone; but, how will all nations of the earth be fcandalifed when they fhall read, in his gofpel, that he hath even delegated this power to his difciples? And, if he be not God, hath the mind of man ever imagined fuch an inftance of temerity and folly? What right, in effect, hath he over confciences, to bind or to unbind them at his pleafure, and to transfer to weak men a power which he himfelf could not exercife without blafphemy?

Thirdly, But this is not all; he promifes to his difciples the gift likewife of miracles; that, in his name, they fhould raife up the dead; that they fhould reftore fight to the blind, health to the fick, and fpeech to the dumb; that they fhould be mafters of all nature. Mofes promifes not to his difciples the gifts with which the Lord had favoured him: he is fenfible that the power is not his own, and that the Lord alone can beftow it on whomfoever he may think fit. Thus, after his death, when Jofhua arrefts the fun in the middle. of his courfe, in order to complete the victory over the enemies of the people of God, it is not in the name of Mofes that he commands that planet to ftand ftill; it is not of him that he holds the power of making even the ftars obedient to him; when he wifhes to exercife it, it is not to him that he addreffes himfelf: but the difciples of Jefus Chrift can operate nothing but in the name of their Mafter; it is in his name that they raife up the dead and make the lame to walk; and, without the affiftance of that divine name, they are equally weak as the reft of men. The miniftry and the power of Mofes terminate with his life; the miniftry and the power of Jefus Chrift only begin, as I may fay, after his death, and we are affured that his reign is to be eternal.

What

What more shall I say? He promises to his disciples the conversion of the universe, the triumph of the cross, the compliance of all the nations of the earth, of philosophers, of Cesars, of tyrants; and that his gospel shall be received by the whole world: but, doth he hold the hearts of all men in his hands thus to answer for a change of which the world had hitherto had no example? You will, no doubt, tell us, that God layeth open the future to his servant. But you are mistaken: if he be not God, he is not even a prophet; his predictions are dreams and chimeras: it is a false spirit which seduces him, and which is concerned in his knowledge of the future, and the sequel hath belied the truth of his promises: he prophecies that all nations, seated under the shadow of death, shall open their eyes to the light; and he sees not that they are on the point of falling into a more criminal blindness in worshipping him: he prophecies that his Father shall be glorified, and that his gospel shall every where form to him worshippers in spirit and in truth; and he sees not that men are going for ever to dishonour him, in placing upon an equality with him, even to the end of ages, that Jesus who ought to have been considered only as his servant and prophet: he prophecies that idols shall be overthrown; and he sees not that he himself shall occupy their place: he prophecies that he will form to himself an holy people of every tongue and of every tribe; and he sees not that

he

he comes only to form a new people of idolaters of every nation, who shall place him in the temple as the living God; whose actions, worship, and homages shall all be directed to him; who shall do all for his glory; who shall depend solely upon him, live only for and through him, and have neither force nor energy but what they receive from him : in a word, who shall worship him, who shall love him a thousand times more spiritually, more intimately, and more universally, than ever the pagans had worshipped their idols. This, then, is not even a prophet ; and his relations, according to the flesh, are guilty of no blasphemy when they say " he is beside himself," and that he bestows, on the dreams of an heated imagination, all the weight and reality of revelations and mysteries.

Behold to what unbelief conducts. Overturn the foundation, which is the Lord Jesus, eternal Son of the living God, and the whole edifice tumbles in pieces : take away the grand mystery of piety, and all the religion is but a dream : deny the divinity of Jesus Christ, and you cut off, from the doctrine of Christians, all the merit of faith, all the consolation of hope, all the motives of charity. Thus, with what zeal did not the first disciples of the gospel oppose those impious men who, from that time, ventured to attack the glory of their Master's divinity? They well knew that it was striking at the heart of their religion ; that it was ravishing from them the only alleviation of

their

their persecutions and sufferings, all confidence in the promises to come, and all the dignity and grandeur of their pretensions; and that, that principle once overthrown, the whole religion dissipated in smoke, and was no longer but a human doctrine and the sect of a mortal man, who, like all the other chiefs, had left nothing but his name to his disciples.

Thus, the pagans themselves then reproached the Christians with rendering divine honours to their Christ. Pliny, a Roman proconsul celebrated for his works, giving an account to the emperor Trajan of their morals and doctrine; after being forced to confess that the Christians were pious, innocent, and upright men, and that they assembled before the rising of the sun, not to concert the commission of crimes, or to disturb the peace of the empire, but to live in piety and righteousness, to detest frauds, adulteries, and even the coveting of the wealth of others; he only reproaches them with chaunting hymns in honour of their Christ, and of rendering to him the same homages as to a god. Now, if these first believers had not rendered divine honours to Jesus Christ, they would have justified themselves against that calumny; they would have rejected that scandal from their religion, almost the only one which shocked the zeal of the Jews and the wisdom of the Gentiles: they would openly have said: We do not worship Jesus Christ; for we know better than to transfer to a creature that honour and worship which are due to God alone. Nevertheless, they make no reply to this accusation. Their apologists refute all the other calumnies with which the pagans endeavoured to blacken their doctrine; they clear up and overthrow the slightest accusations; and their apologies, addressed to the senate, attract to them even the admiration of Rome, and impose silence on their enemies. And, upon the accusation of idolatry towards Jesus Christ, which should be the most crying and the most horrible; upon the reproach of worshipping a crucified person, which was the most likely to discredit them, and which ought indeed to have been the most grievous to men so holy, so declared against idolatry, and so jealous of the glory of God, they are totally silent; and, far from defending themselves, they even justify the accusation by their silence: What do I say, by their silence? They authorise it by their language in professing to suffer for his name, in dying for him, in confessing him before the tyrants, in joyfully expiring upon gibbets, in the sweet expectation of going to enjoy him, and of receiving, in his bosom, a more immortal life than that which they had lost for his glory. They suffered martyrdom rather than bend to the statue of the Cesars, rather than allow their pagan friends, through a human compassion, and to save them from torture, to falsely attest, before the magistrates, that they

had

had offered incense to the idols, and they would have submitted to the accusation of paying divine honours to Jesus Christ, without any attempt to destroy the imputation? Ah! they would have proclaimed the contrary from the house tops; they would have exposed themselves even to death, rather than to have given room to so hateful and so execrable a suspicion. What can unbelief oppose to this? And, if it be an error to equal Jesus Christ to God, it is an error which has been born with the church, and upon which the whole structure hath been reared; which has formed so many martyrs, and converted the whole universe.

But what fruit, my brethren, are we to draw from this discourse? That Jesus Christ is the grand object of Christian piety. Nevertheless, scarcely do we know Jesus Christ: we never consider that all the other practices of piety are, as I may say, arbitrary; but, that this is the ground-work of faith and of salvation; that this is pure and sincere piety; that, continually to meditate upon Jesus Christ, to have recourse to him, to nourish ourselves with his doctrine, to enter into the spirit of his mysteries, to study his actions, to count solely upon the merit of his blood and of his sacrifice, is the only true knowledge, and the most essential duty of the believer. Remember then, my brethren, that piety towards Jesus Christ is the cordial spirit of the Christian religion; that nothing is solid but what you shall build upon that foundation;

tion; and that the principal homage which he expects of you is, that you become like him, and that his life be the model of your own, in order that, through your resemblance to him, you may be included in the number of those who shall be partakers of his glory.

SERMON VIII.

ON THE RESURRECTION OF LAZARUS.

JOHN xi. 34.

Come and see.

THE most hardened sinner could never submit to the horror of his situation, were he able to see and to know himself such as he is. A soul, grown old in guilt, is only bearable to itself, because that the same passion, from which all his miseries spring, conceals them from him, and that his disorder is, at the same time, both the weapon which inflicts the wound, and the fatal bandage which hides it from the eyes of the patient.

Behold wherefore the church, in order to lay the sinner open to himself during this time of penitence, almost continually displays to us, under

various

various images, the deplorable state of a soul who has grown old in his iniquity: one while under the figure of a paralytic young man; that is, to mark to us the insensibility and fatal ease which always follow habitual guilt: another, under the symbol of a prodigal reduced to feed with the vilest animals; and, under these traits, it wishes to make us feel his abasement and his infamy: again, under the image of a person born blind; and that is in order to paint to us the depth and the horror of his blindness: and, lastly, under the parable of a deaf and dumb person possessed with a devil; and that is, more animatedly to figure to us the subjection under which habitual guilt holds all the powers of an unfortunate soul.

To day, in order, as it were, to assemble all these traits under a single image still more terrible and striking, the church proposes to us Lazarus in the tomb, dead for four days, emitting stench and infection, bound hand and foot, his face covered with a napkin, and exciting only horror even in those whom affection and blood had most closely united to him in life.

Come then and see, you, my dear hearer, who live, for so many years past, under the shameful yoke of dissipation, and who are insensible to the misery of your situation. Approach this tomb which the voice of Jesus Christ is now to open before your eyes; and, in that spectacle of infection and putrefaction, behold the true picture of your soul. You

fly

fly to profane spectacles, in order to see your passions represented under pleasing and deceitful colours: approach, and see them expressed here such as they are: come, and, in that infectious and stinking carcase, behold what you are in the sight of God, and how much your situation is worthy of your tears.

But, in exposing here only the horrible situation of a soul who lives in disorder, lest I trouble and discourage, without holding out to him a hand in order to assist him in quitting that abyss; that I may omit nothing of our gospel, I shall divide it into three reflections: in the first, you will see how shocking and deplorable is the situation of a soul who lives in habitual irregularity; in the second, I shall shew to you the means by which he may quit it; and, in the third, what the motives are which determine Jesus Christ to operate the miracle of his resurrection and deliverance. O my God! let thine all-powerful voice be now heard by those unfortunate souls who sleep in the darkness and shadow of death; command these withered bones once more to be animated, and to recover that light and that life of grace which they have lost.

REFLECTION I. I remark, at first, three principal circumstances in the deplorable spectacle which Lazarus, dead and buried, offers to our eyes. 1*stly*, Already become a mass of worms and corruption, he spreads infection and stench: and behold the

profound

profound corruption of a foul in habitual fin. 2*dly*, A gloomy napkin covers his eyes and his face: and behold the fatal blindnefs of a foul in habitual fin. *Laftly*, He appears in the tomb bound hand and foot: and behold the melancholy fubjection of a foul in habitual fin. Now, it is that profound corruption, that fatal blindnefs, and that melancholy fervitude, typified in the fpectacle of Lazarus, dead and buried, which precifely form all the horror and all the wretchednefs of a foul long dead in the eyes of God.

In the firft place, there is not a more natural image of a foul grown old in iniquity, than that of a carcafe already a prey to worms and putrefaction. Thus the holy books every where reprefent the ftate of fin under the idea of a fhocking death; and it feems as if the Spirit of God had found that melancholy image the moft calculated to give us, at leaft, a glimpfe of all the deformity of a foul in which fin dwells.

Now, two effects are produced on the body by death: it deprives it of life; it afterwards alters all its features, and corrupts all its members. It deprives it of life; in the fame manner it is that fin begins to disfigure the beauty of the foul. For, God is the life of our fouls, the light of our minds, and the fpring, as I may fay, of our hearts. Our righteoufnefs, our wifdom, our truth, are only the union of a righteous, wife, and true God with our foul: all our virtues are only the different influences

ences of his Spirit which dwells within us : it is he who exciteth our good defires, who formeth our holy thoughts, who produceth our pure lights, who operateth our righteous propenfities; infomuch that all the fpiritual and fupernatural life of our foul is only, as the apoftle fpeaks, the life of God within us.

Now, by a fingle fin that life ceafes, that light is extinguifhed, that fpirit withdraws, all thefe fprings are fufpended. Thus the foul, without God, is a foul without life, without motion, light, truth, righteoufnefs, or charity; it is no longer but a chaos, a dead body: its life is no longer but an imaginary and chimerical life; and, like thofe inanimate fubftances fet in motion by a foreign influence, it feems to live and to act; but " it is " dead while living."

Behold the firft degree of death which every fin that feparates a foul from God introduces into it; but habitual fin, like inveterate death, goes further. Thus, Lazarus not only is without life in the tomb, but, having been there for four days, the corruption of his body begins to fpread infection. For although the firft fin, which caufes the lofs of grace, leave us, in the eyes of God, without life and without motion; yet we may fay, that certain impreffions of the Holy Spirit, certain feeds of fpiritual life, certain means of recovering the grace loft, ftill remain to us. Faith is not yet extinguifhed; the feelings of virtue not yet effaced; a sense of the truths of salvation not yet lost: it is a dead body in truth; but, life being only just withdrawn, it still preserves, I know not what, of marks of warmth, which seem to spring from some remain of life. But, in proportion as the soul remains in death, and perseveres in guilt, grace withdraws; all extinguishes, all changes, all corrupts, and its corruption becomes universal.

I say universal; yes, my brethren, all changes, all corrupts in the soul, through a continuance of disorder; the gifts of nature, gentleness, rectitude, humanity, modesty, even the mental talents; the blessings of grace, the feelings of religion, the remorses of conscience, the terrors of faith, and faith itself; the corruption penetrates all, and changes, into putrefaction and a spectacle of horror, both the gifts of heaven and the blessings of the earth: nothing remains in its original situation; the loveliest features are those which become the most hideous and the most undistinguishable; the charms of wit become the seasoning of debauchery and the passions; feelings of religion are changed into freethinking; superiority of knowledge into pride, and a vain and shocking philosophy; nobility of mind is no longer but a boundless ambition; generosity and tenderness of heart but a yielding to the sway of impure and profane connections; the principles of glory and honour, handed down to us with the blood of our ancestors, but a vain ostentation, and the source of all our hatreds and animosities; our rank,

rank, our elevation, the caufe of our envies and mean jealoufies; laftly, our riches and our profperity, the fatal inftrument of all our crimes.

But the corruption is not confined to the finner alone; a dead body cannot be long concealed without a fmell of death being fpread around; it is impoffible to live long in debauchery without the fmell of a bad life making itfelf felt. In vain is every precaution employed to conceal the ignominy of a diforderly life; in vain is the fepulchre, full of putrefaction and infection, externally whitened and embellifhed, the ftench fpreads; guilt, fooner or later, betrays itfelf; a black and infectious air always proceeds from that profane fire which, with fo much care, was concealed. A diforderly life betrays itfelf in a thoufand ways; the public, at laft undeceived, opens its eyes, and the more their character becomes blown, the more they difcover themfelves; they become accuftomed to their fhame; they become weary of conftraint and decency: that guilt, which is only to be purchafed with attention and arrangements, appears too dear; they unmafk themfelves; they throw off that remainder of reftraint and modefty which made us ftill cautious of the eyes of men; they wifh to riot in diforder, without precaution or care; and, then, fervants, friends, connections, the city and country, all feel the infection of their irregularities and example. Our rank our elevation, no longer ferve but to render more ftriking

and

and more durable the scandal of our debaucheries: in a thousand places our excesses serve as a model: the view of our manners perhaps strengthens, in secret, consciences whom guilt still rendered uneasy; perhaps they even cite us, and make use of our example in seducing innocence, and in conquering a still timorous modesty: and, even after our death, the fame of our debaucheries shall stain the history of men; shall perhaps embellish lascivious tales; and, long after our day, in ages yet to come, the remembrance of our crimes shall still be an occasion and a source of guilt.

Lastly, But I would not dare to enlarge here, the corruption which habitual guilt sheds through the whole interior of the sinner is so universal, that even his body is infected: debauchery leaves the shameful marks of his irregularities on his flesh: the infection of his soul often extends even to a body which he has made subservient to ignominy. He says, in advance to corruption, like Job, "thou "art my father; and to the worm, thou art my "mother and my sister:" the corruption of his body is a shocking picture of that of his soul.

Great God! can I then flatter myself that thou wilt yet cast upon me some looks of compassion! Wilt thou not groan at the sight of that mass of crimes and putrefaction which my soul presents to thine eyes, as thou now groanest in the spirit over the tomb of Lazarus? Ah! avert thine holy eyes from the spectacle of my profound wretchedness; but,

let

let me no more turn away from it myſelf, and let me be enabled to view myſelf with all that horror which my ſituation deſerves: tear aſunder the veil which hides me from myſelf; my evils ſhall, in part, be done away from the moment that I ſhall be able to ſee and to know them.

And behold the ſecond circumſtance of the deplorable ſituation of Lazarus; a mournful cloth covers his face: that is the profound blindneſs which forms the ſecond character of habitual ſin.

I confeſs that every ſin is an error which makes us miſtake evil for good; it is a falſe judgment which makes us ſeek, in the creature, that eaſe, grandeur, and independence which we can find in God alone: it is a miſt which hides order, truth, and righteouſneſs from our eyes, and, in their place, ſubſtitutes vain phantoms. Nevertheleſs, a firſt falling off from God does not altogether extinguiſh our lights; nor is it always productive of total darkneſs. It is true that the ſpirit of God, ſource of all light, retires, and no longer dwells within us; but ſome traces of light are ſtill left in the ſoul: thus, though the ſun be already withdrawn from our hemiſphere, yet certain rays of his light ſtill tinge the ſky, and form, as it were, an imperfect day; it is only in proportion as he ſinks that gloom gains, and the darkneſs of night at laſt prevails. In the ſame manner, in proportion as ſin degenerates into habit, the light of God retires, darknefs gains, and the profound night of total blindnefs at laſt arrives.

And then all becomes occafion of error to the criminal foul; all changes its afpect to his eyes; the moſt fhameful paffions no longer appear but as weakneffes; the moſt criminal attachments but fympathies brought with us into the world and inherent to our hearts; the exceffes of the table but innocent pleafures of fociety; revenge but a juſt fenfe of injury; licentious and impious converfations but lively and agreeable fallies; the blackeſt defamation but a cuſtomary language of which none but weak and timid minds can make a fcruple; the laws of the church but old-fafhioned cuſtoms; the feverity of God's judgments but abfurd declamations which equally difgrace his goodnefs and mercy; death in fin, inevitable confequence of a criminal life, mere predictions, in which there is more of zeal than of truth, and refuted by the confidence which a return to God, previous to that laſt moment, promifes to us; laſtly, heaven, the earth, hell, all creatures, religion, crimes, virtues, good and evil, things prefent and to come, all change their afpect to the eyes of a foul who lives in habitual guilt; all fhew themfelves under falfe appearances; his whole life is no longer but a delufion and a continued error. Alas! could you tear away the fatal veil which covers your eyes, like thofe of Lazarus, and behold

hold yourfelf, like him, buried in darknefs; all covered with putrefaction, and fpreading around infection and a fmell of death! But now, fays our Saviour, all thefe things are hid from thine eyes; you fee in yourfelf only the embellifhments and the pompous externals of the fatal tomb in which you drag on in fin; your rank, your birth, your talents, your dignities, your titles; that is to fay, the trophies and the ornaments which the vanity of men has there raifed up; but, remove the ftone which covers that place of horror; look within, judge not of yourfelf from thefe pompous outfides, which ferve only to embellifh your carcafe; fee what, in the eyes of God, you are; and, if the corruption and the profound blindnefs of your foul touch you not, let its flavery at leaft roufe and recall you to yourfelf.

Laft circumftance of the fituation of Lazarus dead and buried; he was bound hand and foot; and behold the image of the wretched flavery of a foul long under the dominion of fin.

Yes, my brethren, in vain does the world decry a Chriftian life as a life of fubjection and flavery; the reign of righteoufnefs is a reign of liberty; the foul, faithful and fubmiffive to God, becomes mafter over all creatures; the juft man is above all, becaufe he is unconnected with all; he is mafter of the world, becaufe he defpifes the world; he is dependent neither on his mafters, becaufe he only ferves them for God; nor on his friends, becaufe

he

he only loves them according to the order of charity and of righteousness; nor on his inferiors, because he exacts from them no iniquitous compliance; nor on his fortune, because he rather dreads it; nor on the judgments of men, because he dreads those of God alone; nor on events, because he considers them all as in the order of providence; nor even on his passions, because the charity which is within him is their rule and measure. The just man alone, then, enjoys a perfect liberty: superior to the world, to himself, to all creatures, to all events, he begins, even in this life, to reign with Jesus Christ; all is below him, while he is himself inferior to God alone.

But the sinner, who seems to live without either rule or restraint, is, however, a vile slave; he is dependant on all, on his body, on his propensities, on his caprices, on his passions, on his fortune, on his masters, on his friends, on his enemies, on his rivals, on all surrounding creatures; so many gods to which love or fear subject him; so many idols which multiply his slavery, while he thinks himself more free by casting off that obedience which he owes to God alone; he multiplies his masters, by refusing submission to him alone who renders free those who serve him, and who gives to his servants dominion over the world and over every thing which the world contains.

You often complain, my dear hearer, of the hardships of virtue; you dread a Christian life, as a
life

life of fubjection and forrow : but what, in it, could you find fo gloomy as you experience in debauchery? Ah! If you durft complain of the bitternefs and of the tyranny of the paffions; if you durft confefs the troubles, the difgufts, the frenzies, the anxieties of your foul; if you were candid on the gloomy tranfactions of your heart, there is no lot but what would appear preferable to your own; but you difguife the inquietudes of guilt which you feel; and you exaggerate the hardfhips of virtue which you have never known. But, in order to hold out to you an affifting hand, let us continue the hiftory of our gofpel, and let us fee, in the refurrection of Lazarus, what are the means offered to you, by the goodnefs of God, of quitting fo deplorable a fituation.

REFLECTION II. The power of God, fays the apoftle, is not lefs confpicuous in the converfion of finners than in raifing up the dead; and the fame fupernatural power which wrought upon Jefus Chrift to deliver him from the tomb, ought to operate upon the foul long dead in fin, in order to recall it to the life of grace. I find there only this difference, that the almighty voice of God meets no refiftance from the body which he revives and recalls to life; on the contrary, the foul, dead and corrupted, as I may fay, through the long duration of guilt, feems to retain a remainder of ftrength and motion only to oppofe that powerful voice which is heard even in the abyfs in which it is plunged, and which refounds for the purpofe of reftoring it to light and life. Neverthelefs, however difficult may be the converfion of a foul of this defcription, and however rare fuch examples may be, the fpirit of God, in order to teach us never to defpair of divine mercy when we fincerely wifh to quit the ways of iniquity, points out to us at prefent, in the refurrection of Lazarus, the means of accomplifhing it.

The firft is, confidence in Jefus Chrift: Lord, fays Mary the fifter of Lazarus, if thou hadft been here my brother had not died; but I know that, even now, whatfoever thou wilt afk of God, God will give it thee. I am the refurrection and the life, faid Jefus unto her; believeft thou this? Yes, Lord, faid fhe, I believe that thou art the Chrift, the Son of God, which fhould come into the world. It is through this that the miracle of raifing up Lazarus begins, *viz.* the perfect confidence that Jefus Chrift is able to deliver him from death and corruption.

For, my brethren, the delufion continually employed by the demon, in order to render our defires of converfion unavailing, and to counteract their progrefs, is that of defpondency and miftruft; he warmly retraces to our imagination the horrors of an entire life of guilt: he fays to us, in fecret, that which the fifters of Lazarus fay to Jefus Chrift, though in a different fenfe; that we ought, at a much earlier period, to have checked our career; that

that it is now impoffible, when fo far advanced, to return; that the time for attempting a change is now paft; and that the virulency and age of our wounds no longer admit a refource. Upon this they abandon themfelves to languor and indolence; and, after having incenfed the righteoufnefs of God through our debaucheries, we infult his mercy through the excefs of our miftruft.

I confefs that a foul, long dead in fin, muft fuffer much in returning to God; that it is difficult, after fo many years of diffipation, to form to one's felf a new heart and new inclinations; and that is even fit, that the obftacles, the fufferings, and the difficulties which always attend the converfion of fouls of that defcription, fhould make great finners feel how dreadful it is to have been almoft a whole life-time removed from God.

But I fay that, from the moment a truly contrite foul wifhes to return to him, his wounds however virulent or old, ought no longer to alarm his confidence: I fay that his wretchednefs ought to increafe his compunction but not his defpondency: I fay that the firft ftep of his penitence ought to be that of adoring Jefus Chrift as the refurrection and the life; a fecret confidence that our wants are always lefs than his mercies; a firm perfuafion that the blood of Jefus Chrift is more powerful in wafhing out our ftains than our corruption can be in contracting them: I fay that, the fewer refources of ftrength a criminal foul may

find

find in himself, the more ought he to expect from him who taketh delight in rearing up the work of grace upon the nothingness of nature; and that the more he is inwardly opposed to grace, the more does he, in one sense, become an object worthy of divine power and mercy, for God wisheth that all good shall evidently appear as coming from above, and that man shall attribute nothing to himself.

And in effect, my dear hearer, whatever may be the horror of your past crimes be, the Lord will not long refuse you grace, from the moment that he hath inspired you with the desire and the resofolution of asking it. It is written in Judges, that the father of Samson, terrified by the apparition of the angel of the Lord, who, after announcing to him the birth of a son, commanded him to offer up a sacrifice, and then, like a devouring fire, consumed the victim and the pile, and vanished from his sight; that, terrified, I say, at that spectacle, he was convinced that both himself and his wife were to be struck with death because they had seen the Lord. But his wife, holy and enlightened, condemned his mistrust. If the Lord, said she to him, wished to destroy us, he would not have made fire from heaven to descend on our sacrifice: he would not have accepted it from our hands; he would not have discovered to us his secrets and his wonders, and what we had hitherto been ignorant of.

And

And behold what I now anfwer to you. You believe your death and your deftruction to be inevitable; the ftate of your confcience difcourages you; in vain do fparks of grace and of light fall upon your heart; in vain do they touch you, folicit you, and almoft gain the point of confuming the facrifice of your paffions; you perfuade yourfelf that you are loft beyond refource. But, if the Lord wifhed to abandon and to deftroy you, he would not make fire from heaven to defcend upon your heart; he would not light up within you holy defires and fentiments of penitence: if he wifhed to let you die in the blindnefs of your paffions, he would not manifeft to you the truths of falvation; he would not open your eyes on thofe miferies to come, which you prepare for yourfelf. Befides, how do you know if Jefus Chrift has not permitted your falling into fuch a deplorable ftate for the purpofe of making a prodigy of your converfion an incitement to the converfion of your brethren? How do you know if his mercy has not rendered your paffions fo notorious, in order that thoufands of finners, witneffes of your errors, defpair not of converfion, and be inflamed at the fight of your penitence? How do you know if your crimes, and even your fcandals, have not entered into the defigns of God's goodnefs with regard to your brethren; and if your fituation, which feems hopelefs like that of Lazarus, is not rather an occafion casion of manifesting God's glory than a presage of death to you?

When grace recalls a common sinner, the fruit of his conversion is limited to himself; but, when it singles out a grand sinner, a Lazarus, long dead and corrupted; ah! the designs of its mercy are then much more extensive: in one change it prepares a thousand to come: it raises up a thousand chosen out of one: and the crimes of a sinner become the seed of a thousand just. You give way to despondency in feeling the extremity of your wretchedness: but it is perhaps that very extremity which draws you nearer to the happy moment of your conversion, and which the goodness of God has reserved for you, that you might be a public monument of the excess of his mercies towards the greatest sinners. Only believe, as Jesus Christ said to the sisters of Lazarus, and you shall see the glory of God; you shall see your relations, your friends, your inferiors, and even the accomplices of your debaucheries, become imitators of your penitence; you shall see the most hopeless souls sighing after the happiness of your new life; and the world itself forced to render glory to God, and, in recalling your past errors, to admire the prodigy of your present lot. Take, even from your wretchedness itself, new motives of confidence: bless, in advance, the merciful wisdom of that Being, who, even from your passions, shall know how to extract advantages to his glory; e-

very

very thing co-operates towards the falvation of his chofen, and he permitteth great exceffes only in order to operate great mercies. God ever witheth the falvation of his creature; and, from the moment that we form a wifh of returning to him, our only dread ought to be, not that his juftice reject us, but left our intention be not fincere.

And the fureft proof of our fincerity is the abfenting ourfelves from every occafion which may place an obftacle to our refurrection and our deliverance; obftacle, figured by the ftone which fhut up the mouth of Lazarus's tomb, and which Jefus Chrift orders to be removed before he begins to operate the miracle of his refurrection; remove the ftone. Second mean, marked in our gofpel.

In effect, every day fhews finners, who, tired of diforder, wifh to return to God, but who cannot prevail upon themfelves to quit thofe objects, thofe places, thofe fituations, and thofe rocks, which have been the caufe of their removal from him: they vainly perfuade themfelves that they fhall be able to extinguifh their paffions, to terminate a diforderly life; in a word, to rife from the dead, without removing the ftone, they even make fome efforts; they addrefs themfelves to men of God; they adopt meafures for a change; but, it is of thofe meafures which, not removing the dangers, do not, in the fmalleft degree, forward their fafety; and thus their whole life forrowfully paffes

away

away in detefting their chains, and in the utter inability of breaking them afunder.

Whence comes this, my brethren? It is that the paffions begin to weaken only after the removal of fuch objects as have lighted them up; it is abfurd to fuppofe that the heart can change while every thing around us continues, with regard to us, the fame; you would become chafte, yet you live in the midft of the dangers, the connections, the familiarities, the pleafures, which have a thoufand times corrupted your heart; you would wifh to reflect ferioufly on your eternity, and to place fome interval betwixt life and death, yet you are unwilling to place any betwixt death and thofe debaucheries which prevent you from reflecting on your falvation; and, in the midft of agitations, pleafures, trifles, and worldly expectations, from which, on no account, will you abate, you expect that the inclination and relifh for a Chriftian life will come to you unfought-for: you would that your heart form new propenfities, furrounded by every thing which nourifhes and fortifies the old; and that the lamp of faith and grace blaze up in the midft of winds and tempefts, it which, even in the fanctuary, fo often extinguifhes through want of oil and nourifhment, and, to lukewarm and retired fouls, converts into a danger even the fafety of their retreat.

You come, after that, to tell us that good-will is not wanting; that the moment is not yet come.

How,

How, indeed, fhould it come in the midft of every thing that repels it? But what is that good-will, fhut up within you, which has never any confequence, which never leads to any thing real, and never ferioufly adopts a fingle meafure towards a change? That is to fay, that you would wifh to change could it be done for nothing; you would wifh to work out your falvation by the fame conduct which occafions your deftruction; you would wifh that the fame manners which have feparated your heart from God fhould approach you to him; and that what has hitherto been the caufe of your ruin fhould itfelf become the way and the mean of your falvation. Begin by removing the occafions which fo often have been, and ftill continue to be, the rock of your innocence; remove the ftone which fhuts up the entry of grace to your foul; after that you fhall be entitled to demand of God the completion of his work in you. Then, feparated from thofe objects which nourifhed iniquitous paffions within you, you fhall have it in your power to fay to him, It is thy part now, O my God! to change my heart; to thee I have facrificed every attachment which might ftill fetter it; I have removed all the rocks upon which my weaknefs might ftill have fplit; as much as in me lay, I have changed the outward man; thou alone, O Lord, canft change the heart; it depends upon thee now to complete what yet remains to be done, to break the invifible chains, to overcome all internal obftacles, and totally to triumph over my corruption? I have removed the fatal stone which prevented me from hearing thy voice; let it now resound, even through the abyss in which I am still buried; command me to depart from that fatal tomb, that place of infection and putrefcence, but command me with that almighty word which makes itself to be heard even by the dead, and is to them a word of resurrection and life; give me in charge to thy disciples, to be unloosed from those chains which hold captive all the powers of my soul; and let the ministry of thy church put the last seal to my resurrection and my deliverance.

And behold, my brethren, the last mean held out in our gospel. Immediately, on the removal of the stone, our Saviour cries, with a loud voice, Lazarus, come forth! Lazarus comes forth, still bound hand and foot, and Jesus Christ remits him to his disciples to be unloosed.

Observe here that Jesus Christ doth not order his disciples to unloose Lazarus till after he had entirely quitted the tomb. We must manifest ourselves to the church, says an holy father, before we can, through its ministry, receive the blessing of our deliverance. Lazarus come forth, that is to say, continues that father, how long wilt thou remain concealed and buried inwardly in thy conscience? How long wilt thou conceal thine iniquity within thy breast?

You

You undoubtedly are not ignorant, my brethren, that remission of our sins is only granted through the ministry of the church, and that it is necessary to lay open and to present our bonds to the piety of the ministers, who alone have authority to bind and to unbind on the earth; this is not upon what you require instruction. But, I say, that, in order that the conversion be solid and durable, we must, like Lazarus, shew ourselves quite out of the tomb. An ordinary confession is not the matter in question: an hardened sinner ought to go back even to his infancy; even to the birth of his passions; even to the youngest periods of his life, which have been the commencement of his crimes Neither doubts nor obscurities must longer be left in the conscience, nor mists over the youthful manners, under pretence that they have already been revealed; a general manifestation is required, and whatever may hitherto have been done must be reckoned as nothing; every duty of religion, performed during a disorderly and worldly life, is even to be ranked among our crimes; the conscience must be considered as a chaos, into which no light has, as yet, penetrated, and over which all our fictitious and past penitence has spread only additional darkness.

For, alas! my brethren, a contrite soul, after returning from the errors of the world and the passions, ought to presume that, having to that period lived in criminal habits and propensities, every ry time the facrament has been received in that ftate was only a profanation and a crime.

In the *firſt* place, becauſe, having never felt real contrition for his errors, nor, conſequently, any ſincere defire to purge himſelf of them, the remedies of the church, far from having purified, have only completed his foulneſs, and rendered his diſeaſe more incurable.

2*dly*, Becauſe he has never been known to himſelf; and, conſequently, could never make himſelf known to the tribunal of his conſcience. For, alas! the world, in the midſt of which this ſoul has always lived, and in which he has ever thought and judged like it; the world, I ſay, finding reaſonable and wiſe only its own maxims and manner of thinking, does it ſufficiently know the holineſs of the goſpel, the obligations of faith, and the extent of duties, to be qualified to enter into the detail of thoſe tranſgreſſions which faith condemns?

3*dly*, and *laſtly*, Becauſe that, even admitting he ſhould have known all his wretchedneſs, never having had any real ſorrow for it, he has never been qualified to make it known; for nothing but heartfelt ſorrow can explain itſelf as it ought, or truly repreſent thoſe evils which it feels and abhors; it muſt be a feeling heart that can make itſelf to be underſtood on the wounds and the ſufferings of a heart itſelf. A ſinner, full of a profane paſſion, expreſſes it much more eloquently, and with more animation; nothing is left unſaid of the fooliſh
and

and deplorable fufferings he endures; he enters into all the windings of his heart, his jealoufies, his fears, and his hopes. As the mind of man, fays the apoftle, alone knows what paffes in man, fo likewife it is only the heart which can know what paffes in the heart. Contrition gives eyes to fee, and words to exprefs every thing; it has a language which nothing can counterfeit: thus, in vain may a worldly foul, ftill chained by the heart to all his diforders, come to accufe himfelf, he cannot be underftood; without any abfolute intention of concealing his wounds, he never expofes all their horror, becaufe he neither feels nor is ftruck with them himfelf; his words always relifh of the infenfibility of his heart; and it is impoffible that he fhould expofe, in all their uglinefs, deformities which he knows not, and which he ftill loves: he ought, therefore, to confider the whole period of his paft life as a period of darknefs and blindnefs, during which he has never viewed himfelf but with the eyes of flefh and blood; never judged but through the opinions of paffion and felf-love; never accufed but in the language of error and impenitence; never exhibited himfelf but in a falfe and imperfect light. It is not enough to have removed the ftone from the tomb; the criminal foul muft come forth from it himfelf, that he may exhibit himfelf, as I may fay, in open day; that he may manifeft his whole life; and that, from his earlieft years even to the bleffed hour of his deliverance, nothing

nothing be concealed from the eyes of the ministers ready to unbind him.

But this ſtep, you ſay, has difficulties which may be the occaſion of caſting trouble, embarraſſment, and diſcouragement, through the conſcience, and of ſuſpending the reſolution of a change of life. What! my brethren, you involve yourſelves in diſcuſſions ſo arduous and ſo endleſs, for the purpoſe of clearing up your temporal concerns; and, in order to eſtabliſh regularity and ſerenity in your conſcience, and to leave nothing doubtful in the affair of your eternity, you would cry out from the moment that a few cares and inveſtigations are required? How often do you proclaim, when a deciſive ſtep is in agitation which may determine the ruin or preſervation of your fortune, that nothing muſt be neglected, nothing muſt be left to chance; that one's own eyes muſt look into every thing, that every thing muſt be cleared up, every thing fathomed even to the bottom, that you may have nothing afterwards wherewith to reproach yourſelves; and this maxim, ſo reaſonable when connected with fleeting and frivolous intereſts, ſhould be leſs ſo when applied to the grand and only real intereſt, that of ſalvation?

Ah! my brethren, how poor are we in faith! And what have we, in this life, of more importance than the care of arranging that awful account which we have to render to the eternal Judge, and to the ſearcher of hearts and of thoughts? That is
to

to fay, the care of regulating our confcience, of difpelling its darknefs, of purifying its ftains, of clearing up its eternal interefts, of confirming its hopes, of ftrengthening ourfelves as much as the prefent condition permits, and making ourfelves acquainted, as far as in our power, with its fituation and its difpofitions; and not to make our appearance before God like fools, unknown to ourfelves, uncertain of what we are, and of what we muft for ever be. Such are the means of converfion marked out to us in the miracle of raifing up Lazarus: let us conclude the hiftory of our gofpel, and fee what the motives are which determine Jefus Chrift to operate it.

REFLECTION III. To enter at once into our fubject, without lofing fight of the confequence of the gofpel; the firft motive which our Saviour feems to have, in the refurrection of Lazarus, is that of drying up the tears, and rewarding the prayers and the piety of his fifters. Lord, faid they to him, he whom thou loveft is fick: and behold the firft motive which often determines Jefus Chrift to operate the converfion of a great finner; the tears and the prayers of thofe juft fouls who entreat it.

Yes, my brethren, whether it be that the Lord thereby wifh to render virtue more refpectable to finners, by according favours to them only through the mediation of juft fouls: whether it be that he intend more clofely to knit together his members,

and

and to perfect them in unity and in charity, by rendering the ministry of the one useful and requisite to the other; it is certain, that it is through the prayers of the good, and in their intercession, that the source of the conversion of the greatest sinners springs up. As all is done for the just in the church, says the apostle, so it may be said, that every thing is done through them; and, as sinners are only endured in it to exercise their virtue, or to animate their vigilance, they are also recalled from their errors only to console their faith, and to reward their groanings and prayers.

To love just souls is a beginning, then, of righteousness to the greatest sinners; it is a presage of virtue to respect it in those who practise it; it is a prospect of conversion to seek the society of the good, to esteem their acquaintance, and to interest them in our salvation; and, even admitting that our heart still groan under iniquitous bonds, and that attachment to the world and to pleasures still separate us from God, yet, from the moment that we begin to love his servants, we accomplish, as it were, the first step in his service. It seems as if our heart already becomes tired of its passions, from the moment that we take pleasure in the society of those who condemn them; and that a relish for virtue is on the eve of springing up in us, from the moment that we take delight in those whom virtue alone renders amiable.

Besides,

Besides, the just, instructed by ourselves with regard to our weaknesses, keep them continually present before the Lord; they lament, before him, over those chains which still bind us to the world and to its amusements; they offer up to him some weak desires of virtue which we have intrusted to their charge, in order to induce his goodness to grant more fervent and more efficacious ones; they carry, even to the foot of the throne, some feeble essays towards good which they have noted in us, in order to obtain for us the perfection and plenitude of his mercy. More affected with our evils than for their own wants, they piously forget themselves, in order to snatch from destruction their brethren who are on the point of perishing before their eyes: they alone love us for ourselves, because they alone love in us but our salvation; the world may furnish sycophants, flatterers, social companions in dissipation, but virtue alone gives us friends.

And it is here that you who now listen to me, who, perhaps, like Mary, were formerly slaves of the world and the passions, and who, latterly, touched with grace, like her, quit no more the feet of the Lord; it is here that you ought to remember that, in future, one of the most important duties of your new life is, that of continually demanding, like the sister of Lazarus, from Jesus Christ, the resurrection of your brethren, the conversion of those unfortunate souls who have been accomplices in your criminal pleasures, and who still, under the dominion of death and sin, sorrowly drag on their chains in the ways of the world and of error. You ought continually, in the bitterness of your heart, to be saying to Jesus Christ, like the sister of Lazarus: Lord, he whom thou lovest is sick; those souls to whom I have been a stumbling-block, and who have less offended thee than I, are still, however, in the shadow of death, and in the corruption of sin: and I enjoy a deliverance of which I was more unworthy than they! Ah! Lord, the delight I feel in appertaining to thee shall never be perfect while I behold my brethren thus miserably perishing before mine eyes: I shall but imperfectly enjoy the fruit of thy mercies, while thou refusest them to souls to whom I have myself been the fatal cause of their departure from righteousness: and I shall never think that my crimes are fully forgiven, while I see them existing in those sinners who have been removed from thee only through my example and my passions.

Not, my brethren, that you ought to place your whole dependence on the prayers of the good, or to expect from them alone a change of heart and the gift of penitence. For this is a very general illusion, and more especially among those who are high in the world: they suppose that, by respecting virtue, by shewing favour to the good, and by interesting them to solicit our conversion from God, our chains shall drop off of themselves without

out any effort on our part; they comfort themselves upon that remainder of faith and religion which renders virtue in others still dear and respectable to us; they give themselves credit for not having, as yet, reached that point of free-thinking and impiety, so common in the world, which makes virtue the public butt of its censures and derision. But, alas! my brethren, it availed nothing to king Jehu that he had publicly rendered honour to the holy man Jehonadab; his vices still subsisted with all that respect he had for the man of God. It availed nothing to Herod that he had honoured the piety of John the Baptist, and that he had even loved the holy freedom of his discourses: the deference which he had for the precursor left him still all the excess of his criminal passion. The honours which we pay to virtue attract aids to our weakness; but they do not justify our errors: the prayers of the good induce the Lord to pay more attention to our wants; but they do not render him more indulgent to our crimes: they obtain for us victory over the passions which we begin to detest; but not over those which we still love, and which we still continue to cherish: in a word, they assist our good desires; but they do not authorise our impenitence.

The miracle of raising up Lazarus teaches just souls, then, to solicit the conversion of their brethren; but the conversion and deliverance of their brethren likewise serve to animate their
lukewarmness

lukewarmness and flothfulness. Second motive which Jesus Christ proposes: he wishes, by the novelty of that prodigy, to arouse the faith of his disciples, still dormant and languishing.

And such is the fruit which Jesus Christ continually expects from the miracles of his grace: he operates before your eyes, you who have long walked in his ways, sudden and surprising conversions, in order, by the fervour and the zeal of these newly risen from the dead, to confound your lukewarmness and indolence. Yes, my brethren, nothing is more calculated to cover us with confusion, and to make us tremble over the infidelities which we still mingle with a cold and languishing piety, than the sight of a soul buried, but an instant ago, in the corruption of death and sin, and whose errors had perhaps inflated the vanity of our zeal, and served as a butt to the malignity of our censures; than the sight, I say, of such a soul, vivified, a moment after, by grace, freed from his chains, and boldly walking in the ways of God, more eager after mortification than formerly after pleasure; more removed from the world and its amusements than apparently he was once attached; scrupling to himself the most innocent recreations; allowing almost no bounds to the vivacity and transports of his penitence; and every day making rapid advances in piety: while we, after many years of piety, alas! still languish in the beginning of that holy career; while we, after so many signal

nal favours received, after so many truths known, after so many sacraments and other duties of religion attended, alas! we still hold to the world and to ourselves by a thousand ties; we are yet but in the first rudiments of faith and of a Christian life, and still more distant than at first, from that zeal and that fervour which constitute the whole value and the whole security of a faithful piety.

My brethren, the dreadful prophecy of Jesus Christ is every day fulfilled before our eyes. Publicans and sinners, persons of a scandalous conduct according even to the world, and as distant from the kingdom of God as the east is from the west, are converted, repent, surprise the world with the sight of a retired and mortified life, and shall sit down with Abraham, and Isaac, and Jacob; and perhaps we who are looked upon as children of the kingdom; we, whose manners present nothing to the eyes of the world but what is orderly and laudable; we, who are held out as morals of propriety and piety; we, whom the world canonises, and which we glorified with the reputation and the appearances of piety, alas! we shall perhaps be rejected and confounded with unbelievers, for having always laboured at our salvation with negligence, and having preserved a heart still altogether worldly, in the midst even of our pious works.

Thus, my brethren, you whom this discourse regards, do not judge of yourselves from the comparison which you inwardly make with those souls

whom

whom the world and the paffions hurry away. We may be more righteous than the world, and yet not enough fo for Jefus Chrift : for the world is fo corrupted ; the gofpel is fo little known in it ; faith is fo weakened; the law and truth fo little obferved, that what is virtue, with regard to it, may ftill be a great iniquity in the fight of God.

Rather compare yourfelves with thofe holy penitents who formerly edified the church by the prodigy of their aufterities, and whofe life, even at this day, appears to us fo incredible; with thofe noble martyrs who gave up their body for the truth, and who, amidft the moft cruel torments, were tranfported with joy in contemplating the holy promifes; with thofe primitive believers who fuffered death every day for Jefus Chrift, and who, under perfecution, lofs of property, and of their children, thought themfelves ftill poffeffed of all, as they had neither loft faith nor the hope of a better life : behold the models by whom you ought to meafure your piety, to find it ftill deficient, and all worldly. Unlefs you refemble them, in vain do you not refemble the world, you fhall perifh like it ; it is not enough that you do not imitate the crimes of the worldly, you muft alfo have the virtues of the juft.

Laftly, Not only the goodnefs of Jefus Chrift wifhes, in this miracle, to furnifh to his difciples and to the Jewifh believers a frefh motive for believing in him, but in it his juftice likewife fupplies
a frefh

a frefh occafion of obftinacy and incredulity to the unbelieving Ifraelites ; laft circumftance of our gofpel. They take meafures to deftroy him ; they wifh to put Lazarus himfelf to death, that fo ftriking a teftimony of the power of Jefus Chrift may no longer continue among them. They had weeped his death ; fcarcely is he recalled to life when he appears worthy only of their fury and vengeance. And behold the fole fruit which the generality of you commonly reap from the miracles of grace: that is to fay, from the converfion and the fpiritual refurrection of great finners. Before that the mercy of Jefus Chrift had caft looks of grace and falvation upon a criminal foul, and, while delivered up to the dominion of the paffions, he was not only dead in fin, but fpread every where around the infection and the ftench of his diforders and fcandals, you feemed touched for its errors and fhame ; you deplored the mifery of his lot ; you mingled your tears and regrets with the tears and regrets of his friends and relatives ; and the public irregularity of his conduct experienced from you every forrow and compaffion of humanity ; but, fcarcely hath the grace of Jefus Chrift recalled him to life, fcarcely, come forth from the tomb and that abyfs of corruption in which he was buried, does he render glory to his deliverer by the holy ardours of a tender and fincere piety, than you become the cenfurers even of his piety : you had appeared touched for the excefs of his

vices,

vices, and you publicly deride the excess of his pretended piety. You had blamed his warm pursuits after pleasure, and you condemn the fervor of his love for God. Be consistent, therefore, with yourselves, and decide in favour either of the just or of the sinner.

Yes, my brethren, if the happiness of a soul, who, before your eyes, returns from his errors, excite not your envy; if the contrition of a sinner, who was formerly the companion perhaps of your pleasures and excesses, leave you all your indifference with regard to salvation. Ah! insult not at least his good fortune; despise not in him the gift of God; take not, even from the miracles of grace so proper to open your eyes, a fresh motive of blindness and unbelief; and do not thus change the blessings of God to your brethren, into a dreadful judgment of justice against you.

In reading the history of our gospel, you are sometimes astonished that the obstinacy and blindness of the Jews should be able to resist the most striking miracles of Jesus Christ; you do not comprehend how the raising up of the dead, the curing of persons born blind, and so many other wonders wrought before their eyes, did not force them to acknowledge the truth of his ministry, and the sanctity of his doctrine: you say, that much less would convince you; that any one of all these miracles would suffice, and that you would immediately yield to the truth.

But,

But, my brethren, you condemn yourselves out of your own mouth; for, (without refuting here that absurd manner of speaking, by those grand and sublime proofs which religion furnishes against impiety, and which we have elsewhere employed), candidly, is it not a more arduous and a more astonishing miracle, that a soul, delivered up to sin, and to the most shameful passions, born with every propensity to voluptuousness, pride, revenge, and ambition, and more distant than any one, by the nature of his heart, from the kingdom of God, and from all the maxims of Christian piety; that, all at once, that soul should renounce all his gratifications, break asunder all his warmest attachments, repress his liveliest passions, change his most rooted inclinations, forget injuries, attention to the body and to fortune; no longer have a relish but for prayer, retirement, the practice of the most gloomy and disgusting duties, and hold out to the eyes of the public, in a change, in a resurrection so palpable, the spectacle of a life so different from the former, that the world, that free-thinking itself shall be forced to render glory to the truth of his change, and that they shall no longer know him to be the same; is it not, I say, a more arduous and more astonishing miracle?

Now, doth not the mercy of Jesus Christ operate such miracles almost every day before your eyes? Doth not his holy word, though in a weak and languishing mouth, still raise up, every day, new Lazaruses from the dead? You behold them; you know and you appear astonished at them; yet, nevertheless, do they touch you? Do these wonders which, with so much majesty, the finger of God maketh to shine forth, recall you to truth and to the light? Do these changes, a thousand times more miraculous than the raising up of the dead, convince you? Do they bring you nearer to Jesus Christ, or restore to you that faith which you have lost?

Alas! your whole care, like the Jews, is to stand out against, or to weaken their truth. You deny that grace hath any part in the glory of these wonders; you seek to trace their motives in causes altogether worldly; you consider them as delusions and impositions; you attribute to the artifices of man the most shining operations of the holy Spirit; you insist that such a new life is only a fresh snare to entrap the public credulity, and a new path more securely to attain some worldly purpose. Thus, the works of the almighty power of Jesus Christ harden you; thus, even the wonders of his grace complete your blindness; thus, you make every thing conducive towards your destruction: Jesus Christ becomes to you a stumbling-block, when he ought to have been a source of life and salvation. The examples of sinners slain and corrupt you: their penitence revolts and hardens you.

Great God! suffer then, in order that a life altogether criminal at last be terminated, that I now

raise

raise my voice to thee out of the depths in which I have, for so many years, languished: the impure chains with which I am bound, attach me, by so many folds, to the bottom of the gulf in which I drag on my gloomy days, that, in spite of all my good desires, I still remain fettered, and almost incapable of any effort towards disengaging myself and returning to thee, O my God, whom I have forsaken. But, Lord, out of the depths even in which thou seest me, like another Lazarus, fettered and buried, I have, at least, the voice of the heart free to send up, even to the foot of the throne, my sorrows, my lamentations, and my tears.

The voice of a repentant sinner is always agreeable, O Lord, to thine ear; it is that voice of Jacob which awakens all thy tenderness, even when it offers to thy sight but hands of Esau, and still covered with blood and crimes.

Ah! thine holy ears, O Lord, have now sufficiently been turned away from my licentious and blasphemous words; let them now be attentive to the voice of my supplications; and, let the singularity of the words which I now address to thee, O my God! attract a more favourable attention to my prayer.

I come not here, great God! to excuse my disorders in thy sight, by alleging to thee the occasions which have seduced me, the examples which have led me astray, the misfortune of my engagements,

ments, and the nature of my heart and of my weakness: cover thine eyes, O Lord, upon the horrors of my past life; the only possibility of excusing them is, not to behold or to know them: alas! if I am unable myself to support even their view; if my crimes dread and fly from mine own eyes, and if my terrors and my weakness render it absolutely necessary to turn my sight from them, how, O Lord, should they be able to sustain the sanctity of thy looks, if thou search into them with that eye of severity which finds stains in the purest and most laudable life?

But thou, O Lord, are not a God like unto man, to whom it is always so difficult to pardon and to forget the injuries of an enemy; goodness and mercy dwell in thine eternal bosom; clemency is the first attribute of thy supreme Being; and thou hast no enemies but those who refuse to place their trust in the abundant riches of thy mercy.

Yes, Lord! be the hour what it may when a criminal soul casts himself upon thy mercy; whether in the morning of life or in the decline of age; whether after the errors of youthful manners or after an entire life of dissipation and licentiousness, thou wouldst, O my God! that their hope in thee be not extinguished; and thou assurest us that the highest point of our crimes is but the lowest degree of thy mercy.

But, likewise, great God! if thou listen to my desires; if, once more, thou restore to me that life and

and that light which I have loſt; if thou break a-
ſunder my chains of death which ſtill fetter me; if
thou ſtretch out thine hand to withdraw me from
the gulph in which I am plunged, ah! never, O
Lord, ſhall I ceaſe to proclaim thine eternal mercies: I will forget the whole world, that I may be
occupied only with the wonders of thy grace towards my ſoul: I will every moment of my life
render glory to the God who ſhall have delivered
me: my mouth, for ever ſhut againſt vain things,
ſhall with difficulty be able to expreſs all the tranſports of my love and of my gratitude; and thy
creature, who ſtill groans under the dominion of
the world and of ſin, then reſtored to his true
Lord, ſhall, henceforth and for ever more, bleſs
his deliverer.

SERMON IX.

ON THE DAY OF JUDGMENT.

Luke xxi. 27.

Then shall they see the Son of Man coming in a cloud, with power and great glory.

Such will be that last spectacle which shall terminate the eternal revolutions which the aspect of this world is continually offering to our eyes, and which either amuse us through their novelty, or seduce us by their charms. Such will be the coming of the Son of Man, the day of his revelation, the accomplishment of his kingdom, and the complete redemption of his mystical body. Such the day of the manifestation of consciences, that day of misery and despair to one portion of men, and of peace, consolation, and ineffable delight to the other: the sweet expectation of the just, the dread

of the wicked; the day which is to determine the
destiny of all men.

It was the image, ever present to their minds, of
that terrible day which rendered the first believers
patient under persecution, delighted under sufferance, and illustrious under injury and reproach.
It is that which hath since supported the faith of
martyrs, animated the constancy of virgins, and
smoothed to the anchorite all the horrors of a desert; it is that which still, at this day, peoples those
religious solitudes erected, by the piety of our ancestors, as asylums against the contagion of the age.

Even you, my brethren, when the awful solemnity of that grand event hath sometimes intruded
on your thoughts, have been unable to check feelings of compunction and dread. But these have
been only transitory fears; more smiling and more
agreeable ideas have speedily effaced them, and recalled to you your former calm. Alas! in the
happy days of the church it would have been considered as renouncing faith not to have longed for
the day of the Lord. The only consolation of
those first disciples of faith was in looking forward
to it, and the apostles were obliged even to moderate, on that point, the holy eagerness of believers;
and, at present, the church finds itself under the
necessity of employing the whole terror of our ministry, in order to recall its remembrance to Christians, and the whole fruit of our discourses is confined to making it dreaded.

I mean

I mean not, however, to difplay to you here the whole hiftory of that awful event. I wifh to confine myfelf to one of its circumftances, which has always appeared to me as the moft proper to make an impreffion on the heart: it is the manifeftation of confciences.

Now, behold my whole defign. On this earth the finner never knows himfelf fuch as he is, and is only half-known to men; he lives, in general, unknown to himfelf, through his blindnefs, and to others, through his diffimulation and cunning. In that grand day he will know himfelf, and will be known. The finner laid open to himfelf: the finner laid open to all creatures: behold the fubject upon which I have refolved to make fome fimple and, I truft, edifying reflections.

Part I. "All things are referved for a future "day, fays the fage Ecclefiaftes, and no man know- "eth them here below, for all things come alike "to all: there is one event to the righteous and "to the wicked; to the good and to the clean, "and to the unclean; to him that facrificeth, and "to him that facrificeth not; as is the good, fo is "the finner."

What idea, indeed, fhould we have of Providence in the government of the univerfe, were we to judge of its wifdom and juftice only from the diverfe lots which it provides on this earth for men? What! The good and the evil fhould be difpenfed on the earth, without choice, refpect, or difcrimination?

nation? The juft man fhould almoft always groan under affliction and want, whilft the wicked fhould live furrounded with glory, pleafures, and affluence, and, after fortunes fo different, and manners fo diffimilar, both fhould alike fink into an eternal oblivion; and that juft and avenging God, whom they fhould afterwards meet, would not deign either to weigh their deeds or to diftinguifh their merits? Thou, O Lord, art juft, and wilt render to each according to his works.

This grand point of Chriftian faith, fo confiftent even with natural equity, fuppofed: I fay, that, in that terrible day, when, in the face of the univerfe, the finner fhall appear before that awful tribunal accompanied by his works, the manifeftation of confciences will be the moft horrible punifhment of the unfaithful foul. A rigorous examination fhall, in the firft place, make him known to himfelf: and behold all the circumftances of that awful difcuffion.

I ought, in the firft place, to make you obferve all the titles with which he will be invefted who fhall examine you, and which announce all the rigour with which he fhall weigh in the balance your deeds and thoughts. It will be a rigid legiflator, jealous of the fanctity of his law, and who will judge you only by it; all the foftenings, all the vain interpretations, which cuftom or a falfe knowledge had invented, fhall vanifh; the luftre of the law will diffipate them; the refources with which

which they had flattered the finner, will fink into nothing; and the incenfed legiflator will examine almoft more rigoroufly the falfe interpretations which had changed its purity, than the manifeft tranfgreffions which had violated it. It will be a judge charged with the interefts of his Father's glory againft the finner, eftablifhed to decide betwixt God and man; and that day will be the day of his zeal for the honour of the divinity, againft thofe who fhall not have rendered to him that honour which is his due: a Saviour, who will fhew you his wounds to reproach your ingratitude; all that he hath done for you will rife up againft you; his blood, the price of your falvation, will loudly demand your deftruction; and his defpifed kindneffes will be numbered among your heavieft crimes: the fearcher of hearts, to whofe eyes the moft hidden councils and the moft fecret thoughts will all be laid open: laftly, a God of terrible majefty, before whom the heavens fhall diffolve, the elements fhall be confounded, and all nature overturned; and whofe fcrutiny, with all the terror of his prefence, the finner fhall fingly be forced to fupport.

Now, behold the circumftances of that awful examination. 1*ſtly*, It will be the fame for all men: and, as St Matthew fays, before him fhall be gathered all nations. The difference of ages, countries, conditions, birth, and temperament, fhall no longer be there attended to; and as the gofpel, on which you will be judged, is the law of all times and conditions, and holds out the fame rules to the prince and to the fubject; to the great and to the lowly, to the anchorite and to the man immerfed in the affairs of the world; to the believer who lived in the fervor of the primitive times, and to him who hath the misfortune to live in the relaxation of the prefent age; no diftinction will be made in the manner of proceeding on the examination of the guilty. Vain excufes on rank and birth, on the dangers of his ftation, on the manners of his age, on the weaknefs of temperament, will then be no longer liftened to from you; and, with refpect to modefty, chaftity, ambition, forgivenefs of injuries, renouncement of one's felf; mortification of the fenfes, the juft Judge will demand an exact account, equally from the Greek as from the Barbarian; from the poor as from the powerful: from the man of the world as from the folitary; from the prince as from the humbleft fubject; *laftly,* from the Chriftians of thefe latter times as from the firft difciples of the gofpel.

Vain judgments of the earth, how fhall you then be confounded! And how little fhall we then eftimate nobility of blood, the glory of anceftry, the blaze of reputation, the diftinction of talents, and all thofe pompous titles with which men endeavour on this earth to puff out their meannefs, and to found fo many vain diftinctions and privileges,

leges, when we shall see, amidst that crowd of guilty, the sovereign confounded with the slave; the great with the meanest of the people; the learned promiscuously blended with the ignorant and mean; the gods of war, these invincible and far-famed characters who had filled the universe with their name, at the side of the husbandman and labourer; thou alone, O my God! hast glory, power, and immortality; and, all the titles of vanity being destroyed and annihilated with the world which had invented them, each will appear before thee accompanied solely by his works!

2*dly*, That examination will be universal, that is to say, that it will comprehend all the different ages and circumstances of your life: the weaknesses of childhood, which have escaped your remembrance; the transports of youth, of which almost every moment has been a crime; the ambition and the anxieties of a riper age; the obstinacy and the chagrins of an old age, still perhaps voluptuous. What astonishment, when repassing over the diverse parts which you have acted on the earth, you shall find yourself every where profane, dissolute, voluptuous, without virtue, without penitence, without good works; having passed through a diversity of situations merely in order to amass a more abundant treasure of wrath; and having lived in these diverse states as if, to a certainty, all were to die with you!

The

The variety of events, wnich fucceed each other here below, and divide our life, fix our attention only on the prefent, and do not permit us to recollect it in the whole, or fully to fee what we really are. We never regard ourfelves but in that point of view in which our prefent fituation holds us out; the laft fituation is always the one which leads us to judge of ourfelves; a fentiment of falvation, with which God fometimes indulges us, calms us on an infenfibility of many years; a day, paffed in exercifes of piety, makes us forget a life of crimes; the declaration of our faults, at the tribunal of penitence, effaces them from our remembrance, and they become to us as though they had never been: in a word, of all the different ftates of our confcience we never fee but the prefent. But, in the prefence of the terrible Judge, the whole will be vifible at once; the hiftory will be entirely laid open. From the very firft feeling formed by your heart, even to its laft figh, all fhall be collected before your eyes; all the iniquities, difperfed through the different ftages of your life, will then confront you; not an action, not a defire, not a word, not a thought, will there be omitted; for, if our hairs be numbered, judge of our deeds. We fhall fee fpring up the whole courfe of our years, which, though as if annihilated to us, yet lived in the eyes of God; and there we fhall find, not thofe perifhable hiftories in which our vain actions were to be tranfmitted to pofteri-

ty;

ty; not thofe flattering recitals of our military exploits, of thofe brilliant events which had filled fo many volumes, and exhaufted fo much praife; not thofe public records in which are fet down the nobility of our birth, the antiquity of our origin, the fame of our anceftors, the dignities which have rendered them illuftrious, the luftre which we have added to their name, and all the hiftory, as I may fay, of human illufion and weaknefs; that immortality fo vaunted, which it promifed to us, fhall be buried in the ruins and in the wrecks of the univerfe; but there we fhall fee the moft fhocking and exact hiftory of our heart, of our mind, of our imagination; that is to fay, that internal and invifible part of our life, equally unknown to ourfelves as to the reft of men.

Yes, my brethren: befides the exterior hiftory of our manners, which will be all recalled, what will moft aftonifh us is, the fecret hiftory of our heart, which will then be wholly laid open to our eyes; of that heart which we have never founded, never known; of that heart which continually eluded our fearch, and, under fpecious names, difguifed from us the fhame of its paffions; of that heart whofe elevation, probity, magnanimity, difintereftednefs, and natural goodnefs we have fo much vaunted; which the public error and adulation had beheld as fuch, and which had occafioned our being exalted above other men. So many fhameful defires, which were fcarcely formed
before

before we endeavoured to conceal them from ourselves; so many absurd projects of fortune and elevation, sweet delusions, up to which our seduced heart continually gave itself; so many secret and mean jealousies which were the invisible principle of all our conduct, yet, nevertheless, which we dissembled through pride; so many criminal dispositions which had, a thousand times, induced us ardently to wish, that either the pleasures of the senses were eternal, or that, at least, they should remain unpunished; so many hatreds and animosities which, unknown to ourselves, had corrupted our heart; so many defiled and vicious intentions, with regard to which we were so ingenious in flattering ourselves; so many projects of iniquity to which opportunity had alone been wanting, and which we reckoned as nothing, because they had never departed from the heart: in a word, that vicissitude of passions which, in succession, had possession of our heart: behold what shall all be displayed before our eyes. We shall see, says a holy father, come out, as from an ambuscade, numberless crimes of which we could never believe ourselves capable. We shall be shewn to ourselves; we shall be made to enter into our own heart, where we had never resided: a sudden light shall clear up that abyss: that mystery of iniquity shall be revealed: and we shall see that which of all we knew least, that was ourselves.

To the examination of the evils we have committed will succeed that of the good which we have failed to do. The endless omissions of which our life has been full, and for which we had never felt even remorse, will be recalled; so many circumstances where our character engaged us to render glory to truth, and where we have betrayed it through vile motives of interest, or mean compliances; so many opportunities of doing good, provided for us by the goodness of God, and which we have almost always neglected; so much culpable and voluntary ignorance, in consequence of having always dreaded the light, and even fled from those who could have instructed us; so many events so calculated to open our eyes, and which have served only to increase our blindness; so much good which, through our talents or our example, we might have done, and which we have prevented by our vices; so many souls whose innocence might have been preserved by our bounty, and whom we have left to perish by refusing to abate from our profusions; so many crimes which might have been prevented in our inferiors or equals by prudent remonstrances and useful advice, and which indolence, meanness, and perhaps more culpable views, have made us suppress; so many days and moments which might have been placed to advantage for Heaven, and which we have spent in inutility and an unworthy effeminacy. And what in this is more dreadful, is that, in our own eyes,

that

that was the moſt innocent part of our life, offering nothing to our remembrance, as we think, but a great void.

What endleſs regret, then, to the unfaithful ſoul to ſee ſuch a liſt of days ſacrificed to inutility, to that world which is no more; while a ſingle moment, conſecrated to a God faithful to his promiſes, might have merited the felicity of the holy! To ſee ſo many meanneſſes, ſo many ſubjections for the ſake of riches, and a miſerable fortune which could laſt only for a moment; while a ſingle violence, ſuffered for the ſake of Jeſus Chriſt, would have ſecured to him an immortal crown! What regret, when he now finds that not half the cares and anxieties were required for his ſalvation which he has undergone to accompliſh his deſtruction; and that a ſingle day of that long life, wholly devoted to the world, had ſufficed for eternity!

To that examination will ſucceed, in the fourth place, that of mercies which you have abuſed; ſo many holy inſpirations either rejected or only half proſecuted; ſo many watchful attentions of Providence to your ſoul rendered unavailing; ſo many truths, declared through our miniſtry, which, in many believers, have operated penitence and ſalvation, but have always been ſterile in your heart; ſo many afflictions and diſappointments, which the Lord had provided for you, in order to recall you to him, and of which you have always made ſo unworthy an uſe; even ſo many natural gifts which once

once were blossoms of virtue, and which you have turned into agents of vice; ah! if the unprofitable servant be cast into utter darkness for having only hidden his talent, with what indulgence can you flatter yourself, you who have received so many, and who have always employed them against the glory of that Master who had entrusted them to you?

Here, indeed, it is that the reckoning will be terrible. Jesus Christ will demand from you the price of his blood. You sometimes complain that God doth not enough for you; that he hath brought you into the world weak, and of a temperament of which you are not the master; and that he bestoweth not the necessary grace to enable you to resist the many opportunities which drag you away. Ah! you will then see that your whole life has been a continued abuse of his mercies; you will see that, among so many infidel nations which know him not, you have been privileged, enlightened, called to faith, nourished in the doctrine of truth and the virtue of the sacrament, incessantly supported by his inspirations and his grace; you will be shocked to see all that God hath done for you, and the little that you have done for him; and your complaints will quickly be changed into an utter confusion, destitute of every resource but in the horrors of your own despair.

Hitherto the just Judge hath examined you only on those crimes which are especially your own;

but

but what will it be when he shall enter into a reckoning with you on the sins of others, of which you have been either the occasion or the cause, and which will, consequently, be charged to your account? What a new sink! All the souls to whom you have been a subject of scandal and ruin will be presented to you; all the souls whom your discourses, your counsels, your example, your solicitations, your immodesties, have precipitated, with yourself, into eternal destruction; all the souls whose weakness you have either seduced, or whose innocence you have corrupted, whose faith you have perverted, whose virtue you have shaken, whose free-thinking you have authorised, or whose impiety you have strengthened by your persuasions, or by the example of your life. Jesus Christ, to whom they belonged, and who had purchased them with his blood, will demand them at your hands, as a dear heritage, as a precious conquest, which you have unjustly ravished from him; and, if the Lord marked Cain with the sign of reprobation in demanding account from him of the blood of his brother, judge with what sign you shall be marked when you shall be brought to a reckoning for his soul.

But this is not all. Were you a public character, and high in authority, what abuses authorised! What iniquities glanced over! What duties sacrificed, either to your own interests, or to the passions and interests of others! What respect of persons, in opposition to equity and conscience! What

iniquitous

iniquitous undertakings counselled! What wars, perhaps, what confusions, what public evils, of which you have either been the author or the infamous agent! You will see that your ambition or your counsels have been as the fatal source of an infinity of miseries, of the calamities of your age, of those evils which are perpetuated, and pass from father to son; and you will be surprised to find that your iniquities have survived yourself, and that, even long after death, you were still culpable, before God, of an infinity of crimes and disorders which took place on the earth. And now it is, my brethren, that the danger of public stations shall be known, the precipices which surround the throne itself, the rocks of authority, and with what reason the gospel denominated happy those who live in the obscurity of a private station; with what it was that religion wished to inspire us with so much horror at ambition, so much indifference towards the grandeurs of the earth, so much contempt for all that is exalted only in the eyes of men, and so frequently recommended to us to love only what we ought for ever to love.

But, exempted perhaps from all these vices which we have just been mentioning, and attached, for a long time past, to the duties of a Christian life, you presume, that this terrible examination will either not regard you, or, at any rate, that you will appear there with more confidence than the criminal soul. Undoubtedly, my dear hearer,

hearer, that will be the day of triumph and glory for the juſt; the day which will juſtify theſe pretended exceſſes of retreat, mortification, modeſty, and delicacy of conſcience, which had furniſhed to the world ſo many ſubjects of cenſure and profane deriſion: the juſt ſhall, no doubt, appear before that awful tribunal with more confidence than the ſinner; but he will alſo appear there, and even his righteouſneſs ſhall be judged: your virtues, your holy works, will be ſubmitted to that rigorous examination. The world, which often refuſes the praiſes due to the trueſt virtue, too often likewiſe grants them to the ſole appearances of virtue: there are even ſo many juſt who deceive themſelves, and who are indebted, for that name and that reputation, merely to the public error. Thus, it is not only Tyre and Sidon that I ſhall viſit in the day of my wrath, ſayeth the Lord; that is to ſay, thoſe ſinners whom their crimes ſeemed to confound with the unbelievers and the inhabitants of Tyre and Sidon: I ſhall carry the light of my judgments even to Jeruſalem; that is to ſay, I will examine, I will ſearch into, I will fathom the motives of thoſe holy works which ſeem to equal you with the moſt faithful of the holy Jeruſalem.

I will trace, even to the ſource, the motive of that converſion which made ſo much noiſe in the world; and it ſhall be ſeen whether I find not its origin in ſome ſecret diſguſt, in the declenſion of youth and fortune, in private views of favour and

preferment,

preferment, rather than in the deteſtation of ſin and love of righteouſneſs.

I will balance thoſe liberalities poured out on the boſom of the poor, thoſe compaſſionate viſits, that zeal for pious undertakings, that protection granted to my ſervants with complaiſance, a deſire of eſteem, oſtentation, and worldly views which have infected them; and, in my ſight, they ſhall perhaps appear to be rather the fruits of pride, than the conſequences of grace and the work of my Spirit.

I will recall that train of prayer and other holy practices of which you had made a kind of habit, which no longer rouſed within you any feeling of faith and compunction; and you ſhall know whether lukewarmneſs, negligence, the little fruit which attended them, and the little diſpoſition within you previous to them, have not, before me, conſtituted ſo many infidelities for which you ſhall be judged without mercy.

I will ſearch into that removal from the world and from pleaſures, that ſingularity of conduct, that affectation of modeſty and regularity; and, perhaps, I ſhall find them more the conſequence of humour, temperament, and indolence, than of faith; and that, in a life more regular and more retired, in the opinion of men, you ſhall ſtill have preſerved all your ſelf-love, your attachment to the fleſh, all the niceties of ſenſuality; and, in a word, all the ſins of the moſt worldly ſouls.

I will

I will fearch, even to the bottom, that pretended zeal for my glory which made you fo deeply lament over the fcandals of which you were a fpectator, which led you to condemn them with fuch confidence and pride, and to blaze out, with fuch warmth, againft the irregularities and weakneffes of your brethren; and, perhaps, fhall that zeal be no longer in my fight but a natural feverity of temper, a malignity of difpofition, an inclination towards cenfure and upbraiding, an indifcreet warmth, a vain oftentatious zeal; far from finding you full of zeal for my glory, and for the falvation of your brethren, you fhall no longer appear before me, but unjuft, obftinate, malicious, and rafh.

I will demand an account from you of thofe fplendid talents which, it would appear, you employed only for my glory and for the inftruction of believers; and which had drawn upon you the bleffings of the juft, and the acclamations even of the worldly; and, perhaps, that continual attention to, and gratification of your own pride, the defire of furpaffing others, and your fenfibility of human applaufe, will prove the prominent features of your works to be only the works of man and the fruits of pride; and that I fhall curfe thofe labours which had fprung from fo impure a fource.

Great God! What works, upon which I had fo firmly depended, fhall then be found dead in thine eyes! How terrible fhall be that difcrimination!

And

And, of all the actions which we have performed even for heaven, how few wilt thou acknowledge as thine, and which thou wilt deem worthy of reward!

Do not from thence conclude, my brethren, that it is then needless to labour for salvation, seeing the just Judge shall seek only the condemnation of men: only their condemnation. My brethren? He is come solely to save them, and his mercies will far surpass even his justice. But behold the conclusion which you ought rather to draw. Those righteous souls whom you so frequently accuse of excess, of scrupulosity in the practice of the duties of a Christian life, as though they carried things too far; these souls, exposed to the light of God, shall appear lukewarm, sensual, imperfect, and perhaps criminal: and you, who live in the dangers and pleasures of the world; you, who devote to religion and your salvation only the most idle moments of your life; you, who scarcely mingle a single work of piety with an entire year of dissipation and inutility, in what situation shall you then be, my dear hearer? If those, who shall have only laudable works to present, shall yet be in danger of rejection, what shall be your destiny? You, who have only a life entirely worldly to offer? If the tree full of blossoms be treated with such rigour, what shall become of the withered and barren tree? And, if the just be even with difficulty saved; I speak not of the sinner, for

he

he is already judged; but the worldly foul, who lives without either vice or virtue, how shall he dare to appear?

You after fay, my dear hearer, that your confcience does not reproach you with great crimes: that, if not good, neither are you bad, and that your only fin is indolence and sloth. Ah! you shall then know yourself before the tribunal of Jesus Christ. You shall fee whether the testimony of your confcience, which reproached you not with crimes, and left you fcarcely any thing culpable to confefs, were not a terrible blindnefs, up to which the juftice of God had always delivered you. From the dread in which you shall fee the juft, you shall find what ought to be your own fears; and whether the confidence in which you have always lived, fprung from the peace of a good confcience, or from the falfe fecurity of a worldly one.

O my God! cries St Auguftin, could I but fee, at this moment, the ftate of my foul as thou fhalt then lay it open to me! Could I defpoil myfelf of thofe prejudices which blind me; miftruft thofe examples which confirm me; thofe cuftoms which quiet me; thofe talents which dazzle me; thofe praifes which feduce me; that rank and thofe titles which deceive me; and thofe complaifances of a facred guide, which form all my fecurity; could I but defpoil myfelf of that felf-love which is the fource of all my errors, and behold myfelf alone at thy feet, in thy light: O my God! what horror would I not feel for myself? And what measures would I not take, in humbling myself before thee, to prevent the public shame of that awful day, when the councils of hearts, and the secrecy of thoughts, shall be manifested? For, my brethren, not only shall the sinner be shewn to himself, but he shall likewise be shewn to all creatures.

PART II. That mixture of good and wicked, inevitable on this earth, gives birth to two disorders. In the first place, through favour of that mixture, concealed vice escapes that public ignominy which is its due; virtue, not known, receives not the applause it merits. In the second place, the sinner, high in honours, frequently fills the most distinguished offices, while the good and pious man lives in humiliation, and crawls like a slave at his feet. Now, on that terrible day, a double manifestation shall be made, which will repair that two-fold disorder. In the first place, the sinful will be marked out from the just by the public exposition of their conscience. In the second place, they will be discerned by separation from them, and the difference of their stations before the throne of glory.

In order fully to comprehend all the shame and confusion with which the criminal soul shall then be covered, when shewn to all creatures, and all his vices, the most secret, expofed to the light, it requires only to pay attention: 1*stly*, To the number and character of the spectators who shall witness nefs his fhame: 2*dly*, To the care he had taken to conceal his weakneffes and debaucheries from the eyes of men, while on the earth: 3*dly*, and *laftly*, To his perfonal qualities, which will render his confufion ftill more deep and overwhelming.

Here figure to yourfelves, then, my brethren, the criminal foul before the tribunal of Jefus Chrift, furrounded by angels and men; the juft, the finful, his relations, his fubjects, his mafters, his friends, his enemies, all their eyes fixed on him; prefent at the terrible fcrutiny which the juft Judge will make into his actions, his defires, and his thoughts; forced, in fpite of themfelves, to affift at his judgment, and to witnefs the juftice of the fentence which the Son of Man fhall pronounce againft him. All the refources which, on this earth, might foften the moft humiliating confufion, fhall fail, on that day, to the unfaithful foul.

Firft refource. On this earth, when guilty of a fault which has funk us into contempt, the whole has turned on a certain number of witneffes confined to our nation, or to the place of our birth; we may have removed ourfelves from them, in the courfe of time, to avoid continually reading, in their eyes, the remembrance and reproach of our paft fhame; we may have changed our place of dwelling to go elfewhere among ftrangers, to recover a reputation which we had already loft. But, on that grand day, all men affembled fhall be acquainted with the fecret hiftory of your manners

and

and of your confcience: you fhall no longer have it in your power to go, to hide yourfelf far from the looks of the fpectators, to feek new countries, and, like Cain, to fly into the defert. Each fhall be fixed immovable in the place marked out for him, bearing on his forehead the fentence of his condemnation and the hiftory of his whole life, obliged to fuftain the eyes of the univerfe, and the whole fhame of his weakneffes. There fhall no longer, then, be any hidden fpot wherein to conceal himfelf from the public regard; the light of God, the fole glory of the Son of Man, will fill the heavens and the earth; and, in all that immenfity of fpace around you, you will, in every part, difcover from afar only watchful eyes fixed on you.

Second refource. On the earth, when our fhame is even public, and, when degraded in the minds of men, in confequence of fome ftriking fault, yet there are always fome friends grounded in our favour, whofe efteem and fociety recompenfe us, in fome meafure, for the public contempt, and whofe kindnefs affifts us in fuftaining the inveteracy of the general cenfure. But, on this occafion, the prefence of our friends will be the object by far the moft infupportable to our fhame. If finners, like ourfelves, they will caft up to us our common pleafures and our example, which, perhaps, have been the firft rock upon which their innocence fplit: if juft, as they had believed us to be children of light, ah! they will reproach to us their

good

good opinion abufed, and their friendfhip feduced.
You loved the juft, fhall they fay to us, and you
hated righteoufnefs; you protected virtue, yet, in
your heart, you placed vice on the throne: in us
you fought that probity, that fidelity, and that
fecurity which you found not in your worldly
friends, but you fought not the Lord who formed
all thefe virtues in our heart: ah! did not the author of all our gifts deferve to be more loved,
more fought after than we!

And behold the third refource, which fhall fail,
to the confufion of the criminal foul. For, fhould
no friends be found on this earth to intereft themfelves in our misfortunes, there are always, at leaft,
indifferent perfons whom our faults do not wound
or excite againft us. But, on that terrible day,
we fhall have no indifferent fpectators. The juft,
fo feeling on this earth to the calamities of their
brethren, fo ingenious in excufing their faults, and
fo ready in covering them with the veil of charity,
in order, at leaft, to foften, if they cannot find an
apparent excufe for them in the eyes of men; the
juft, then, defpoiled, like the Son of Man, of that
indulgence and pity which they had exercifed towards their brethren on the earth, fhall hifs at the
finner, fays the prophet, fhall infult him, and fhall
demand his punifhment from the Lord to avenge
his glory; they fhall enter into the zeal and the
interefts of his juftice; and, becoming judges themfelves, they fhall mock him, fays the prophet, and
fay,

fay, "Lo, this is the man that made not God his
"ftrength; but trufted in the abundance of his
"riches, and ftrengthened himfelf in his wicked-
"nefs. Behold, now, that foolifh man, who be-
"lieved himfelf the only fage on the earth, and
"who confidered the life of the juft as a folly;
"who made to himfelf, in the favour of the great,
"in the vanity of titles and dignities, in the ex-
"tent of his lands and poffeffions, in the good o-
"pinion and applaufes of men, fupports of dirt,
"which were to perifh with him. Where, now,
"are your gods, your rock in whom you trufted?
"Let them rife up and help you, and be your
"protection."

Nor fhall finners be more indulgent to his mifery; they will feel for him all that horror which
they fhall be forced to feel for themfelves; the fel-
lowfhip of misfortune, which ought to unite, will
be only an eternal hatred which fhall divide them;
only a cruel inveteracy, which fhall fill their hearts
with nothing but fentiments of cruelty and fury a-
gainft their brethren; and they will hate, in others,
the fame crimes from which all their miferies
fpring. In a word, the men moft diftant from us,
the moft favage nations, to whom the name of Jefus Chrift hath never been announced, come then,
but too late, to the knowledge of truth, fhall rife
up againft you, and reproach to you, that, if the
miracles which God had, in vain, operated amongft
you had been wrought before their eyes; that if

they,

they, like you, had been enlightened by the gofpel, and fuftained by the fuccours of faith, they would have done penance in fackcloth and afhes, and put to advantage, for their falvation, thofe favours which you have abufed for your deftruction.

Such fhall be the confufion of the reprobate foul. Accurfed before God, he will find himfelf, at the fame time, the outcaft of heaven and of earth, the fhame and curfe of all creatures: even the inanimate, which he had forced to be fubfervient to his paffions, and which groaned, fays St Paul, in the expectation of deliverance from that fhameful fervitude, fhall, in their way, rife up againft him. The fun, of which he had abufed the light, fhall be darkened, as if it were not to fhine on his crimes: the ftars fhall difappear, as if to tell him that they have too long witneffed his iniquitous paffions: the earth fhall crumble from under his feet, as if to eject, from its bofom, a monfter which it could no longer bear: and the whole univerfe, fays Solomon, fhall arm againft him to avenge the glory of the Lord whom he has infulted. Alas! we fo dearly love to be lamented in our misfortunes: indifference alone irritates and wounds us: here, not only fhall all hearts be fhut to our misfortunes, but all beholders fhall infult our fhame, and the only portion left to the finner fhall be his confufion, his defpair, and his crimes. Firft circumftance of the confufion of the criminal foul: *viz*, the multitude of witneffes.

I take

I take the second from the care and anxiety they had taken, whilst living on the earth, to disguise and conceal themselves from the eyes of men. For, my brethren, the world is a grand theatre on which almost every one acts a borrowed character. As we are full of passions, and as all passions have always in them something mean and despicable, our whole attention is employed in concealing their meanness, and in endeavouring to give ourselves out for what we are not: iniquity is always treacherous and deceitful. Thus, your whole life, you, above all, who listen to me, and who considered the duplicity of your character as knowledge of the world and of the court; your whole life has been only one train of dissimulation and artifice; even your sincerest and most intimate friends have only, in part, known you; you were beyond the reach of the world, for you changed character, sentiment, and inclination, according to circumstances and the disposition of those to whom you wished to make yourselves agreeable; through these means you had acquired the reputation of ability and wisdom; but there shall be seen, in its native colours, a mean and treacherous soul destitute of probity and truth, and whose principal virtue had been the concealment of its baseness and meanness.

You, likewise, unfaithful soul, whom a sex more jealous of honour had rendered still more attentive to conceal your weaknesses from the eyes of men, you

you were so artful in saving yourself from a discovery; you took from so far, and so surely, your measures to deceive the eyes of a husband, the vigilance of a mother, and, perhaps, the probity of a confessor: you would not have survived the accident which had therein betrayed your precautions and artifices. Vain cares! you only covered your lewdnesses, says the prophet, with a spider's web, which, on that great day, the Son of Man shall dissipate with a single blast of his mouth. In the presence of all assembled nations, sayeth the Lord, I will gather around thee all thy lovers. They shall see that eternal train of artifices, disguises, and meannesses; that shameful traffic of protestations and oaths which you made instrumental to so many different passions, and, at the same time, to lull their credulity; they shall see them, and, tracing even to the source those criminal favours which you had bestowed on them, they shall find them not in their pretended merit as you had wished to make them believe, but in your own infamous character, in a heart naturally lewd; you, who pique yourselves on having a heart so noble, so sincere, and so incapable of being touched but by merit alone. And all this shall take place before the eyes of the universe; of those friends whom an appearance of regularity had preserved to you; of your relations who were ignorant of the disgrace with which you covered them;

them; of that hufband who had fo much depended on your affection and fidelity.

O my God! is there an abyfs fufficiently profound in the earth in which the unfaithful foul would not then wifh to hide himfelf? For, in the world, men never fee but the outfide and the fcandal of our vices; and, befides, our confufion is fhared and countenanced by thofe who are continually culpable of the fame faults. But, before the tribunal of Jefus Chrift, your weakneffes fhall be feen even in your heart; that is to fay, their birth, their progrefs, their moft private motives, and a thoufand fhameful and perfonal circumftances, which, even more than the crimes themfelves, fhall cover you with fhame: it will be a confufion in which none fhall bear a fhare, and, confequently, will be entirely your own.

Laftly, The final circumftance, which fhall render the fhame of the finner overwhelming, is his perfonal qualities.

You paffed in the world for a faithful, fincere, and generous friend: it will be feen that you were vile, perfidious, interefted, without faith, honour, probity, confcience, or character. You gave yourfelf out for a towering mind above all the vulgar prejudices; and you fhall unfold the moft humiliating meanneffes and circumftances, at which the vileft foul would almoft expire with fhame. In the world you were regarded as a man of integrity, and of an approved probity in the adminiftration

of

of your charge; that reputation had perhaps attracted fresh honours, and acquired to you the public confidence; you, neverthelefs, abufed the credulity of men; thofe pompous fhews of equity concealed an unjuft and fervile foul, and a thoufand times had your fidelity been in fecret betrayed, and your confcience corrupted by views of fortune and motives of intereft; you were apparently adorned with fanctity and righteoufnefs; you had always affumed the femblance of the juft; you were believed to be the friend of God, and the faithful obferver of his law; yet your heart was not upright before the Lord; under the cloak of religion you covered a defiled confcience and ignominious concealments; you walked in the way of holy things more fecurely to attain your purpofes. Ah! on that day of revelation you go to undeceive the whole univerfe; thofe who had feen you on the earth, aftonifhed at your unexpected lot, fhall fearch among the reprobate to difcover the upright man; the hope of the hypocrite fhall then be overthrown: you unjuftly had enjoyed the efteem of men; you fhall be known and God avenged. Laftly, Yet fhall I dare to fay it; and here reveal the fhame of my brethren? You were perhaps the difpenfer of holy things, high in honour in the temple of God; the charge of faith, of doctrine, and of piety, was intrufted to you; you appeared every day in the fanctuary, clothed in the formidable tokens of your dignity, offering

up

up pure gifts and sacrifices without stain; you were intrusted with the secrecies of consciences; you sustained the weak in faith; you spoke of wisdom among the instructed; and, under all that religion hath most august or most holy, you perhaps concealed whatever the earth has most execrable. You were an impostor, a man of sin seated in the temple of God; you instructed others, and you taught not yourself; you inspired horror against idols, and your days were only numbered by your sacrileges. Ah! the mystery of iniquity shall then be revealed; and you shall at last be known for what you have always been, the curse of heaven and the shame of the earth.

Behold, my brethren, all the confusion with which the criminal soul shall be overwhelmed. And it will not be a transitory confusion. In the world we have only the first shame of a fault to undergo: the noise of it gradually dies away; new adventures at last take place of ours; and the remembrance of our disgrace fades away, and disappears with the rumour which had published them. But, at the great day, shame shall eternally remain upon the criminal soul; there shall no longer be any fresh events to obliterate his crimes and his confusion; nothing shall more change: all shall be fixed and eternal: that which he shall have appeared before the tribunal of Jesus Christ, that will he for ever appear: even the nature of his torments shall incessantly publish the nature of his crimes;

crimes; and his shame shall every day be renewed in his punishment. My brethren, reflections here are needless; and, if some remains of faith still exist within you, it is for you to found your own consciences, and, from this moment, to adopt such measures as may enable you to sustain the manifestation of that great day.

But, after having shewn to you the public confusion with which the sinner shall be covered; why may not I expose to you here what shall be the glory and the consolation of the truly just man, when the secrecies of his conscience shall be laid open to the universe; when the whole mystery of his heart shall be unfolded; of that heart, of which all the loveliness, concealed from the eyes of men was known only to God; of that heart in which he had always supposed stains and defilements; and of which his humility had concealed from himself all the holiness and innocency; of that heart in which God alone had always dwelled, and which he had taken pleasure in adorning and enriching with his gifts and grace! What new wonders shall that divine sanctuary, hitherto so impenetrable, then offer to the eyes of the beholders, when the veil shall be removed from it! What fervent desires! What secret victories! What heroical sacrifices! What pure prayers! What tender lamentations! What faith! What grandeur! What elevation above all those vain objects which form all the desires and hopes of men! Then it shall indeed

deed be feen, that nothing was fo great, or fo worthy of admiration in the world, as a truly juft man; as thofe fouls who were confidered as ufelefs, becaufe they were fo to our paffions; and whofe obfcure and retired life was fo much defpifed. It fhall be feen that the heart of the faithful foul poffeffed more luftre and grandeur than all thofe great events which take place on the earth, was alone worthy of being written down in the eternal books, and offered to the eyes of God a fight more worthy of angels and men than all the victories and conquefts, which here below, fill the vanity of hiftories, to which pompous monuments are erected in order to eternife their remembrance, and which, then, fhall no longer be confidered but as puerile fquabbles, or the fruit of pride and the human paffions. Firft diforder repaired on that great day: vice concealed here below from public fhame, and virtue from the applaufes its merits.

The fecond diforder, which the mixture of the good and of the bad gives birth to in the world, is the inequality of conditions, and the unjuft exchange of their lots. It is with the prefent age as with the image of which Daniel explained the myftery: the juft, like the clay which we trample under our feet, or, like iron hardened in the fire of tribulation, in general occupy, here below, only the meaneft and moft contemptible ftations; while, on the contrary, the finful and the worldly, typified

fied by the gold and silver, vain objects of their passions, almost always find themselves placed at the head of affairs, and in the most eminent places. Now, this is a disorder; and, although the good be thereby exercised, and the wicked hardened; although this confusion of good and evil enter into the order of Providence; and that, by ways and means impenetrable to man, God make use of them to lead the just and the sinner to his purposes, yet it is necessary that the Son of Man gather together all things; and that it shall at last be discerned between the righteous and the wicked; between him that serveth God, and him that serveth him not. Now, behold the grand spectacle of that last day: order shall be re-established; the good separated from the wicked: the sheep set on his right hand, and the goats on the left.

Separation, 1*stly*, altogether new. It will not be demanded from you, in order to determine what rank you ought to hold in this awful scene, what were your names, your birth, your titles, or your dignities; these were but a vapour, which had no reality but in the public illusion; you will be examined only to prove whether you be an unclean animal or an innocent sheep: the prince shall not be separated from the subject; the noble from the peasant; the poor from the powerful; the conqueror from the vanquished; but the chaff from the good grain; the vessels of honour from the vessels of shame; the goats from the sheep.

The

The Son of Man shall be seen from on high, casting his regards over all the mingled nations and people assembled at his feet; recalling, in that view, the history of the universe, that is to say, of the passions or of the virtues of men; he shall be seen gathering together his chosen from the four quarters; choosing them from among every tongue, every station, and every nation; re-uniting the children of Israel dispersed through the universe; unfolding the secret history of an holy and new people; bringing forth to view heroes of faith till then unknown in the world; no more distinguishing ages by the victories of conquerors, by the establishment or the fall of empires, by the politeness or the barbarity of the times, by the great characters who have blazed in every age, but by the diverse triumphs of grace, by the hidden victories of the just over their passions, by the establishment of his reign in a heart, by the heroical fortitude of a persecuted believer. You shall see him change the face of all things, create a new heaven and a new earth, and reduce that infinite variety of people, titles, conditions, and dignities to a people holy, and a people reprobate, to the goats and the sheep.

Separation, 2*dly*, cruel. The father shall be separated from his child; friend from friend; brother from brother: the one shall be taken, the other left. Death, which deprives us of the dearest friends, and whose loss occasions to us so many sighs and tears, leaves us, at least, a consolation in the hope of being one day re-united to them. Here, the separation is eternal; no hope of re-union shall more exist; we shall no more have relatives, father, child, friend; no other ties than everlasting flames, which shall for ever unite us to the reprobate.

Separation, 3*dly*, ignominious. We are so touchy on a preference, when neglected, or left blended with the crowd on any splendid occasion; we are so peevish and so irritated, when, in the distribution of favours, we see novices carrying off the palm and the principal offices; our services forgotten, and those, whom we had always seen far below us, now exalted and placed over our heads: but, on that grand day it is that preference shall be accompanied with circumstances the most humiliating and the most galling to the criminal soul. In that universal silence, in that dreadful expectation, in which each one shall be for the decision of his destiny. You shall see the Son of Man advancing in the heavens, with crowns in one hand and the rod of wrath in the other, to carry off, from your side, a just soul whose innocence you, perhaps, had blackened by rash discourses, or whose virtue you had insulted by impious pleasantries; a believer who was, perhaps, born your subject; a Lazarus who in vain, perhaps, had importuned you with the recital of his wants and poverty; a rival whom you had always beheld with an eye of scorn, and upon whose ruins your intrigues and artifices had perhaps exalted you. You shall see the Son of Man place a crown of immortality on his head, seat him at his right hand, while you, like the proud Haman, rejected, humbled, and degraded, shall no longer have before your eyes but the preparation of your punishment.

Yes, my brethren, every galling and overwhelming circumstance shall attend that preference. A savage converted to faith shall be ranked among the sheep, while a Christian inheritor of the pronises shall be left among the goats. The layman shall ascend, like the eagle over its prey, while the minister of Jesus Christ shall grovel on the earth, covered with shame and reproach. The man of the world shall pass to the right hand, while the recluse passes to the left. The wife, the learned, the critic of the age, shall be driven to the side of the unclean; and the ideot, who knew not how to answer even the common salutations, shall be placed on a throne of glory and light. Rahab, a sinful woman, shall mount up to the heavenly Sion along with the true Israelites; while the sister of Moses, and the spouse of Jesus Christ, shall be driven from the camp and the tents of Israel, and shall appear covered with a shameful leprosy. Thou art determined, O my God! that nothing shall be wanting towards the despair of the criminal soul. It is not sufficient that he shall be overwhelmed under the weight of his own misery; thou shalt

create

create for him a new punishment in the felicity of the just, who, preferred to him, shall be seen conducted by angels into the bosom of immortality.

What change of scene, my brethren, in the universe! It is then that, all scandals being plucked out from the kingdom of Jesus Christ, and the just wholly separated from the sinful, they shall form a holy nation, a chosen race, and the church of firstborn, whose names were written down in heaven. It is then that the commerce of the wicked, inevitable on this earth, shall no longer occasion their faith to lament, or their innocence to tremble. It is then that their lot, no longer connected with the unfaithful or the hypocrite, shall no more constrain them to be witnesses of their crimes, and sometimes even the involuntary agents of their passions. It is then that, all the bonds of society, of authority, or dependence, which attached them on this earth to the impious and to the worldly, being broken asunder, they shall no longer say, with the prophet, " Lord, why lengthenest thou out here " our banishment and our sojourning? How long " shall the land mourn, and the herbs of every " field wither for the wickedness of them that " dwell therein?" Lastly, Then it is that their tears shall be changed into joy, and their sighs into thanksgivings; they shall pass to the right hand as the sheep, while the left shall be reserved for the goats and the impious.

The

The difpofition of the univerfe thus laid out; all nations of the earth thus divided; each one fixed in the place allotted to him; ,furprife, terror, defpair, and confufion marked in the countenance of one part; on that of the other, joy, ferenity, and confidence: the eyes of the juft raifed on high towards the Son of Man, from whom they await their deliverance; thofe of the impious frightfully fixed on the earth, and almoft piercing the abyfs with their looks, as if already to mark out the place which is deftined for them: the King of glory, fays the gofpel, placed in the middle of two nations, fhall come forward; and, turning towards thofe who fhall be at his right hand, with an afpect full of fweetnefs and majefty, and fufficient of itfelf to confole them for all their paft fufferings, he will fay to them, " Come, ye bleffed of my Fa-
" ther, inherit the kingdom prepared for you from
" the foundation of the world. The finful had
" always confidered you as the outcaft, and the
" moft ufelefs portion of the earth; let them now
" learn that the world itfelf exifted only for you,
" that all was created for you, and that all hath
" finifhed from the moment that your number was
" completed. Quit, then, an earth where you had
" always been travellers and ftrangers; follow me
" into the immortal ways of my glory and felici-
" ty, as you have followed me in thofe of my hu-
" miliation and fufferings. Your toils have en-
" dured

"dured but for an inftant; the happinefs you go to enjoy fhall be without end."

Then, turning to the left hand, vengeance and fury in his eyes, here and there cafting the moft dreadful looks, like avenging thunderbolts, on that crowd of guilty; with a voice, fays a prophet, which fhall burft open the bowels of the abyfs to fwallow them up, he fhall fay, not as upon the crofs, Father, pardon them, for they know not what they do, but, "Depart from me, ye curfed, into everlafting fire, prepared for the devil and his angels. You were the chofen of the earth, you are the curfed of my Father; your pleafures have been fleeting and tranfitory, your anguifh fhall be eternal." The juft, then, mounting with the Son of Man, fhall begin to fing this heavenly fong, Thou art rich in mercy, Lord, and thou haft crowned thy gifts in recompenfing our good actions. Then fhall the impious curfe the Author of their being, and the fatal day which brought them forth; or, rather, they fhall enter into wrath againft themfelves, as the authors of their mifery and deftruction. The abyfs fhall open; the heavens fhall bow down; the reprobate, fays the gofpel, fhall go into everlafting punifhment, and the juft into life eternal. Behold a lot which fhall change no more.

After a relation fo awful, and fo proper to make an impreffion on the moft hardened hearts, I cannot

not conclude without addressing to you the same words which Moses formerly addressed to the Israelites after having laid before them the dreadful threatenings, and the soothing promises contained in the Book of the Law. "Children of Israel, be-
"hold I set before you this day a blessing and a
"curse: a blessing, if ye obey the commandments
"of the Lord your God which I command you
"this day; and a curse, if ye will not obey the
"commandments of the Lord your God, but turn
"aside, out of the way which I command you this
"day, to go after other gods which ye have not
"known."

Behold, my brethren, what I say to you in concluding a subject so terrible. It now belongs to you to choose and to declare yourselves: the right hand and the left are before you: the promises and the threatenings: the blessings and the curses. Your destiny turns on this awful alternative: you either shall be on the side of satan and his angels, or you shall be chosen with Jesus Christ and his saints. Here there is no middle way: I have pointed out the path which leads to life, and that which leads to perdition. In which of these two do you now walk? And on which side do you believe that you should find yourselves, were you, at this moment, to appear before the awful tribunal? We die as we have lived: tremble lest your destiny of this day be your everlasting destiny. Quit, and,

and, from this moment, the ways of the finful; begin now to live like the juft, if you wifh, on that laft day, to be placed at the right hand, and to mount, along with them, into the abode of a bleffed immortality.

SER-

SERMON X.

THE HAPPINESS OF THE JUST.

MATTHEW v. 4.

Bleſſed are they who mourn, for they ſhall be comforted.

Sire,

If the world were to ſpeak to you in place of Jeſus Chriſt, it undoubtedly would not ſay, " bleſſed " are they who mourn."

Happy, would it ſay, the prince who has never fought but to conquer, and whoſe mind has always been ſuperior either to the danger or to the victory: who, during the courſe of a long and a proſperous reign, has enjoyed, and ſtill continues to enjoy, at his eaſe, the fruits of his glory, the love of his people, the eſteem of his enemies, the advantage of his conqueſts, the ſplendour of

his

his actions, the wisdom of his laws, and the august prospect of a numerous posterity; and who has nothing left now to desire, but the continuance of what he possesses.

In this manner would the world speak; but, Sire, Jesus Christ does not speak like the world.

Happy, says he to you, not him who is the admiration of his age; but he who makes his study of the age to come, and lives in the contempt of himself and of all the things of the earth; for to him is the kingdom of heaven. Not him whose reign and actions history will immortalize in the remembrance of men; but he whose tears shall have effaced the history of his sins from the remembrance even of God; for he shall be for ever consoled. Not him who, by new conquests, shall have extended the bounds of his empire; but he who has succeeded in confining his desires and his passions within the limits of the law of God; for he shall inherit a kingdom more durable than the empire of the universe. Not him who, exalted by the voice of nations above all preceding princes, tranquilly enjoys his greatness and his fame; but he who, finding nothing even on the throne worthy of his heart, seeks no perfect happiness on this earth but in virtue and in righteousness; for he shall be filled. Not him to whom men have given the pompous titles of great and invincible; but he to whom the wretched shall give, before the tribunal of Jesus Christ, the title of father and of

merciful;

merciful; for he shall be treated with mercy. Lastly, Happy, not him who, always disposer of the lot of his enemies, has more than once given peace to the earth; but he who has been able to give it to himself, and to banish, from his heart, all the vices and disorderly inclinations which disturb its tranquility; for he shall be called a child of God.

Such, Sire, are those whom Jesus Christ calls happy: and the gospel acknowledges no other happiness on the earth than virtue and innocence.

Great God! it is not then that long train of unexampled prosperities, with which thou hast favoured the glory of his reign, that can render him the happiest of kings. He is thereby great; but he is not thereby happy. His felicity has commenced with his piety. Whatever does not sanctify man, can never make the happiness of man. Whatever does not place thee, O my God! in an heart, places only vanities which leave it empty, or real evils which fill it with disquiet; and a pure conscience is the only resource of real enjoyments.

It is to this truth that the church, on the occasion of this solemnity, confines its whole fruit. As the common error, that the life of the saints has been gloomy and disagreeable, is one of the principal artifices employed by the world in order to prevent us from imitating them, the church, in renewing their memory on this day, gives us to remember, at the same time, that not only they

now

now enjoy an immortal felicity in heaven, but alfo that they have been the only happy of the earth, and that he who carries iniquity in his bofom always carries terror and anxiety; and that the lot of the godly is a thoufand times more tranquil and more fatisfactory, even in this world, than that of finners.

But, in what does the happinefs of the juft in this life confift ? It confifts, 1*ſtly*, In the manifeſtation of truth concealed from the fages of the world. 2*dly*, In the relifh of charity denied to the lovers of the world. In the lights of faith which foften all the fufferings of the believing foul, and which render thofe of the finner ftill more bitter: this is my firft point. In the comforts of grace which calm all the paffions, and which, denied to a corrupted heart, leave it a prey to itfelf: is the laft. Let us examine thefe two truths fo calculated to render virtue amiable, and the example of the faints beneficial.

PART I. Our forrows proceed, in general, from our errors; and we are unhappy only becaufe we are inadequate judges of what is really good and evil. The juft, who are children of light, are, therefore, much happier than finners, becaufe they are more enlightened. The fame lights which correct their judgments alleviate their fufferings: and faith, which fhews the world to them fuch as it is, changes, into fources of confolation for them, the very fame events in which fouls, delivered up

to

to the paffions, find the principle of all their difquiets.

And, in order to make you fenfible of a truth fo honourable to virtue, obferve, I pray you, my brethren, that, whether a contrite foul recall the paft, and thofe times of error which preceded his penitence; whether he pay attention to what paffes before his eyes in the world; or, laftly, whether he look forward to the future, every thing confoles, every thing ftrengthens him in the caufe of virtue which he has adopted, every thing unites in rendering his condition infinitely more pleafing than that of a foul who lives in diffipation, and who finds, in thefe three fituations, only bitternefs and inward terrors.

For, in the *firft* place, however the finner may be delivered up to all fervency of his heart, he is not fo violently hurried away, by prefent gratifications, but that he fometimes gives a look back to thofe years of iniquity which he amaffes behind him. Thofe days of darknefs, which he has confecrated to debauchery, have not fo completely perifhed, but that, in certain moments, they obtrude themfelves up his remembrance. Gloomy and troublefome images force themfelves upon his foul, and, from time to time, aroufe him from his lethargy by holding out, as if collected into one point, that fhocking mafs of crimes which make lefs impreffion, during their commiffion, becaufe he only fees them in fucceffion. At one glance of

his

his eye he fees favours always contemned, infpirations always rejected, a vile perverfion of a difpofition naturally good and originally formed, it appears, for virtue; weakneffes at which he now blufhes, phantoms and horrors againft which he would wifh for ever to fhut his eyes.

Such is what the finner leaves behind him. He is miferable if he look back to the paft. His whole happinefs is, as it were, fhut up in the prefent moment; and, to be happy, he muft never think, but allow himfelf, like the dumb creation, to be led away by the attraction of the prefent objects; and, to preferve his tranquility, he muft either extinguifh or brutify his reafon. And thence thofe maxims fo unworthy of humanity, and fo circulated in the world; that too much reafon is a forry advantage; that reflections fpoil all the pleafures of life; and, that, to be happy, the lefs we think the better. O man! was it for thy mifery then that Heaven had given thee that reafon by which thou art enlightened, or to affift thee in fearch of the truth, which alone can render thee happy? Could that divine light, which embellifhes thy being, be a punifhment rather than a gift of the Creator? And, fhould it fo glorioufly diftinguifh thee from the beaft only that thy condition may be more wretched?

Yes, my brethren, fuch is the lot of an unbelieving foul. Intoxication, delirium of paffion, and the extinction of all reafon alone can render him happy;

happy; and, as that situation is merely momentary, the inltant the mind becomes calm and regains itself, the charm ceafes, happinefs takes wing, and man finds himfelf alone with his confcience and his crimes.

But how different, O my God! is the lot of a foul who walks in thy ways, and how much to be pitied is the world which knows thee not! In effect, the fweeteft thoughts of a righteous foul are thofe by which the paft is recalled. He there encounters, it is true, that portion of his life which had been engroffed by the world and the paffions; and the remembrance, I confefs, fills him with fhame before the fanctity of his God, and forces from him tears of compunction and forrow. But, what confolation in his tears and in his grief!

For, my brethren, a contrite foul can never retrace the whole train of his paft errors without difcovering all the proceedings of God's mercy upon him. The fingular ways by which his wifdom hath gradually, and, as it were, ftep by ftep, conducted him to the bleffed moment of his converfion. So many unexpected favourable circumftances, fo many accidents of difgrace, of lofs, of death, of treachery, and of affliction; all provided by a watchful Providence to facilitate the means of breaking afunder his chains. Thofe fpecial attentions of God, even when in the paths of iniquity. Thofe difgufts, even in the midft of his pleafures, provided for him by his goodnefs. Thofe inward calls

calls which inceffantly whifpered to him, return to virtue and to duty. That internal monitor, which, go where he would, never left him, and unceafingly repeated to him, as formerly to St Auguftin: Fool! How long wilt thou hunt after pleafures which can never make thee happy? When, by terminating thy crimes, wilt thou terminate thy troubles? What more is yet required to open thine eyes upon the world, than thine own experience itfelf, of thy wearinefs and unhappinefs while ferving it? Try if, in belonging to me, thou fhalt not be more happy, and if I fuffice not to fill the foul which poffefles me?

Such is what the paft offers to a contrite foul. It there fees the accomplices of its former pleafures ftill delivered up, by God's juftice, to the errors of the world and of the paffions, and it alone chofen, feparated, and called to the knowledge of the truth.

With what peace and confolation does that reflection fill the believing foul! " How infinite, O
" my God," cries he with the prophet, " are thy
" mercies! Thou haft covered me in my mother's
" womb: Thou haft compafled my path, and my
" lying down, and all my ways have been known
" to thee: what have I done for thee more than
" fo many other finners whofe eyes thou deigneft
" not to open, and to manifeft the feverity of thy
" judgments and of thy juftice? How marvellous,
" O God! are all thy works, and that my foul
 " knoweth

" knoweth right well." First advantage of righteous souls: the remembrance even of their past infidelities consoles them.

But, secondly, if they find sources of solid consolations in reviewing the past, their piety is not less comforted while viewing the present occurrences of the world. And here, my brethren, you will presently see how essentially requisite is virtue to the happiness of life, and how that very world, which gives birth to all the passions, and, consequently, to all the disquietudes of sinners, becomes the sweetest and most consolatory exercise of the faith of the just.

What indeed is the world even to the worldly themselves, who love it, who seem intoxicated with its delights, and who cannot do without it? The world? It is an eternal servitude where no one lives for himself, and where, in order to be happy, we must bring ourselves to hug our chains, and to love our slavery. The world? It is a daily revolution of events, which successively arouse, in the hearts of its partisans, the most violent and the most melancholy passions; cruel antipathies, hateful perplexities, torturing fears, devouring jealousies, and corroding cares. The world? It is a land of curse, where even its pleasures are productive only of bitterness and thorns. Gaming fatigues and exhausts by its frenzies and by its caprices: conversation becomes wearysome through the contrariety of tempers and the opposition of sentiments:

ments : paſſions and criminal attachments are followed with their difgufts, their difappointments, and their unpleaſant reports : theatres, no longer having as fpectators but fouls grofsly diffolute and incapable of being roufed but by the moſt ſhocking exceſſes of debauchery, become infipid while moving only thofe delicate paſſions, which only ferve to ſhew guilt from afar, and to lay fnares for innocence. Laftly, the world is a place where hope itfelf, confidered as a paſſion fo fweet and fo pleafing, renders all men unhappy ; where thofe, who have nothing more to hope, believe themfelves ftill more miferable ; where every thing that pleafes foon ceafes to pleafe ; and where inanity or liftlefs infipidity is almoſt the beſt and moſt fupportable lot to be expected. Such is the world, my brethren ; nor is this that obfcure world, to which neither the great pleafures, nor the charms of profperity, of favour, and of affluence are known : it is the world in its moſt brilliant point of view ; it is the world of the court ; it is you yourfelves who now liften to me. Such is the world ; nor is this one of thofe fanciful paintings of which the reality is no where to be found. I paint the world after your own heart, that is to fay, fuch as you know it to be, and fuch as you yourfelves continually experience it.

Such, neverthelefs, is the place in which all finners feek their happinefs. That is their country. There they would willingly eternife themfelves.

Such is that world which they prefer to the eternal inheritance, and to all the promises of faith. Great God! how just art thou in punishing man through his passions themselves, and to permit that, wishing to seek his happiness elsewhere than in thee who alone art the true peace of his heart, he form for himself a ridiculous felicity of his fears, his disgusts, his wearinesses, and his disquietudes!

But that which is so fortunate here for virtue, is that the same world, so tiresome and so insupportable to sinners who seek their happiness in it, becomes a source of the most soothing reflections to the righteous, who consider it as an exilement and a foreign land.

For, in the *first* place, the inconstancy of the world, so dreaded by those delivered up to it, supplies a thousand motives of consolation to the believing soul. Nothing appears to him either constant or durable upon the earth; neither the most flourishing fortunes, nor the warmest friendships, nor the most brilliant reputations, nor the most envied favour. He sees a sovereign wisdom through all, which delights, it would appear, in making a sport of men, by alternately exalting them on the ruins of each other; by hurling down those at the top of the wheel, in order to elevate those who, only a moment before, were groveling at the bottom; by introducing, every day, on the theatre of life new heroes to eclipse all those who formerly played on it so brilliant a part; by incessantly giving
new

new scenes to the universe. He sees men passing their whole life in ferments, projects, and plots; ever on the watch to surprise each other, or to avoid being surprised; always eager and active to profit of the retreat, the disgrace, or the death of a rival; and of these grand lessons, so fitted to inculcate contempt of the world, make only fresh motives of ambition and cupidity: always engrossed either by their fears or by their hopes; always uneasy either for the present or for the future; never tranquil, all struggling for quiet, yet every moment removing themselves farther and farther from it.

O man! why art thou so ingenious in rendering thyself miserable? Such is, then, the reflection of the believing soul. That happiness thou seekest is more easily attained. It is necessary neither to traverse seas nor to conquer kingdoms. **Depart not from thyself and thou wilt be happy.**

How sweet do the sorrows of virtue then appear to the godly man, when he compares them with the cruel chagrins and the endless agitations of sinners! How transported to have at last found a place of rest and of safety, while he sees the lovers of the world still sadly tost about at the mercy of the passions and of human hopes! Thus the Israelites formerly escaped from the danger of the Red sea, seeing from afar Pharaoh and all the nobility of Egypt still at the mercy of the waters, felt all the luxury of their own safety, thought the barren

paths

paths of the desert delightful, and were insensible to every hardship of their journey; and, comparing their lot with that of the Egyptians, far from giving vent to a complaint or a murmur, they sung with Moses that divine hymn of praise and of thanksgiving in which are celebrated, with such magnificence, the wonders and the tender mercies of the Lord.

2*dly*, The injustice of the world, so humbling to those who love it, when they see themselves forgotten, neglected, and sacrificed to unworthy rivals, is also a fund of soothing reflections to a soul who despises it and fears only the Lord. For, what resource is left to a sinner who, after having sacrificed his ease, his conscience, his wealth, his youth, and his health, to the world and to his masters; after having submitted in silence to every circumstance the most mortifying to the mind, sees at once, and without knowing why, the gates of favour and advancement for ever shut against him; sees places snatched from him to which he was entitled by his services, and of which he thought himself already certain; threatened, should he dare to murmur, with the loss of those he still enjoys; forced to crouch to more fortunate rivals, and to be at the beck of those whom, only a little before, he had deemed unworthy of even receiving his orders? Shall he retire far from the world, to evaporate, in continual invectives against it, the spleen and the rancour of his heart, and thus revenge

himself

himself of the injustice of men? But of what avail will be his retirement? It will afford only more leisure for retrospection, and fewer relaxations from chagrin. Shall he try to console himself with similar examples? But our misfortunes never, as we think, resemble those of others; and, besides, what consolation can it be to have our sorrows renewed by seeing their image reflected from others? Shall he entrench himself in strength of mind, and in a vain philosophy? But, in solitude, reason soon descends from its pride; we may be philosophers for the public, but we are only men with ourselves. Shall he fly, as a resource, to voluptuousness, and to other infamous pleasures? But, in changing the passion, the heart only changes the punishment. Shall he seek, in indolence and inactivity, an happiness he has never been able to find in all the fervency of hopes and pretensions? A criminal conscience may become indifferent, but it is not thereby more tranquil. One may cease to feel misfortune and disgrace, but infidelities and crimes must always be felt. No, my brethren, the unhappy sinner is so without resource. Every comfort is for ever fled from the worldly soul from the moment that he is deserted by the world.

But the righteous man learns to despise the world even in the contempt which the world has for him. The injustice of men, with respect to him, only puts him in mind that he serves a more equitable Master, who can neither be influenced nor prejudiced;

prejudiced; who sees nothing in us but what, in reality, there is; who determines our destinies upon our hearts alone, and with whom we have nothing but our own conscience to dread: consequently, that they are happy who serve him; that his ingratitude is not to be feared; that every thing done for him is faithfully recorded; that, far from concealing or neglecting our sufferings and our services, he gives us credit even for our good wishes; and that nothing is lost with him but what is not done solely for him.

Now, in these lights of faith, what a fresh fund of consolation for a believing soul! How little is the world, in this point of view, with all its scorns and ill usage, capable of affecting him! Then it is that, throwing himself into the bosom of God, and viewing, with Christian eyes, the nothingness and vanity of all human things, he feels in a moment all his inquietudes, inseparable from nature, changed into the sweetest peace; a ray of light shines in his soul, and re-establishes serenity; a trait of consolation penetrates his heart, and every sorrow is alleviated. Ah! my brethren, how sweet to serve him, who alone can render happy those who serve him! Why, O blessed condition of virtue, art thou not better known to men! And wherefore art thou held out as a disagreeable and sorrowful lot, thou who alone canst console the miseries and alleviate all the sufferings of this banishment?

Lastly,

Laſtly, The judgments of the world, ſource of ſo many chagrins for the wordly, complete ſtill more the conſolation of the believing ſoul. For the torture of the lovers of the world is that of being continually expoſed to the judgments, that is to ſay, to the cenſures, to the deriſions, to the malignity of each other. In vain do we deſpiſe the men : we wiſh to be eſteemed even by thoſe we deſpiſe. In vain are we exalted above others : the more we are exalted, we are only the more expoſed to the criticiſms and to the obſervations of the multitude, and we much more poignantly feel the cenſures of thoſe from whom homages alone were to have been expected. In vain may the ſuffrage of the public be in our favour ; contempt is ſo much the more ſtinging as it is unuſual and rare. In vain may we retaliate with cenſures yet more biting and keen ; reſentment and revenge always ſuppoſe a ſenſe of guilt ; and, beſides, the chagrin of having encountered ſcorn is much more lively than any pleaſure that can accrue from retorting it. Laſtly, From the moment that you live ſolely for the world, and that your pleaſures or your vexations depend wholly on it, the judgments of the world can never be indifferent to you.

Neverthelefs, it is in the midſt of all theſe vexations that happineſs muſt be at leaſt profeſſed. Every thing attributed to you, either by truth or vanity, is called in queſtion : your birth, your talents,

lents, your reputation, your services, your success, your prudence, and even your honour. If you go to wreck, your incapacity accounts for it: if successful, the honour is given to chance, or to your inferiors: if you enjoy the good opinion of the public, the judgment of the more knowing is appealed to from the popular error; if possessed of the art of pleasing, it is immediately said that you have made a thorough use of your talents, and that you have been only too agreeable: if your conduct be superior to any attack, the most poignant ridicule is directed against your temper. Lastly, Be whom ye may, high or low, prince or subject, the most desirable situation for your vanity is that of being unacquainted with the world's opinion of you. Such is the life of the world. The same passions which bind us together, disunite us: envy and destruction blacken our noblest qualities; and our gratifications find censurers even in those who copy them.

But a believing soul is sheltered from all these uneasinesses. As he courts not the esteem of men, neither does he fear their scorn; as he has no intention of laying himself out to please, neither is he surprised to find that he has not done it. God, who sees him, is the only Judge he fears, and who, at the same time, consoles him for the judgments of men. His glory is the testimony of his own conscience. His reputation he seeks in the fulfilment of his duty. He considers the suffrages of
the

the world, as the rock of virtue, or as the reward of vice; and, without even paying attention to its judgments, he is satisfied with giving it good examples. But what do I say, my brethren? The world itself, all worldly as it is, so full of censures, malignity, and contempt for its own worshippers, is forced to respect the virtue of those who hate and despise it. It appears that virtue imprints, on the person of a real righteous man, a dignity, a something I know not what, of divine, which attracts the veneration and almost the worship of worldly souls: it appears that his intimate union with Jesus Christ occasions his being irradiated, as I may say, like the three disciples on the holy mount, with a part of that celestial splendour which the Father shed around his well-beloved Son, and by which all liberty ceases of refusing homage. It is an inalienable right which virtue has over the heart of men; and, by a deplorable caprice, the world despises the passions it inspires, and respects the virtue it strives against. Not that the esteem of the world, so worthy itself of being despised, can be any great consolations to the believing soul. But his consolation is, that he sees the world condemned even by the world, its pleasures decried even by those who hunt after them, sinners become the apologists of virtue, and the life of the world to pass sorrowfully away in doing what they condemn, and flying from what they approve.

Such is the manner in which the present age becomes a source of consolatory reflections to a Christian soul; but, in the thought of futurity, he also finds consolations which are changed into inward and continual terrors for sinners: Last advantage drawn by the just from the lights of faith. The magnificence of its promises sustains and consoles them: they await the blessed hope, and that happy moment when they shall be associated with the church of heaven, reunited to their brethren whom they had left on the earth, received eternal citizens of the heavenly Jerusalem, incorporated in that immortal assembly of the elect, where charity will be the law that shall unite them; truth, the flame that shall enlighten them; and eternity, the measure of their felicity.

These thoughts are so much the more consoling to the godly, as they are founded on the truth of God himself. They know that, in sacrificing the present, they sacrifice nothing; that, in the twinkling of an eye all shall have passed away; that, whatever must have an end cannot long endure; that this moment of tribulation ought to be reckoned as nothing, when put in competition with that eternal weight of glory which he prepareth for us; and that the rapid passage of present things scarcely deserves that we should be at the pains of numbering the years and the ages.

I know that faith may subsist with criminal manners; and that the sanctifying grace is often

lost

lost without losing a sincere submission to the truths revealed to us by the Spirit of God. But the certitude of faith, so consoling to the righteous soul, is no longer for the sinner who still believes but an inexhaustible fund of inward anxieties and cruel terrors. For, the more that sinners like you, who bear upon your conscience the sink of a whole life of irregularity, are convinced of the truths of faith, the more inevitable must the punishments and the misery appear with which it threatens such sinners. All the truths offered to your faith, in the holy doctrine, excite fresh alarms in your breast. Those divine lights, which are the source of all consolation to believing souls, become, within you, only avenging lights which disquiet, agonise, and judge you; which, like a mirror, hold up continually to your sight what you would wish never to see; which enlighten you, in spite of yourselves, on what you would wish to be for ever ignorant. Your faith itself constitutes your punishment before-hand. Your religion is, here below, if I may venture to say so, your hell; and, the more you are convinced of the truth, the more unhappy do you live. O God! how great is thy goodness towards man, in having rendered virtue necessary even to his quiet, and in thus attracting him to thee, by making it impossible for him to be happy without thee!

And here, my dear hearer, allow me to recall you to yourself. When the lot of a criminal soul

should

should not be so fearful for the age to come, see if, even in this world, it appears much to be envied: his afflictions are without resource, his evils without consolation, even his pleasures without enjoyment; his anxieties upon the present endless, his reflections on the past and on the future gloomy and sad; his faith is the source of all his anguish; his lights of all his despair. What a situation! What a miserable lot! What shocking changes are operated, by a single act of guilt, both internally and outwardly on man! How dearly does he purchase eternal misery! And, is it not true that the way of the world and of the passions is still infinitely more arduous and painful than that of the gospel; and that there is more toil and vexation of spirit in gaining the kingdom of hell, if it be proper to speak in this manner, than in gaining the kingdom of heaven? O innocence of heart, what blessings dost thou not bring with thee to man! O man, what losest thou not when thou losest thine innocence of heart! Thou losest all the consolations of faith, the sweetest occupation of the piety of the righteous; but thou also deprivest thyself of all the comforts of grace by which the lot of the godly is rendered so truly enviable here below.

PART II. When comforts and consolation, says St Augustin, are promised to worldly souls in the observance of the law of God, they consider our promises as a pious mode of speaking employed to

give

give credit and confequence to virtue; and, as a heart which has never tafted of thefe chafte delights is alfo incapable of comprehending them, we are obliged, continues that holy father, to reply to them, " How wouldft thou that we convince " thee?" We cannot fay unto thee: " O tafte " and fee that the Lord is good!" feeing a difeafed and vitiated heart can have no relifh for the things in heaven. Give us an heart that loves, and it will feel the truth of every thing we fay.

My defign, therefore, here, is not fo much to enlarge upon all the inward operations of grace in the heart of the juft, as to contraft the happy fituation in which it places them, here below, with the melancholy lot of finners, and, by this comparifon, to overwhelm vice and to encourage virtue. Now, I fay, that grace provides two kinds of confolations here below to the godly: the one internal and fecret, the others external and fenfible; both of them fo effential to happinefs in this life, that no earthly gratification can ever compenfate for them.

The firft internal benefit accruing to the believing foul from grace, is the eftablifhment of a folid peace in his heart, and a reconciliation with himfelf. For, my brethren, we all bear within us natural principles of equity, of modefty, and of rectitude. We come into the world, as the apoftle fays, with the precepts of the law written in the heart. If virtue be not our firft bent, we, at leaft, feel that it is our firft duty. In vain does paffion

fometimes

sometimes undertake secretly to persuade us that we are born for pleasure; and that, after all, tendencies implanted by nature, and which every one finds within himself, can never be crimes. This foreign persuasion is ineffectual in quieting the criminal soul. It is a desire, for we would heartily wish to be lawful whatever pleases us; but it is not a real conviction. It is a saying, for it appears honourable to be above all vulgar prejudices; but it is not a feeling. Thus we always carry within us an incorruptible judge, who incessantly adopts the cause of virtue against our dearest inclinations; who blends with our most headstrong passions the troublesome ideas of duty; and, who renders us unhappy even amidst all our pleasures and abundance.

Such is the state of an impure and a sullied conscience. The sinner is the secret and constant accuser of himself; go where he will, he carries a torment within which the hand of man cannot allay. Unhappy in being unable to conquer his lawless tendencies: more unhappy still in being unable to stifle his incessant remorses. Enticed by his weakness, and withheld by his lights, the permission of every crime is a conflict with himself: he reproaches himself for the iniquitous gratification, even in the moment of its enjoyment. What shall he do? Shall he combat his lights in order to appease his conscience? Shall he suspect his faith to sin in tranquility? But unbelief is still a more horrible

rible state than even guilt. To live without **God**, without worship, without principle, and without hope! To believe that the most abominable transgressions and the purest virtues are merely names! To consider all men as only the vile and fantastical puppets of a low theatre, and merely intended for the amusement of the spectators! To consider himself as the offspring of chance, and the eternal possession of nonentity! These thoughts have something, I know not what, of gloomy and horrible, that the soul cannot look upon without horror; and it is true that unbelief is rather the despair of the sinner than the refuge of the sin. What, then, shall he do? Continually obliged to fly himself, lest he find himself alone with his conscience, he ranges from object to object, from passion to passion, from precipice to precipice. He thinks to compensate the emptiness and the insufficiency of pleasures by their variety; there is none which he does not try. But in vain is his heart successively offered to all the created; all the objects of his passions reply to him, says St Augustin, " Deceive not thy-
" self in loving us; we are not that happiness of
" which thou art in search; we cannot render thee
" happy: raise thyself above the created, and,
" mounting to heaven, see if he who hath formed
" us be not greater and more worthy of being lov-
" ed than we." Such is the lot of the sinner.

Not that the heart of the just enjoys a tranquility so unalterable but that they, in their turn, experience

perience troubles, difgufts, and anxieties here below. But thefe are paffing clouds, which fhade, as I may fay, only the furface of their foul. A profound calm always reigns within; that ferenity of confcience, that fimplicity of heart, that equality of mind, that lively confidence, that mild refignation, that calm of the paffions, that univerfal peace, which begins, even from this life, the felicity of innocent fouls. Vain creatures, what can ye, over an heart which you have not made, and which is not made for you? Firft confolation of grace, viz. peace of heart.

The fecond is love, which mollifies to the juft all the rigours of the law, and, according to the promife of Jefus Chrift, changes his yoke, fo infupportable to finners, into a fweet and confoling yoke for them. For a believing foul loves his God ftill more fervently, more tenderly, and more truly, than he had ever loved the world. Every thing, therefore, even the moft rigorous, that he undertakes for him, is either no longer a trial to his heart, or becomes its fweeteft care. For the attribute of the holy love, when mafter of the heart, is either to mollify the fufferings it occafions, or to change them even into holy pleafures. Thus a foul enamoured of God, if I may dare to fpeak in this manner, pardons with joy, fuffers with confidence, mortifies itfelf with pleafure, flies from the world with delight, prays with confolation, and fulfils every duty with an holy fatisfaction. The
more

more his love increases, the more does his yoke become easy. The more he loves the happier he is: for it is the height of happiness to love what is become essential and necessary to us.

But, the sinner, the more he loves the world the more unhappy he is: for the more he loves the world the more do his passions multiply, the more do his desires inflame, the more do his schemes get perplexed, and the more do his anxieties become sharpened. His love is the cause of all his evils: its vivacity is the source of all his sufferings; because the world, which is the cause of them, is incapable of furnishing him with their cure. The more he loves the world the more is his pride stung by a preference; the more does his haughtiness feel an injury, the more does he sink under a disconcerted project; the more does a disappointed desire afflict him, the more does an unexpected loss weigh him down. The more he loves the world the more do pleasures become necessary to him; and, as no one can fill the immensity of his heart, the more insupportable does his weariness become: for weariness is the inseparable attendant of every pleasure; and, with all its amusements, the world, ever since it was a world, complains of its lassitude.

And think not that, to accredit virtue, I here affect to exaggerate the misery of worldly souls. I know that the world seems to have its happiness; and that, amid all that whirlwind of cares, motions, fears, and anxieties, a small number of fortunate individuals is seen, whose happiness is envied, and who seem, in appearance, to enjoy a smiling and tranquil lot. But investigate these vain outsides of happiness and gladness, and you will find real sorrows, distracted hearts, and agitated consciences. Draw near to these men who, in your eyes, appear the happy of the earth, and you will be surprised to find them gloomy, anxious, and sinking under the weight of a criminal conscience. Hear them in those serious and tranquil moments, when the passions, more cooled, allow some influence to reason: they all confess that they are any thing but happy, that the blaze of their fortune shines only at a distance, and appears worthy of envy only to those who know it not. They confess that, amidst all their pleasures and prosperity, they have never been able to taste any pure and unadulterated joy; that the world, a little searched into, is nothing; that they are astonished themselves how it can be loved when known; and that happy are they alone, here below, who can do without it and serve God. Some long for the opportunity of an honourable retreat; others are continually proposing to themselves more orderly and more Christian manners. All admit the happiness of the godly; all wish to become so; all bear testimony against themselves. They are the forced rather than the voluntary followers of pleasure. It is no longer inclination, it is habit, it is weakness which retains them in the shackles of the world

and

and of fin. They feel this; they lament it; they acknowledge it; and they give way to the current of so wretched a lot. Deceitful world! render happy, if in thy power, those who serve thee, and then will I forsake the law of the Lord to attach myself to the vanity of thy promises.

You yourself, my dear hearer, since the many years that you serve the world, have you greatly forwarded your happiness? Put in a balance, on the one side, all the agreeable moments and days you have passed in it, and, on the other, all the sorrows and vexations you have there experienced, and see which scale will preponderate. In certain moments of pleasure, of excess, and of frenzy, you have, perhaps, said, "It is good for us to be here;" but that was only a momentary intoxication, the illusion of which the following moment discovered to you, and plunged you into all your former anxieties. Even now, when speaking to you, question your own heart: are you at peace within; is nothing wanting to your happiness? Do you fear, do you wish for nothing? Do you never feel that God is not with you? Would you wish to live and die such as you are? Are you satisfied with the world? Are you unfaithful to the Author of your being without remorse? There are twelve hours in the day; are they all equally agreeable to you? And have you, as yet, been able to succeed in fashioning a conscience so as to remain tranquil in guilt?

Even

Even then, when you have plunged to the very bottom of the sea of iniquity to extinguish your remorses, and have succeeded, as you thought, in stifling that remnant of faith which still pleads in your heart for virtue, hath not the Lord commanded the serpent, as he saith in his prophet Amos, to follow and sting you even in the abyss where you had fled for shelter? And, even there, have you not felt the secret gnawings of the ravenous worm? Is it not true that the days you have consecrated to God by some religious duty have been the happiest of your life; and that you have never lived, as I may say, but when your conscience has been pure, and that you have lived with God? No, says the prophet with an holy pride, the God whom we worship is not a deceitful God, nor is he, like the gods which the world worships, unable to reward those who serve him: let the worldly themselves be the judges here.

Great God! What then is man, thus to wrestle his whole life against himself, to wish to be happy without thee, in spite of thee, in declaring himself against thee; to feel his wretchedness, and yet to love it; to know his true happiness, and yet to fly from it? What is man, O my God! and who shall fathom his ways, and the eternal contradiction of his errors?

Would I could finish what I had at first intended, and prove to you, my brethren, that the lot of the godly is still more worthy of all our wishes for

this

this reafon, that, when the internal confolations happen even to fail them, yet they have the external aids of piety to ftrengthen and to affift them: the fupport of the facrament, which, to the reluctant finner, is no longer but a melancholy tribute to decency, equally tirefome and embarraffing: the example of the holy, and the hiftory of their wonders, from which the finner averts his eyes, left he fee in them his own condemnation: the holy thankfgivings and prayers of the church, which, to the finner, become a melancholy fatigue: and, laftly, the confolation of the divine writings, in which he no longer finds but menaces and anathemas.

What invigorating refrefhment, in effect, my brethren, to the mind of a believer, when, after quitting the vain converfations of the world, where the only fubjects have been the exaltation of a family, the magnificence of a building, the individuals who act a brilliant part on the theatre of the univerfe, public calamities, the faults of thofe at the head of affairs, the events of war, and the errors with which the government is continually accufed; laftly, where, earthly, they have fpoken only of the earth; what a refrefhment after quitting thefe, when, in order to breathe a little from the fatigue of thefe vain converfations, a believing foul takes up the book of the law, and finds every where in it; that it matters little to man to have gained the whole world, if he thereby lofe his foul; that the moft vaunted conquefts fhall fink into ob-

livion

livion with the vanity of the conquerors; that the heavens and the earth fhall pafs away; that the kingdoms of the earth and all their glory fhall wafte away like a garment; but that God alone will endure for ever; and, confequently, that to him alone we ought to attach ourfelves! The foolifh have repeated vain things to me, O my God! fays then this foul with the prophet; but O how different from thy law!

And certainly, my brethren, what foothing promifes in thefe holy books! What powerful inducements to virtue! What happy precautions againft vice! What inftructive events! What fublime ideas of the greatnefs of God, and of the wretchednefs of man! What animated paintings of the deformity of fin, and the falfe happinefs of finners! We have no need of thine affiftance, wrote Jonathan and all the Jewifh people to the Spartans, for, having the holy books in our hands to comfort us, we have no occafion for the aid of men. And who, think you, my brethren, were thefe men who fpeak in this manner? They were the unfortunate remains of Antiochus's cruelty, wandering in the mountains of Judea, defpoiled of their property and fortunes, driven from Jerufalem and the temple where the abomination of idols had taken place of the worfhip of the holy God; and, fcarcely emerged from fo afflicting a fituation, they are in need of nothing, for they have the holy books

in

in their hands. And, in an extremity fo new, furrounded on all hands by nations of enemies, having no longer, in the midſt of their army, either the ark of Iſrael or the holy tabernacle; their tears ſtill flowing for the recent death of the invincible Judas, who was alike the ſafeguard of the people and the terror of the uncircumciſed; having feen their wives and children murdered before their eyes; they themſelves on the point every day of finking under the treachery of their falſe brethren, or the ambuſcades of their enemies; the book of the law is alone ſufficient to comfort and to defend them; and they think themſelves in a fituation to difclaim that affiſtance which an ancient treaty and alliance entitled them to demand.

I am not furpriſed after this, that, in the confolation of the fcriptures, the firſt difciples of the gofpel ſhould forget all the rage of perſecution; and that unable to bring themſelves to loſe fight of that divine book during life, they ſhould defire it to be incloſed in their tomb after death, as if to guarantee to their aſhes that immortality it had always promiſed to them; and likewiſe, as it would appear, to preſent it to Jeſus Chriſt on the day of revelation, as the facred claim by which they were entitled to heavenly riches, and to all the promiſes made to the righteous.

Such are the confolations of believing fouls upon the earth. How terrible then, my brethren, to
live

live far from God under the tyranny of sin; always at war with one's self; destitute of every real joy of the heart; without relish often for pleasures alike as for virtue; odious to men through the meanness of our passions; insupportable to ourselves through the capriciousness of our desires; hated of God through the horrors of our conscience: deprived of the comforts of the sacrament, seeing our crimes permit us not to approach it; deprived of all consolation from the holy books, seeing we find in them only threatenings and anathemas; without the resource of prayer, seeing the practice of it is forbidden, or, at least, the habit of it lost by a life wholly dissolute. What then is the sinner but the outcast of heaven and of the earth!

Thus, know ye, my brethren, what shall be the regrets of the reprobate on that great day, when to each one shall be rendered according to his works? You probably think that they will regret their past felicity, and shall say, " Our days of
" prosperity have slipt away like a shadow, and
" that world, in which we had spent so many
" sweet moments, is now no more: the duration
" of our pleasures has been like that of a dream:
" our happiness is flown, but, alas! our punish-
" ments are to begin." You are mistaken; this will not be their language. Hear how they speak in the book of Wisdom, and such, as we are assured

ed by the Spirit of God, they shall one day speak,
" We never tasted pure delight in guilt; we have
" erred from the ways of truth, and the Sun of
" righteousness hath never rose upon us: alas!
" and yet that was only the beginning of our mis-
" fortunes and sufferings; we wearied ourselves
" in the way of wickedness and destruction; our
" passions have always been a thousand times
" more intolerable to us than could ever have
" been the most austere virtues; and we have suf-
" fered more in working our own destruction, than
" would have been necessary to secure our salva-
" tion, and to be entitled to mount up now with
" the chosen into the realms of immortality.
" Fools that we are! by a sorrowful and unhappy
" life to have purchased miseries which must en-
" dure for ever!"

Would you then, my dear hearer, live happy
on the earth; live Christianly. Piety is universally beneficial. Innocence of heart is the source of
true pleasures. Turn to every side; there is no
rest, says the Spirit of God, for the wicked. Try
every pleasure; they will never eradicate that dif-
ease of the mind, that fund of lassitude and gloom
which, go where you will, continually accompanies
you. Cease then to consider the lot of the godly
as a disagreeable and sorrowful lot; judge not of
their happiness from appearances which deceive
you. You see their countenance bedewed with
tears; but you see not the invisible hand which

wipes them away: you see their body groaning under the yoke of penitence; but you see not the unction of grace which mollifies it: you see sorrowful and austere manners; but you see not a conscience always cheerful and tranquil. They are like the ark in the desert: it appeared covered only with the skins of animals: the exterior is mean or disgusting; it is the condition of that melancholy desert. But, could you penetrate into the heart, into that divine sanctuary; what new wonders would rise to your eyes! You would find it clothed in pure gold: you would there see the glory of God with which it is filled: you would there admire the fragrance of the perfumes, and the fervor of the prayers which are continually mounting upwards to the Lord; the sacred fire which is never extinguished on that altar; that silence, that peace, that majesty which reigns there; and the Lord himself, who hath chosen it for his abode, and who hath delighted in it.

Let their lot inspire you with an holy emulation. It depends wholly on yourself to be similar to them. They perhaps have formerly been the accomplices of your pleasures; why could you not become the imitator of their penitence? Establish, at last, a solid peace in your heart: begin to be weary of yourself. Hitherto you have only half-lived; for it is not living to live at enmity with one's self. Return to your God who calls and who expects you: banish iniquity from your soul, and you will

banish

banish the source of all its sorrows; you will enjoy the peace of innocence; you will live happy upon the earth; and that temporal happiness will be only the commencement of a felicity which shall never fade nor be done away.

SERMON XI.

ON THE DISPOSITIONS FOR THE COMMUNION.

LUKE iii. 4.

Prepare ye the way of the Lord, make his paths straight.

BEHOLD what the church is continually repeating to us during this holy time, in order to prepare us for the birth of Jesus Christ: prepare, says she to all her children, prepare the way of the Lord who descends from heaven to visit and to redeem his people; make his paths straight; let the hollows be filled up and the mountains levelled; let the crooked ways become straight and the rugged even. Or, to express the same meaning without metaphor; prepare yourselves, says she to us, to gather the fruit of that grand mystery which we are

are going to celebrate, by humiliation of heart, meekness and charity, rectitude of intention, uniformity of living, renunciation of your own wisdom and of your own righteousness; mortifying the flesh and humbling the spirit.

Allow me to hold the same language to you Christians, my brethren, who, on this solemn occasion, come to purify yourselves in the penitential tribunals, in order to give a new birth to Jesus Christ in your hearts, on receiving him at the sacred table: prepare the way of the Lord. The deed you are going to perform is the most holy act of religion, and the source of the most special favours: undertake it not, therefore, without all the cares and all the precautions which it requires; do not expose yourselves, through your own fault, to lose the inestimable advantages which ought to accrue to you from it.

The communion ought to give birth to Jesus Christ in our hearts; but where would be the difference between the righteous man and the sinner, between the soul who discerns the body of the Lord, and him who treats it as a common food, were he equally to have birth in the heart of all who receive him? Deceive not yourselves then, my brethren; there is a way of receiving Jesus Christ, by which his presence is rendered useless to us; and would to God that, in thus receiving him, we deprived ourselves only of those favours which follow an holy communion! Ah! my brethren,

thren, unlefs the communion gives birth to Jefus Chrift in our hearts, it brings death to him there; if it do not render us participators of his fpirit and of his grace, it is the fentence of our condemnation; if it be not a fruit of life to our foul, it is a fruit of death: terrible alternative which ought to excite our fears, but which ought not entirely to keep us away from the facred table. The bread which is there diftributed is the true nourifhment of our fouls, the ftrength of the ftrong, the fupport of the weak, the confolation of the afflicted, the pledge of a bleffed immortality: how dangerous would it then be to abftain from it? But, infinitely more fo would it be to eat it without preparation. On that account I again repeat to you, my deareft brethren, with the church, " Prepare " the way of the Lord:" let your preparations for receiving him be of long ftanding; banifh from your hearts whatever may offend him; inftruct yourfelves in the difpofitions which he exacts of thofe who receive him; ufe every effort to acquire them; there is no other mean of avoiding the rifk of an unworthy communion, and of attracting Jefus Chrift into your fouls.

This is an important matter, which demands all your attention. On one fide, there is queftion of making you fhun the horrible crime of profaning the body and the adorable blood of Jefus Chrift; on the other, of inftructing you how to reap from the communion all the grace which it is capable
of

of bringing forth in our hearts. What, then, are those preparations so essential towards a profitable and worthy communion? I reduce them to four, which shall be the subject and the division of this discourse.

REFLECTION I. The eucharist is an hidden manna; it is the food of the strong, a sensible and permanent testimony of the love of Jesus Christ, the continuation and the fulfilment of his sacrifice. Now, it is necessary to know how to discern this hidden manna from common food, lest it be taken unworthily: first preparation. It is the food of the strong; we ought, therefore, to examine ourselves before we venture to make use of it: second preparation. The testimony of the love of Jesus Christ; it can be received, therefore, only in remembrance of him, that is to say, in feeling aroused in his presence every tender and exquisite sensation which can be excited by the remembrance of a dear and beloved object: third preparation. It is the fulfilment of his sacrifice; every time, therefore, that we participate in it, we shew his death, and we ought to bring there a spirit of the cross and of martyrdom: fourth preparation. A respectful faith which enables us to discern, a prudent faith which makes us to examine, an ardent faith which enables us to love, an exalted faith which makes us to immolate; this is the summary of the apostle's doctrine, in relating to us the institution of the eucharist, and likewise that of all the saints with regard to the use of that adorable sacrament.

First preparation: a respectful faith which makes us to discern. Think not, my brethren, that I mean here to speak of that faith which distinguishes us from unbelievers. Where is the merit of believing when the prejudices of childhood have accustomed reason to it, and when belief is, as it were, born with us? Exertion would even be necessary to cast off its yoke; and, to pass from faith to error, a greater effort is perhaps required than to return from error to the truth. I speak of that lively faith which pierces through the clouds, which surround the throne of the Lamb; which sees him not mystically, and, as it were, through a glass, but face to face, if I may venture to say so, such as he is: of that faith which, in spite of the veil with which the true Moses covers himself on this holy mountain, fails not, however, to perceive all his glory, and to feel the inability of supporting his presence: of that faith which, without rashly examining into his majesty, is, nevertheless, overpowered with its lustre; which sees the celestial legions covering themselves with their wings, and the pillars of the firmament shaking before this King of terrible majesty: of that faith to which the senses could add nothing, and which is blessed, not because it believes without seeing, but because it almost sees in believing. I speak of that respectful faith which is seized with a religious trembling

at

at the sole presence of the sanctuary, which approaches the altar as Moses did the burning bush and the Israelites the thundering mountain; of that faith which feels the whole weight of God's presence, and, in fear, cries out like Peter, " De-
" part from me, for I am a sinful man, O Lord."
I speak of that faith of which the respect approaches almost to dread, and which it is even necessary to comfort; which, from the farthest spot that it discovers Jesus Christ upon the altar, feels an eclat of majesty which strikes and agitates it, and overpowers it with the dread of having ventured to come there without his order.

Behold, my brethren, what that discernment of faith is which the apostle demands of you. Great God! but doth any faith like this still remain upon the earth? Ah! in vain dost thou still manifest thy presence to the world; it knows thee no better than formerly: thy disciples themselves often know thee but according to the flesh; and, by being constantly with thee, their eyes become habituated, and almost no longer discern thee. When thou shalt shew thyself in the heavens upon a bright cloud, men shall be consumed with terror, and the impious shall seek to hide themselves in the deepest caverns, and shall entreat the mountains to cover their heads: ah! art thou not the same in the sanctuary as upon a cloud of glory? Are the heavens not opened above thee? When the priest pronounces the awful words, do not the heavenly spirits come down from heaven to officiate as thy servants, and to furround thee with their homages? Doſt thou not judge men upon that myſterious tribunal, and caſt looks of difcernment upon that multitude of worſhippers which fills thy temples? Doſt thou not feparate the goats from the ſheep? Doſt thou not there pronounce fentences of life and death? In one hand doſt thou not hold thy wrath, and in the other crowns? Doſt thou not feparate me there, and ſtamp, with an inviſible hand, upon my forehead the mark of my election or of my eternal reprobation? Alas! and, while thou art perhaps condemning me, I have the prefumption to draw near; while thou art caſting me off from before thee, I boldly prefent myfelf there; while thou perhaps layeſt open the abyfs to mark out my place, I impudently come to take it at thy table; while thou perhaps art ranging me with the children of wrath, I come to feat myfelf among the children of thy love: thy body, which giveth life, to me is a body of death; the Lamb without ſtain, which breaks the feven feals of the book of death, is the laſt feal which fills up and clofes that of mine iniquities; and thou, who ſhouldſt be my Saviour, becomeſt my guilt.

Ah! my brethren, God could not be feen in former times without inſtant death being the confequence. A whole people of Bethſhamites was exterminated for having only too curiouſly examined the ark: the angel of the Lord covers Heliodorus

liodorus with wounds, because he had dared to enter into the sanctuary of Jerusalem : the Israelites in the desert were not permitted even to approach the holy mountain from whence the Lord gave out his law ; the thunders of heaven defended its access ; terror and death every where preceded the face of the God of Abraham. What! because whirlwinds of fire no longer burst forth to punish the intruders and the profaners of our sanctuaries, respect and dread no longer accompany us there! Weak men, over whom the senses have such dominion, and who are never religious but when the God whom they worship is clothed in terror! For, say, were we to discern the body of the Lord ; did the faith of his presence make those grand impressions upon us which it would undoubtedly do were we openly to see him ; ah! would we tranquilly and almost unfeelingly come to seat ourselves at his table? Should a few moments, employed in reciting, with a languid heart and an absent mind, some slight formula, prepare us for an action so awful? Should a communion be the business of an idle morning perhaps gained from a customary slumber, or the vain cares of dress? Ah! the thoughts of it should long previously occupy and affect us: time should even be necessary to strengthen us, if I may venture to say so, against our own feelings of respect, and against the idea of his majesty : the days previous to this sacred festival should be days of retirement, of silence,

lence, of prayer, and of mortification : every day which brings us nearer to that bleffed term, fhould witnefs the increafe of our anxieties, our fears, our joy. The thoughts of it fhould be mingled with all our affairs, all our converfations, all our meals, all our relaxations, and even with our fleep itfelf: our mind, filled with faith, fhould feel its inability to pay attention to any thing elfe ; we fhould no longer perceive but Jefus Chrift : that image alone fhould fix all our attention. Behold what is called to difcern the body of the Lord.

I know that a worldly foul experiences inward agitations at the approach of a folemnity in which decency, and perhaps the law, require his prefence at the altar. But, O my God ! thou who fathom-eft thefe troubled hearts, are fuch thofe religious terrors of faith which fhould accompany an humble creature to thy altar? Ah! it is a fadnefs which operates death ; thefe are inquietudes which fpring from the embarraffments of a confcience which requires to be cleared. They are gloomy and fad, like the young man of the gofpel, whom thou orderedft to follow thee : they dread thefe bleffed days as fatal days : they look upon, as dark and gloomy myfteries, all the folemnities of Chriftians: the delights of thy feaft become a fatigue to them: they only partake of it like the blind and the lame of the gofpel : that is to fay, that the laws of thy church muft drag thefe faithlefs fouls, as if by force, from the public places, from the pleafures

of

of the age, and from the high way of perdition, and bring them, in spite of themselves, into the hall of thy feast : they delay, as much as possible, this religious duty ; the sole thought of it empoisons all their pleasures. Thou seest these unbelieving souls dragging on the load of a wavering conscience ; long hesitating betwixt their duties and their passions ; softening at last, by the choice of an indulgent confessor, the bitterness of this step ; appearing before thee, O God, who becomest their nourishment in this mystery of love, with as much reluctance as if they went to face an enemy ; and, perhaps, in the course of a whole year, experiencing no other circumstance to grieve them than that of receiving a God who gives himself to them. Ah ! Lord, therefore, thou invisibly rejectest these guilty victims who oblige themselves to be dragged by force to the altar, thou who willest none but voluntary sacrifices : therefore, thou reluctantly givest thyself to these ungrateful hearts who unwillingly receive thee ; and, wert thou still capable of being troubled in the spirit, as thou permittedst to be visible over the tomb of Lazarus, ah! we should once more see thee groaning when thou enteredst those profane mouths which, in thy sight, are only open sepulchres, as they have long been troubled before they could prevail upon themselves to appear here to pay thee that homage.

Let us acknowledge then, my dearest brethren, that the faith which makes us to discern the body of Jesus Christ is very rare. We believe, but with a superficial faith, which only skims the surface, as I may say, without entering into the efficacy and the mysteries of this sacrament: we believe, but with an indolent faith, which grounds its whole merit in submitting without opposition: we believe, but with an inconstant faith, which professes to believe, but denies it in works: we believe, but with an human faith, which is the gift rather of our fathers according to the flesh, than of the Father of light: we believe, but with a popular faith, which leaves us only weak and puerile ideas: we believe, but with a superstitious faith, which tends to nothing but vain and external homages: we believe, but with a faith merely of custom, which feels nothing: we believe, but with an insipid faith, which no longer discerns: we believe, but with a convenient faith, which is never followed with any effects: we believe, but with an ignorant faith, which fails either in respect through familiarity, or in love through its backwardness: we believe, but with a faith which enchains the mind, and leaves the heart to wander: lastly, we believe, but with a tranquil and vulgar faith, in which there is nothing either animated, grand, sublime, or worthy of the God which it discovers to us. Ah! to discern thy body, Lord, through faith, it is to prefer this heavenly bread to all the luxuries of Egypt; it is to render it the only consolation of our exilement, the tenderest soother of our sufferings,

ngs, the sacred remedy of all our evils, the continual desire of our souls; it is, through it, to find serenity under all the frowns of fortune, peace in all our troubles, and equanimity under all the stings of adversity; it is to find in it an assylum against our disgraces, a buckler to repel the flaming darts of Satan, a renovated ardour against the unavoidable lukewarmnesses of piety. To discern thy body, Lord, it is to devote more cares, more attention, and more circumspection towards worthily receiving thee, than to all the other actions of life. To discern thy body, Lord, it is to respect the temples in which thou art worshipped, the ministers who serve thee, and our bodies which receive thee. Let every man examine himself, let him thereupon listen to the testimony of his own conscience; and this is the second preparation, a prudent faith, which makes us to prove ourselves: let a man examine himself.

REFLECTION II. I know that we are unacquainted with our own heart: that the mind of man is not always informed of what takes place in man: that the passions seduce, examples harden, and prejudices drag us away; that our inclinations are always victorious over our lights; that the heart is never in the wrong; that, to examine one's self, is frequently only to harden one's self in error. Such is man, O my God! delivered up to his own understanding: he is continually deceived, and nothing appears to his eyes but under fictitious

ous colours: he but imperfectly knows thee; he hardly knows himself: he comprehends nothing in all that surrounds him; he takes darkness for light; he wanders from error to error; he quits not his errors when he returns to himself: the lights alone of thy faith can direct his judgments, open the eyes of his soul, become the reason of his heart, teach him to know himself, lay open the folds of self-love, expose all the artifices of the passions, and exalt him to that spiritual man, who conceives and judges of all. By the rules of faith, then, my brethren, must we examine ourselves; all human doctrines, the mollifications of custom, the examples of the multitude, our own understanding, are all deceitful guides: if ever it was of importance not to be deceived, it surely is in a conjuncture where sacrilege is the consequence of mistake.

But upon what shall we examine ourselves? Upon what! Upon the holiness of this sacrament, and upon our own corruption. It is the body of Jesus Christ, it is the bread of angels, it is the Lamb without stain, who admits none around his altar but those who either have not defiled their garment or who have purified them in the blood of penitence. And what art thou, forward soul, whom I see approaching with so much confidence? Bringest thou there thy modesty, thine innocence? Hast thou always possessed the vessel of thy body in honour and in holiness? Hath thy heart not been

been dragged through the filth of a thousand paffions? In the sight of God, is not thy soul that blackened brand of which the prophet speaks, which impure flames had blasted and consumed from thine earliest years, and which is no longer but a shocking vestige of their fury? Art thou not totally covered with shameful wounds? Is there a spot upon thy body free from the mark of some crime? Where wilt thou place the body of the Lamb? What! it shall rest upon thy tongue; that pure and immaculate body upon a tomb which hath never exhaled but infection and stench; that body immolated with so much gentleness upon the instrument of all thy vengeances and bitterness; that crucified body on the seat of all thy sensualities and debauches. What! he shall descend to thy heart? But will he therein find where to repose his head? Hast thou not changed that holy temple into a den of thieves? What! thou art going to place him among so many impure pleasures, profane attachments, ambitious projects, emotions of hatred, of jealousy, and of pride; it is amidst all these monsters that thou hast prepared his dwelling-place? Ah! thou deliverest him up to his enemies, thou once more puttest him into the hands of his executioners.

You have examined yourselves, say you to me. Before drawing near you have made your confession. Ah! my brethren, and, with the same mouth from which you have so lately vented all

your iniquities, you go to receive Jesus Christ?
And, the heart still reeking with a thousand ill-extinguished passions, and which to-morrow shall see in all their wonted vigour, you dare to approach the altar with your present, and to participate in the holy mysteries? And, the imagination still stained with the ideas of those recent excesses which you have just been recounting to the priest, you go to eat of the pure bread of the chosen? What! on your departure from the tribunal the communion, in your eyes, supplies the place, and answers the purposes of penitence? From guilt you rush headlong to the altar? In place of dissolving in tears with the penitent, you come to rejoice with the righteous? In place of nourishing yourself with the bread of tribulation, you run to a delicious feast? In place of lingering at the gate of the temple, like the publican, you confidently draw near to the holy of holies? In former times, a penitent came not to the table of the Lord but after whole years of humiliation, of abstinence, of prayer, and of austerity, and they purified themselves in tears, in grief, and in the public exercises of a painful discipline: they became new men; an heart-felt regret was the only vestige of their former life: no traces of their past crimes were to be recognised but in the grace of penitence, and of the macerations which, at last, had expiated them; and the eucharist was that heavenly bread which no man, a sinner, then eat but with the

sweat

sweat of his brow. And, at present, to have confessed crimes is believed to have already punished them; that an absolution, which is only given under the suppofition of an humbled and contrite heart, actually creates, and renders it so; that all the purity required of thofe who receive the body of Jefus Chrift, is, that they have laid open all the virulence and infection of their fores. Unworthy communions, my brethren; you eat and you drink your damnation: in vain may we comfort you; can man juftify when God condemns?

Befides, it is pure and without leaven; it requires to be exempted from leaven to eat of it: now, candidly, have thofe worldly perfons, whom the circumftances of a folemnity determine to approach the holy table, quitted the old leaven in prefenting themfelves at the altar? Do they not bring along with them every paffion ftill living in its roots? Judge thereof from the confequences. On their departure from thence they find themfelves exactly the fame; hatreds are not extinguifhed, the empire of voluptuoufnefs is not weakened, animation in the purfuit of pleafures is not blunted, inclination for the world is not lefs violent; in a word, cupidity has loft nothing of its rights. We fee no greater precautions than before againft dangers already encountered: the fociety of the world again refumes its influence; converfations are renewed; the paffions awaken; every thing refumes its former train, and, in addition to their former

state,

state, they have now to add the profanation of this awful mystery. How is this? It is that a simple confession is no examination of one's self.

Again, it is the food of the strong. A weak, sickly, and wavering soul, who turns with every wind; who gives way to the first obstacle; who founders upon the first rock; who escapes every moment from the guidance of grace; who has a long experience of his own fragility; who never brings to the altar but promises an hundred times violated, but momentary sensations of devotion, which the very first pleasure stifles; who, from his earliest years, has been in the alternate practice of weaknesses and holy things, and who has seen a constant succession of crimes to repentance, and of the sacrament to relapses: is a soul of this description a strong soul? Is it not its duty to examine itself, to increase, to strengthen, and to exercise itself in charity? Scarcely in a state to digest milk, ought it to load itself with solid food, and such as can serve the purposes of nourishment only to the perfect man?

It is written in the law that, if the sin-offering be placed in an earthen vessel, the vessel shall immediately be broken; but, if in a brazen vessel, it shall be both scoured and rinsed in water. Would these circumstances, so carefully and minutely marked, be worthy of the holy Spirit, did they not contain instructions and mysteries? Doth not a weak soul, who receives the true victim, resemble
that

that earthen veſſel which falls in pieces, as I may ſay, being unable to endure the violence of this ſacred fire? On the contrary, the firm ſoul, like the braſs, is purified, loſes in it all its ſtains, and comes out from it more beautiful and brilliant than before. What is the conſequence, according to Jeſus Chriſt, of putting new wine into old bottles; do they not burſt, and allow the wine to be loſt upon the ground? What is the application of this parable? You put the myſtical wine, that wine whoſe ſtrength operates an holy intoxication in pure ſouls, into a decayed and worn-out heart, which long-eſtabliſhed paſſions have almoſt conſumed. Ah! I am not ſurpriſed that it is unable to endure its ſtrength, that the blood of Jeſus Chriſt cannot tarry there, and that, on the firſt occaſion, you ſhed and trample it under foot; it required to have gradually accuſtomed your heart to it, to have prepared it by retirement, by prayer, by daily conqueſts over yourſelf; and, through the means of theſe continued and ſalutary trials, to have ſtrengthened and rendered it capable of receiving Jeſus Chriſt.

It is the paſſover of Chriſtians: now, Jeſus Chriſt celebrates his paſſover with his diſciples alone.

Now, what is it to be his diſciples? It is to renounce one's ſelf, to carry his croſs, to follow him. Are you mortified in your deſires, patient under your afflictions? Do you walk in the ways in which Jeſus Chriſt hath walked before you? To be be his disciples is mutually to love each other; and how often have you come to eat of this bread of union, how often have you made your appearance at this banquet of charity, your heart inwardly loaded with gall and bitterness against your brother? How often have you come to offer up your present at the altar without having reconciled yourself with him?

Lastly, It is a God so pure, that the stars are dimmed in his presence; so holy, that, after the fall of the angel, heaven was rent and the abyss opened that he might place an eternal chaos between sin and him; so jealous, that a single wandering desire injures and offends him. Thus, my brethren, it is necessary that you examine yourselves upon your own inclinations: are not those desires of the age, of which the apostle speaks, still nourished within you? Render glory to God, and, in his presence, search your hearts to the bottom. I go to eat of the body of Jesus Christ, and to convert it into my own substance; but, when he shall have entered into my soul, he who knows and discerns its intentions and most secret inclinations, will he find nothing there unworthy of the sanctity of his presence? He will immediately proceed to the spring and to the causes of my wanderings; he will examine whether their source be dried up, or their course only suspended; he will perceive what are still the dominant inclinations of my soul, and what is the weight which still turns the

balance

balance of my heart: Alas! will he be enabled to say, as formerly when entering into the house of Zaccheus, "This day is salvation come to this house?" Have I sincerely cast off that passion so fatal to my innocence; that bitterness of heart of which I have so lately expressed my detestation at the feet of the priest; that idolising of riches which leads me to grasp at even iniquitous profits; that madness of gaming by which my health, my affairs, and my salvation are injured; that vexatious and variable temper which the slightest contradiction inflames; that vanity which leads me to soar above the rank in which my ancestors had left me; that envy which, with malignant eyes, has always viewed the reputation and the prosperity of my equals; that proud and censorious air which judges upon all, and never judges itself; that supreme influence over me of effeminacy and voluptuousness, which are, as it were, interwoven with the foundation and principle of my being? Has the avowal, which I come from making, of my weaknesses, to the minister of Jesus Christ, rooted them out from my heart? Am I a new creature? He alone who is regenerated can aspire to this heavenly bread which I am going to eat: in thine eyes am I so, O my God? Do I not bear the name of living, though still, in effect, dead? Will the Mighty, entering into my soul, possess it in peace, and will he not find there seven unclean spirits who shall chase him from it? Instruct me, Lord, and suffer not that
thy

thy Christ, that thy holy descend into corruption. Such, my brethren, is the way to examine ourselves. The Lord had formerly forbidden the Jews to offer up honey and leaven in the sacrifices: see if, in approaching the altar, you bring not with you the leaven of your crimes, and the honey of voluptuousness: that is to say, both that relish for the world and for pleasure, and that effeminate and sensual character, enemy of the cross, and incompatible with salvation. Approach not, if you do not feel yourself sufficiently pure: this holy body, says the prophet, would not purge your iniquity, it would only increase it; your religion would be vain, your heart idolatrous, your sacrifice a sacrilege.

Examine, therefore, yourself, and afterwards eat of the heavenly bread. But we are not to stop at the simply discerning and examining. Hitherto you have only removed the obstacles; but you have not settled the last preparations: you have lopt off whatever might repel Jesus Christ from your soul; but you have not acquired what might attract him to it: you have arranged so as not to receive him unworthily; but you have not so as to receive him with fruit: it is not sufficient to be free from guilt; it is necessary to be clothed with righteousness and sanctity: it is little not to betray him like Judas; it is necessary to love him with the other disciples: it is little, in a word, to be no longer profane, worldly, voluptuous, effeminate,

nate, proud, and revengeful; it is neceſſary to be ſedate, meek, humble, firm, chaſte, believing, Chriſtian. " As oft as ye do this do it in remembrance " of me:" this is the third diſpoſition to communicate in remembrance of Jeſus Chriſt.

REFLECTION III. What is it to communicate in remembrance of Jeſus Chriſt? It is, in the *firſt* place, internally to deſcribe all that paſſed in the heart of Jeſus Chriſt in inſtituting this adorable ſacrament. " With deſire," ſaid he to his diſciples, " I have deſired to eat this paſſover with you be- " fore I ſuffer." He ſighed for that bleſſed moment; he never loſt ſight of it; in the remembrance of it he was comforted for all the bitterneſs of his paſſion. What did he thereby mean to teach us? Ah! that we ought to bring to this divine table an heart enflamed, penetrated, conſumed; an eager, earneſt, and impatient heart; an hunger and a thirſt after Jeſus Chriſt; an inclination rouſed by love: in a word, what I have termed a burning deſire which impels us to love. This bread, ſaid a father, requires a famiſhed heart. Ah! Lord, ſays then the believing ſoul with St Auguſtin, who will give me that thou mayſt enter into my heart to take poſſeſſion of it; wholly to fill it; to reign there alone; to dwell there with me even to the conſummation of ages; to be mine all; there to conſtitute my pureſt delights; to ſhed through it a thouſand inward conſolations; to ſatiate, to gladden it, to make me forget my miſeries, mine anxieties, my vain pleasures, all mankind, the whole universe, and to leave me wholly to thee, to enjoy thy presence, thy conversation, and all the delights which thou preparest for those who love thee? Perhaps, Lord, the tenement of my soul is not yet sufficiently embellished to receive thee; but come and be thyself all its ornament. Perhaps thou perceivest stains which repel thee from it; but thy divine touch will purify them all. Perhaps thou discoverest invisible enemies still there; but art not thou the mighty? Thy sole presence will disperse them, and peace alone will reign there when once thou shalt be in possession of it. Perhaps it has wrinkles which render it forbidding; but thou wilt renew its youth like that of the eagle. Perhaps it is still stained with the blemishes of its former infidelities; but thy blood will wash them entirely out. Come, Lord, and tarry not; every blessing will attend me with thee: despised, persecuted, afflicted, despoiled, calumniated, I will consider as nothing my sorrows from the moment that thou shalt come to alleviate them: honoured, favoured, exalted, surrounded with abundance, these vain prosperities will cease to interest me, will appear as nothing from the moment thou shalt have made me to taste how sweet thou art. Such are the desires which ought to lead us to the altar.

But, alas! many bring there only a criminal disgust and repugnance: occasions are required to
induce

induce them to determine upon it; of themselves they would never have thought of it. But, what do I fay, occafions? Thunders and anathemas are required. Good God! that the church fhould be reduced, through the lukewarmnefs of Chriftians, to make a law to them of participating in thy body and in thy blood! That penalties and threatenings fhould be required to lead them to thy altar, and to oblige them to feat themfelves at thy table! That the Chriftian's only felicity upon earth fhould be a painful precept to him! That the moft glorious privilege with which men can be favoured by thee fhould be an irkfome reftraint to them! Others approach it with an heavy heart, a pallid appetite, a foul wholly of ice: people who live in the commerce of pleafures and of the facrament; who participate at the table of Satan and at that of Jefus Chrift; who have ftated days for the Lord and days alloted for the age: people to whom a communion cofts only a day of reftraint and refervation; who, on that day, neither gamble, fhew themfelves, fee company, nor fpeak evil. But this exertion goes no further; all devotion ceafes with the folemnity; it is a deed of ceremony; after this fhort fufpenfion they are at eafe with themfelves; they tranquilly return to their former ways; for that was a point agreed upon with themfelves; they fmoothly continue to live in this mixture of holy and of profane: the facrament calms us upon pleafures; pleafures to be more tranquil on the

fide

side of the conscience lead us to the sacrament; and they are almost good in order to be worldly without scruple. Thus they bring to the altar a taste cloyed with the amusements and the delights of the age, with the embarrassments of affairs, with the tumult of the passions: they feel not the ineffable sweets of this heavenly food; they retrace, even at the foot of the throne of grace, the images of those pleasures they have so lately left: interests which occupy us, projects which puzzle us, ideas which force us from the altar to drag us back to the world, make much deeper impressions upon the heart than the presence of Jesus Christ. But is it not, Lord, against those monsters of Christians that thy prophet, incensed, formerly said to thee, " Ah! Lord, let thy table become a snare before " them; and that which should have been for " their welfare, let it become a trap."

In the *second* place, to communicate in remembrance of Jesus Christ, is to wish to awaken, through the presence of this sacred pledge, every impression which his memory can make upon an heart which loves him. The firmest bonds are loosened by absence: Jesus Christ well foresaw that, ascending up to heaven, his disciples would insensibly forget his kindnesses and his divine instructions. Alas! Moses remains only forty days upon the mountain, and already the Israelites cease to remember the miracles that he had wrought to deliver them from Egypt. We wot not, said they
among

among themselves, what is become of this Moses, the man that brought us out of the land of Egypt; let us make gods who shall go before and defend us against our enemies. Jesus Christ, to guard against these inconstancies of the human heart, wished, in ascending to the heavenly Sion, to leave us a pledge of his presence: it is there that he wishes we should come to console ourselves for his sensible absence ; it is there that we ought to find a more lively remembrance of his wonders, of his doctrine, of his kindnesses, of his divine person ; it is there that, under mysterious signs, we come to see him born at Bethlehem, brought up at Nazareth, holding discourse with men, and traversing the cities of Judea, working signs and miracles which no one before him had ever done, calling as followers rude disciples, in order to make them masters of the world, confounding the hypocrisy of the Pharisees, announcing salvation to men, leaving marks every where of his power and goodness, entering in triumph into Jerusalem, led to mount Calvary, expiring upon a cross, conqueror of death and of hell, leading with him into heaven those who were captives as the trophies of his victory, and forming afterwards his church with the overflowing of his spirit and the abundance of his gifts ; in a word, we shall there find him in all his mysteries.

You envy, said St Chrysostom, the lot of a woman who touches his garments, of a sinful one who bathes his feet with her tears, of the women of Galilee who had the happiness to follow and to serve him in the course of his ministry, of his disciples with whom he familiarly conversed, of the people of those times who listened to the words of grace and of salvation which proceeded from his mouth; you call blessed those who saw him; many prophets and kings have vainly wished it; but you, my brethren, come to the altars and you shall see him; you shall touch him; you shall give him an holy kiss, you shall bathe him with your tears, and your bowels shall bear him even like those of Mary. Alas! our fathers went into the holy land to worship the traces of his feet, and the places that he had consecrated with his presence. Here, they were told, he proposed the parable of the good shepherd and the lost sheep; here he reconciled an adulteress; here he comforted a sinful woman; here he sanctified the marriage and the feast with his presence; here he multiplied the loaves to fill a famished multitude; here he checked his disciples who wanted to bring fire from heaven upon a criminal city; here he deigned to hold converse with a woman of Samaria; here he suffered the children around him, and rebuked those who wanted to drive them away; here he restored sight to the blind, made the lame to walk, delivered those possessed with devils, made the dumb to speak, and the deaf to hear. At these words our fathers felt themselves transported with an holy joy; they shed tears of tenderness and of

religion

religion upon that bleſſed land; this ſight, theſe images, carried them back to the times, to the actions, to the myſteries of Jeſus Chriſt, inſpired them with freſh ardour, and conſoled their faith; ſinners found there a ſweet truſt, the weak a new force, and the righteous new deſires.

Ah! Chriſtians; no, it is not neceſſary to croſs the ſeas; ſalvation is at your hand; the word which we preach to you will be, if you wiſh it, upon your mouth and in your heart: open the eyes of faith, behold theſe altars; they are not places conſecrated formerly with the preſence, it is Jeſus Chriſt himſelf: approach in remembrance of him; come to rekindle all that your heart hath ever felt of tender, affecting, and lively, for this divine Saviour. Let the remembrance of his meekneſs, which would not permit him to break the reed already bruiſed, nor to extinguiſh the yet glimmering lamp, quiet your tranſports and your impatiencies: let the remembrance of his toils and of his troubleſome life overwhelm you for your effeminacy: let the remembrance of his modeſty and of his humility, which made him fly when they wanted to make him king, cure you of your vanities, of your ſchemes, of your frivolous pretenſions: let the remembrance of his faſt for forty days reproach you for your ſenſualities: let the remembrance of his zeal againſt the profaners of the temple teach you with what reſpect, and with what holy dread you ought to enter there: let the remembrance of the

ſimplicity

simplicity and the frugality of his manners condemn the vain superfluities and the excesses of yours: let the remembrance of his retirement and of his prayers warn you to fly the world, to retire sometimes into the secrecy of your house, to pass, at least, some portion of the day in the indispensible practice of prayer: let the remembrance of his tender compassion for a famished people give you bowels of commiseration for the unfortunate: let the remembrance of his holy discourses teach you to converse innocently, holily, and profitably with men: in a word, let the remembrance of all his virtues, there more lively, more present to the heart and to the mind, correct you of all your weaknesses: this is what is called to communicate in remembrance of him.

But, to bring continually to the altar the same weaknesses; to familiarise ourselves in such a manner with the body of Jesus Christ, that it no longer awakens in us a new sentiment, but leaves us always such as we are; to nourish ourselves with a divine food, yet not to increase; frequently to approach this burning furnace without any additional heat to your lukewarmness; to appear there with faults an hundred times detested yet still dear, with habits of imperfection, which, though light in themselves, are no longer so, however, through the attachment and the bent which render them inevitable to us, and through the circumstance of the sacrament which there is the risk of profaning; to

make

make profession of piety, of estrangement from the world, to be almost every day in the commerce of holy things, and to have determined, as it were, upon a limited point of virtue beyond which never to rise, and, after ten years exercise of piety, to be no farther advanced than at first, on the contrary, to have rather relaxed from the first fervour; to be continually applying to this divine remedy, yet to feel no alteration for the better in the disease; to heap sacrament upon sacrament, if I may dare to say so, yet never to empty the heart in order to make room for this heavenly food; to nourish envies, animosities, secret attachments, a fund of sensuality, of vain desires to please, to be courted, to be prosperous; to permit, in conversation, the habit of witticisms and every freedom of speech upon others, of endless nothings, of sentiments wholly profane, of quibbles which wound sincerity, of concealments by which falsehood becomes familiar, of hastinesses and bursts of passion; to be jealous to an extreme wherever self is concerned; to rise indignant at the smallest appearance of neglect, and to be incapable of digesting a single disobliging gesture; and yet, with all this, to feed upon the bread of angels; O my God! how much less than this ought to make us tremble!

But, is it to eat of this bread unworthily, to eat it with so many imperfections and weaknesses? Who knows this, O Lord, but thee? All that we know is, that it is not communicating in remembrance of thee; that many righteousnesses shall appear in thy sight, at the great day, as a soiled cloth; that many, who had even prophesied in thy name, shall be rejected; and that every thing is to be dreaded in this state. Peter is not admitted to thy supper till after thou hadst washed his feet; nevertheless, thou assurest us that he was altogether pure. Magdalene is sent away, and thou sayest unto her, " Woman, touch me not," because a too sensible affection was the cause of her eagerness; and, nevertheless, her love had been great, and she had washed thy sacred feet and her own sins with her tears. And we, Lord, full of wants, empty of sincere fruits of penitence, made up wholly of effeminacy and sensualities, lukewarm and without desire, fixed in a certain state of languishing and imperfect piety, more sustained by habitude and the engagements of an holy profession than by thy grace, or by a lively and solid faith, alas! we make thy body our ordinary food. What inexplicable gulphs, Lord! What a train of crimes, perhaps, not known, unrepented of, multiplied to infinity, and which are as the shoot upon which a thousand new profanations are afterwards grafted! What gulphs, once more! And what terrible secrets shall thy light make manifest to us at the great day! In thy sight, O my God, what am I! I can neither offend nor please thee by halves; my condition admits not of those middle states of virtue which hold, as it were, a mid way betwixt innocence and guilt;

guilt; if not a faint, I am a monster; if not a vessel of honour, I am a vessel of shame; if not an angel of light, there is no room to hesitate, I am an angel of darkness; and, if not a living temple of thy spirit, I must be its profaner. Good God! what powerful motives for vigilance, for self-examination, for circumspection, for approaching thine altars with trembling; for humility, tears, and compunction, while waiting the manifestation of thine adorable judgments! But still, my brethren, it is not enough to communicate in remembrance of Jesus Christ; and, in order to retrace his life, it is likewise necessary, and this is the last disposition, to renew the remembrance of his death, and to shew him whenever we eat of his body and drink of his blood; and this is what I call a noble faith which leads us to sacrifice.

REFLECTION IV. As oft as you shall eat of the body and drink of the blood of the Lord, you will shew his death until the kingdom of God shall come. How this? Literally speaking his death is shewn, because this mystery was a prelude to his passion; because Judas there determined to betray him; because Jesus Christ, eager to undergo that baptism of blood with which he was to be baptised, anticipated its fulfilment, and sacrificed himself beforehand by the mystical separation of his body and of his blood; because the eucharist is the permanent sacrifice of the church, the fruit and the fulness of that of the cross: lastly, because Jesus Christ

Christ is there as in a state of death; he hath a mouth and speaks not; eyes and uses them not; feet and walks not. But, my brethren, in that sense the impious, equally as the just man, shews the death of the Lord as oft as he eats of his body: it is a mystery, and not a merit; it is the nature of the sacrament, and not the privilege of him who receives it; it is a consequence of its institution, and not a disposition for approaching it. Now, the design of the apostle here, is to prevent the abuses, to instruct believers how to eat worthily of the body of the Lord, to explain to them, in the mysteries contained in this sacrament, the dispositions which it requires. There is a way, therefore, of shewing the death of the Lord, which should be wholly in our hearts, which disposes and prepares us, which fits the situation of our soul to the nature of this mystery, which makes us to bear upon our body the mortification of Jesus Christ, which immolates and crucifies us with him. Let us resume the reasons we have touched upon, and change the letter into spirit.

1*stly*, The death of the Lord is shewn, because this mystery was a prelude to his passion. In former times the eucharist was a prelude to martyrdom. From the moment that the rage of the tyrant was declared, and the persecution begun, all the believers run to provide themselves with this bread of life; they carried this precious trust into their houses: death seemed less terrible to them

when

when they had before their eyes the beloved pledge of their immortality : they even defired it ; and the ineffable confolations which the prefence of Jefus Chrift, hidden under myftical veils, already fhed through their foul, made them to long for that torrent of delight with which he will overflow his chofen when they fhall behold him face to face. Were they dragged to prifon, and, like felons, loaded with irons, they of whom the world was unworthy; they carefully concealed the divine eucharift in their bofom ; they feafted upon it in the hope of martyrdom ; they grew fat upon this heavenly food like pure victims, that their facrifice might be more pleafing to the Lord. Chafte virgins, fervent believers, holy minifters, partook altogether of the bleffed bread : and what delight even in their chains ! What ferenity of mind in thefe dark and gloomy abodes ! What fongs of thankfgiving in thefe horrible places where the eye encountered nothing but the fad images of death, and preparations for the moft cruel tortures ! How often did they fay to Jefus Chrift, prefent with them in this adorable facrament: Ah ! we fear no ill, Lord, fince thou art with us: though hofts furround us yet will we not be afraid ; our enemies may deftroy our bodies, but thou wilt reftore them to us glorious and immortal ; for who can deftroy thofe whom the Father hath beftowed upon thee ? Bleffed chains which thou deigneft to fuftain ! Holy prifons which thou confecrateft with

thy

thy prefence! Beloved dungeons in which thou filleft our fouls with fo many lights! Precious death which is to unite us with thee, and to withdraw the veil which conceals thee from our fight! Thence what fortitude under their tortures! Filled with the body of Jefus Chrift, wafhed in his blood, they quitted their prifons, fays an holy father, like lions out of their den ftill raging and thirfting for death and carnage; they flew upon the fcaffolds, and, with an holy pride, launched here and there looks of confidence and magnanimity which appalled the moft ferocious tyrants, and even difarmed their executioners: they fhewed then the death of the Lord in preparing themfelves for martyrdom by the communion.

The tranquility of our ages, and the religion of the Cefars leave us no longer the fame hope; death is no longer the reward of faith, and the eucharift makes no more martyrs: but have we not domeftic perfecutors? Has our faith only tyrants to dread? And is there not a martyrdom of love as well as of blood? In approaching the altars then, my brethren, a believing foul fighs for the diffolution of his mortal body; for, could he love this life, and fhew the death of Jefus Chrift, and renew, in thefe myftical figns, his quitting the world to go to his Father? He complains of the length of his exilement; he bears, to the foot of the fanctuary, a fpirit of death and of martyrdom: " Ah!
" Lord, fince thou art dead and crucified to the
" world,

" world, why detain me there? What can I find
" upon the earth worthy of my heart, feeing thou
" art no longer there? The myftery itfelf, which
" fhould confole me through thy prefence, recalls
" to me thy death: thefe covers which veil thee
" are an artifice of thy love; and thou half con-
" cealeft thyfelf only to infpire my heart with the
" defire of fully beholding thee. Vain things,
" what offer ye to me but an empty fhadow of the
" God whom I feek? What anfwer do ye make
" when my foftened heart bends towards you to
" foothe its anxieties? Return, fay you, to him
" who hath made us; we groan in awaiting his
" coming to deliver us from this fervitude, which
" makes us fubfervient to the paffions and to the
" errors of men: feek him not among us, thou wilt
" not find him, he is rifen, he is no longer here;
" if he appear it is only to die again; recall the
" defires and the affections which thou meant to
" place upon us, and turn them towards heaven;
" the bridegroom hath been carried away, the
" earth is no longer for a Chriftian now but a
" vale of mourning and tears: fuch is what they
" anfwer to me. What then detains me here,
" Lord? What are the ties and the charms which
" can attach me to the world? Reftlefs in plea-
" fures, impatient in abfence, tired of the conver-
" fations and the commerce of men, afraid of foli-
" tude; without relifh for the world, without relifh
" for virtue; doing the evil I would not, and leav-
" ing

" ing undone the good that I would; what keeps
" me here? What delays the diffolution of this
" body of fin? What prevents me from foaring
" with the wings of the dove upon the holy moun-
" tain? I feel that I fhould then be happy; I could
" then feaft at all times upon this delicious bread:
" I tafte no real delight but at the feet of thy al-
" tars; thefe are, indeed, the happieft moments
" of my life: but they are fo fhort, and I muft fo
" foon return to the infipidities and to the difgufts
" of the world; I am under the neceffity of being
" fo long abfent from thee: no, Lord, there is no
" perfect happinefs on the earth, and death is a
" gain to whoever knows to love thee."

Are thefe our fentiments, my brethren, when we draw near to the altars? Where are now the Chriftians who, like the firft believers, await the bleffed hope, and haften, by their fighs, the end of their banifhment, and the coming of Jefus Chrift? This is a refinement of piety of which they have no idea; it is merely a language of the fpeculift; it is, however, the ground-work of religion, and the firft ftep of faith. The neceffity of dying is confidered as a cruel punifhment; the fole idea of death, with which our fathers were fo comforted, makes us to fhudder; the end of life is the term of our pleafures in place of being that of our fuf-ferings; the attentions paid to the body are end-lefs; our precautions extend even to abfurdity; or, if it fometimes happen that this laft moment is defired,

tired, it is in confequence of being wearied of life and of its chagrins; it is a difgrace, an habitual infirmity preying upon us, a revolution in our worldly matters which leaves no more pleafures to be expected here below, the difappointment of an eftablifhment, a death, an accident, or, laftly, a difguft and a wifh of felf-love; we tire of being unfortunate, but we are not eager to go to be reunited with Jefus Chrift: and, with all this, they come to eat of the Lord's fupper, to renew the remembrance of his paffion, and to fhew his death until he fhall come; what an outrage!

2*dly*, His death is fhewn in this myftery, becaufe Judas there finally determined upon delivering him up. Now, what does this remembrance exact of us? Ah! my brethren, an ardent defire of repairing, by our homages, the impiety of fo many fhocking communions which crucify Jefus Chrift afrefh. So many impure, revengeful, worldly, and extortioning finners, of every people and of every nation, receive him into profane mouths: we ought to feel the infults which Jefus Chrift thereby fuffers; to humble ourfelves before him, feeing that his moft fignal bleffing is become the occafion of the greateft crimes; to tremble for ourfelves; to admire his goodnefs, which, for the profit of a fmall number of chofen, hath gracioufly been willing to fubmit to the indignities of that endlefs multitude of finners, of all ages and of all times, who have, and ftill continue to difhonour him; to avert, by the tears of our heart and a thousand inward lamentations, the scourges which unworthy communions never fail to draw down upon the earth. For, if the apostle formerly lamented that general plagues, epidemical diseases, and sudden deaths were only a consequence of the profanation of the sacrament; ah! thy finger has long been upon us, Lord; the cup of thy wrath is poured out upon our cities and provinces; thou armest kings against kings, and nations against nations: nothing is now spoken of but battles and the rumours of war; our fields are stricken with sterility; our families are consumed by the sword of the enemy, and the father is deprived of the only prop and consolation of his old age; we groan under burdens, which, though keeping the enemy of the state from our walls, yet leave us a prey to famine and want; the arts are now almost of no avail to the people; commerce languishes, and industry can hardly supply the common necessaries of life; yet what are even the public calamities, when compared with the private miseries known to thee alone? We have seen our citizens mowed down by hunger and death, and our cities turned into frightful deserts; the enemy of thy name takes advantage of our dissentions, and usurps thine inheritance.

Whence proceed these scourges, great God! so continued and so terrible? Where are formed those clouds of wrath and indignation which have so long been pouring out their torrents upon us? Is it it not to punish the sacrilegious that thou art armed? Do not the outrages which are every day committed against thy body, at the feet of the altars, draw down upon us these marks of thy wrath? O strike us then, Lord, and avenge thy glory; stop not the arm of thy angel who hovers over us; let the houses where the traces of a profane blood are still imprinted not be spared; thine anger is just. But no, give us not the water of gall to drink because we have sinned against thee; give peace in our days; listen to the cries of the righteous who entreat it of thee: " Lord," say they with the prophet, " we looked for peace, but no good came; " and for a time of health, and behold trouble." Terminate the profanations which are ever the attendants of wars; cease to punish sacrileges by multiplying them on the earth; once more restore majesty to so many temples profaned, worship and dignity to so many churches despoiled, peace to our cities, abundance to our families, consolation and gladness of heart to Israel; let the child be restored to his father, and the husband to the desolate wife; and, if our evils touch thee not, O pay attention to the miseries of thy church.

3*dly*, The death of the Lord is shewn in this mystery, for Jesus Christ sacrifices himself in it, by the mystical separation of his body and of his blood. What follows from thence? That we must be at the foot of the altar as if we were at the foot of the cross: that we must enter into the dispositions

of

of the disciples and of the women of Jerusalem who received the dying sigh of Jesus, and were present at the consummation of his sacrifice. Now, what hatred had they not against a world which had crucified their Master? What measures did they think it necessary to keep with his murderers? Were they afraid of declaring themselves the disciples of him who had so openly declared himself their Saviour, and that at the price of his blood? Did they not say to the heavenly Father, Ah! strike us, Lord, who are the guilty, and spare the innocent. What horror at their past faults, which had attached so good a Master to the cross! What a lively impression in their heart of his sufferings! Thus, my brethren, still to keep measures with the age, to be afraid of declaring openly for piety, to be ashamed of the cross of Jesus Christ, to calculate your works of devotion in such a way that an air and a favour of the world may still pervade the whole: not boldly to confess Jesus Christ; to be afraid of abstaining from a theatre where he is insulted, from an assembly where he is offended, from a proceeding by which innocence must suffer, from I know not what train of life of which the world makes a necessity to you, from certain maxims which wound the gospel, and which custom has established as laws; to pretend to keep up all these conciliatory measures with the world, and yet to come to eat the passover with the disciples of Jesus Christ; to preserve a correspondence with

his

his enemies, and yet to feat yourselves at his table; to esteem the maxims which crucify him, and yet to wish to be the spectators and the faithful companions of his cross; ah! it is a contradiction.

He hath overcome the world; he hath fixed it to his cross: along with himself he hath given death to its maxims and errors: consequently, to shew his death in the communion is to renew the memory of his victory. And, if the world lives and still reigns in your heart, my brother, do you not annihilate the fruit of his death? Do you not contest with Jesus Christ the honour of his triumph? And, in place of shewing his death, do you not come to renew it with his enemies?

Besides, in the *fourth* place, his death is shewn in this mystery, for it is the consummation of the sacrifice of the cross, and he applies the fruit of it to us. Now, what gives us a right to the fruit of the cross, and, consequently, to the communion? Sufferance, mortification, and a penitent and inward life. For, say, living in delights, shall you dare to nourish a body, like yours, enervated by pleasures, flattered, caressed; shall you dare, I say, to nourish it with a crucified body? Shall you dare to incorporate Jesus Christ, dying and crowned with thorns, with delicate and sensual members? Would this connection not be horrible? Will you dare, by converting his body into your own substance, to transform it into an effeminate and voluptuous body? Ah! it would be the perfection

of

of iniquity. To be nourished with the body of Jesus Christ your members must become his members; his body must take the figure of your body. Now, his body is a crucified body; his members are suffering members: and, if you live without suffering; if you bear not upon your body the mortification of Jesus Christ; if, perhaps, you have never practised a single instance of self-denial; if your days are passed in a tranquil effeminacy; if afflictions excite impatience; if you feel hurt at every thing which opposes your humour; if you prescribe to yourself no works of mortification; if those sent to you by heaven are unwillingly and unthankfully received; how will you that you unite your body to that of Jesus Christ? This is never reflected upon, my brethren; and, nevertheless, a soft and sensual life can be a presage only of an unworthy communion.

Lastly, The death of the Lord is shewn in this mystery, for he is there himself as in a state of death. He hath a mouth and speaketh not; eyes and useth them not; feet and walketh not. View then, my brother, and act according to this model; behold how you ought to shew his death in partaking of his body: you must bring there eyes instructed to be closed for the earth; a tongue accustomed to silence, or to sayings of God, as St Paul says; feet and hands immovable for the works of sin; senses either extinguished or mortified: in a word, to bring there an universal death over your body: the state of Jesus Christ in the eucharist is the state of the Christian on earth; a state of retreat, of silence, of patience, of humiliation, of divorce from the senses. For, what is Jesus Christ in the eucharist? He is in the world as if not there; he is in the midst of men, but invisible; he hears their vain discourses, their chimerical plans, their frivolous expectations, but he enters not into them; he sees their solicitudes, their agitations, and their enterprises, and he allows them to act; divine honours are paid to him, and he is insulted; and, ever the same, he seems insensible alike to the insults as to the homages: he looks on while families, empires, and ages are renewed; manners are changed; the taste of men and of ages are incessantly fluctuating: he sees customs sink into decay and then revive; the figure of this world in an eternal revolution; his inheritance divided; wars, seditions, and unexpected revolutions; the whole universe shaken; and he is tranquil upon its ruins; and nothing withdraws him from his close and ineffable study of his Father; and nothing interrupts the divine quiet of his sanctuary, where he is always living for the purpose of interceding for us. Once more, consider and act according to this model: let us bring to the sacred table eyes long since closed upon every thing which may hurt our soul; a tongue surrounded with a guard of circumspection and of modesty; ears chaste and impenetrable

to

to the hissings of the serpent, and to the luxury of those sounds and voices so calculated to soften the heart; a soul alike insensible to scorn or to praise; a soul beyond the reach of the things of this earth, and proof against all the revolutions of life; the same in good or in bad fortune; viewing, with indifferent eyes, every occurrence here below; esteeming the good or the evil which occur to him as a matter that does not regard him; and, through all the agitations of the earth, the tumult of the senses, the contradiction of tongues, the vain enterprises of men, always watchful to guard over his peace of heart, to move continually with a steady pace towards eternity, never to lose sight of his God, and to have his conversation always in heaven.

Not that I would exclude from the altar all those who have not yet attained to this state of death: alas! it is the business of a whole life; and the body of Jesus Christ is an aid established to fortify and to assist us in this undertaking. But, our inclination ought to bend to it, lest we approach the altar unworthily; we must be at open war with the senses, with our own corruption, with our own weaknesses, and be continually gaining the advantage in some article; Christian self-denial must be practised; the daily victories, which the impressions of the world and of the senses gain over us, must be expiated by retirement, by silence, by tears, and by prayer; we must rise with fresh vigour

gour from every backsliding. But, I mean you to understand that a communion is not the concern of a day, or of a solemnity; that our whole life ought to be a preparation for the eucharist; that all our actions should be as steps which lead us up to the altar; that the life of too many in the world, even of those who are not in debauchery, who restrict themselves upon nothing, who live according to the senses, who are warm only on the interests of the earth, is a life which shews not the death of the Lord, and which, consequently, excludes you from this mystery. I mean you to comprehend, that the eucharist is a festival, if I dare to say so, of mourning and death; that delights, pleasures, and vain decorations disfigure this sacred table, and occasion your being rejected equally as him who appears there without the wedding-garment: that the meats of the earth and the bread of heaven cannot be eaten at the same time; and that, on the morrow after the Israelites had eaten of the old corn of the land of Canaan, the manna ceased, neither had they any more of that heavenly food. I mean you to comprehend, that this sacrament is the fruit and not the mark of penitence; that those communions, determined by a solemnity, give rise to more profaners than true worshippers; that the body of Jesus Christ cannot be eaten without living by his spirit; that the plenitude of the holy spirit must even rest upon a soul, as upon Mary, before Jesus Christ can

Vol. III. 3 M enter

enter into it, as it were, to assume once more the human nature. I mean you to comprehend, that the reading of the holy books, and the salutary rigours of penitence, should prepare an abode in our hearts for Jesus Christ, to the end that we may be like holy arks, and that this heavenly manna may rest there amidst the tables of the law and the rod of Aaron. I mean you to understand, that nothing should alarm you more, you who live in the dangers of the age and who love them, than all the communions of which you have partaken without preparation. I mean you to understand, that the bread of life becomes a poison to the majority of believers; that the altars witnesses almost more crimes than the theatre; that Jesus Christ is more insulted in his sanctuary than in the assemblies of sinners; and that the solemnities are no longer but mysteries of mourning for him, and days set apart to dishonour him. I mean you, in a word, to understand, that, in order to approach it worthily, a respectful faith is required which enables us to discern; a prudent faith which leads us to examine ourselves; a lively faith which causes us to love; a noble faith which induces us to sacrifice ourselves: without these it is rendering one's self guilty of the body and of the blood of the Lord; it is eating and drinking their own condemnation.

Ah, Lord! how little have I hitherto known the innocence and the extreme purity which thou requirest of those who come to eat of this heavenly ly food! The Centurion, that man of so fervent, so humble, and so enlightened a faith; that man so rich in good works, who loved thy people, who raised up edifices to thy name, and appropriated them to public prayers, and to the interpretation of thy scriptures; that man does not think himself worthy even to receive thee in his house: even the purest of virgins, when informed by thy angel that thou wert to descend into her womb, is terrified at it; she contemplates her own nothingness; and, if the power of speech still remains to her, it is to ask, how can this be? And who am I, Lord, to dare to seat myself at thy table with so little precaution? I, who come to appear empty before thee; who have nothing to offer to thee but the refuse of an heart so long engrossed by the world; who am thine only by intervals, and who still leaves to the created and to the passions the main part of my heart; who bring to thine altars only weak essays of salvation, and consummated works of sin; who have nothing above other sinners but the abuse of thy blessings; but unavailing lights; but sentiments which evaporate in vain wishes; but a thousand inspirations, which gain nothing from me but fruitless steps to conversion; but an heart incapable of familiarising itself either with sin or with virtue; but a disposition naturally good, and almost intuitively inimical to excess and to vice, and which I, however, have spoiled.

Ah,

Ah, Lord! the fruits of an holy communion are so abundant, so sensible; the soul quits it so overflowed with thy blessings and thy grace, that, when I had no other proof of the unworthiness of my communions than their inefficacy, I ought to tremble and be humbled. When thy body is eaten worthily, we are told that the hunger is not allayed; and I withdraw from that sacred table wearied out, and tired of mine homages: I breathe, on quitting it, as on quitting a drudgery, or an affair to which ceremony alone calls me; I congratulate myself that it is over, as I would do on being rid of a painful undertaking; and, if I feel any relish excited, it is for the world and for pleasures. When thy body is eaten worthily, we abide in thee, and thou abidest in us; that is to say, that thy precious blood, which still flows in our veins, leaves us thy inclinations, thy traits, thy resemblance, and that we are another thee; noble and heavenly inclinations should alone be seen in us, and sentiments worthy of the blood we have received: and, nevertheless, I always find in me only terrestrial desires, mean and groveling tendencies, and an heart still crawling in the dirt, and incapable of soaring above the created, and of returning to thy bosom from whence it came. When thy body is eaten worthily, thou tellest us that we live for thee, and eternally; and I have continued to live for the world, for myself, for those around me, for my pleasures, for my schemes of advancement,

for

for mine affairs, for a family, for children, for my glory; for you, scarcely a single moment in the day. What then must I do, Lord? Must I retire from thy table? What! this fruit of life should be forbidden me? What! the bread of consolation should no longer be broken for me? No, Lord, thou dost not mean to exclude me from it, but only that I be prepared for it; thou refusest me not the bread of children, but thou wouldst that mine unworthiness force thee not to give me a serpent in place of it. Prepare then thyself in mine heart an abode worthy of thee; make the rough and crooked ways of it smooth, and let the heights be levelled; purify my desires; correct my inclinations, or rather create within me new ones. Thou alone canst be thy precursor, and prepare the way for thee in souls. Fill us then, Lord, with thy spirit, to the end that we may eat of thy body worthily, and live eternally for thee.

Now, to God, &c.

F I N I S.

www.ingramcontent.com/pod-product-compliance
Lightning Source LLC
Chambersburg PA
CBHW032002300426
44117CB00008B/865